Praise for *War & Homecoming*

"A compelling dissection of the veteran's identity in the American consciousness that veterans may feel instinctively but that nonveterans need to understand. Martin uncovers both the academic and the visceral aspects of the veteran's identity and how veterans grapple with their own narratives. His work should be read widely, for we all shape veterans' military experiences, their homecoming, and their place in the wider culture. In place of 'Thank you for your service,' works like this remind us to delve into a more complex veteran's experience than most are willing to consider."—Lt. Col. Elizabeth Barrs, US Army (Ret.)

"Part personal narrative, professional memoir, and pop-culture analysis, Martin's *War and Homecoming* guides readers through an accessible and constructive conversation about how society makes military heroes, victims, and storytellers. If you work with or alongside people who once served in uniform, pack it in the rucksack as a multipurpose tool, along with such contemporary titles as Sebastian Junger's *Tribe.*"—Randy Brown, coeditor of *Why We Write: Craft Essays on Writing War*

"In his first, highly anticipated book, Martin offers readers a true gift by sharing his vulnerability—by trusting readers with the intimacy of his personal experiences as both a military veteran and an established scholar. Supported by interdisciplinary scholarship and examples from popular culture and American literature, Martin provides both argument and action plan for fostering veterans' connection and belonging in society. A much-needed, foundational text for the field of veterans studies"—Mariana Grohowski, editor in chief of the *Journal of Veterans Studies*

"Amassing scholarship and research from across the humanities and social sciences, Martin dissects the myths and stereotypes of veteran identity in American culture, politics, and society. All veterans have stories to tell, stories we need to hear; *War & Homecoming* tells a damn good one."—Corrine E. Hinton, associate professor of English at Texas A&M University–Texarkana

"A must-read for anyone who wants to understand personal civil-military relations as seen through the eyes of a veteran."—Brig. Gen. Jim Iacocca, US Army (Ret.)

"Martin's foundational work on veteran studies and veteran identity is truly groundbreaking. His contribution to this field of study is magnified by his knowledge and personal experience as a veteran. He is one of the many reasons Eastern Kentucky University excels at supporting its student veterans and their families."—David McFaddin, president of Eastern Kentucky University

"As both soldier and scholar, Martin is as familiar with the concussive rattle of an IED blast as with the societal mythmaking that tells veterans who they're expected to be. Presented with hollow labels of hero or wounded warrior, veterans are often left to choose between accommodating assumptions or keeping quiet. *War and Homecoming* guides us away from that binary choice, exploring the empowerment and importance of storytelling, which enables veterans to define for themselves what it means to serve, and to come home."—Brian Mockenhaupt, author of *The Living and the Dead: War, Friendship, and the Battles that Never End*

"Travis L. Martin posits that a nation that continues to fail to recognize the value and importance of exploring veteran identities is a nation that will remain ignorant to lessons that can be learned from war and loss." —Jason Poudrier, Iraq War poet

"*War & Homecoming* provides a scholarly and much-needed invitation to get down to the hard work of listening to our veterans, of hearing their nuanced and varied stories, of moving beyond the stereotypes and the superficial. Travis L. Martin convincingly explains that encouraging an authentic discourse with our veterans not only provides a crucial act of self-definition on the part of the veteran; it also deepens our social understanding of veterans as individuals."—Mark Wilkerson, author of *Tomas Young's War*

War & Homecoming

War & Homecoming

Veteran Identity and the Post-9/11 Generation

TRAVIS L. MARTIN

UNIVERSITY PRESS OF KENTUCKY

Scholarly publisher for the Commonwealth, serving Bellarmine University, Berea College, Centre College of Kentucky, Eastern Kentucky University, The Filson Historical Society, Georgetown College, Kentucky Historical Society, Kentucky State University, Morehead State University, Murray State University, Northern Kentucky University, Spalding University, Transylvania University, University of Kentucky, University of Louisville, and Western Kentucky University.

Editorial and Sales Offices: The University Press of Kentucky
663 South Limestone Street, Lexington, Kentucky 40508-4008

www.kentuckypress.com

Library of Congress Cataloging-in-Publication Data

Names: Martin, Travis L., author.
Title: War & homecoming : veteran identity and the post-9/11 generation / Travis L. Martin.
Other titles: War and homecoming, veteran identity and the post-9/11 generation
Description: Lexington : The University Press of Kentucky, 2022. | Includes bibliographical references and index.
Identifiers: LCCN 2022004979 | ISBN 9780813195643 (hardcover) | ISBN 9780813195650 (pdf) | ISBN 9780813195667 (epub)
Subjects: LCSH: Veterans—United States. | Veterans in motion pictures. | Veterans in literature. | Identity (Psychology)—United States. | Afghan War, 2001—Veterans—United States. | Iraq War, 2003–2011—Veterans—United States.
Classification: LCC UB357 .M367 2022 | DDC 362.860973—dc23/eng/20220207
LC record available at https://lccn.loc.gov/2022004979

This book is printed on acid-free paper meeting the requirements of the American National Standard for Permanence in Paper for Printed Library Materials.

Manufactured in the United States of America.

ASSOCIATION of UNIVERSITY PRESSES

Member of the Association of University Presses

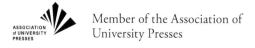

For Dogs Everywhere
"Thank You for Your Service"

Contents

Preface

This book was published exactly twenty years after I enlisted in the US Army. As a private, I wouldn't have been able to point out Iraq or Afghanistan on a map. I knew Kuwait was to the south and Baghdad was somewhere in the middle. And I knew how to do my job. Maybe the subsequent waves of troops who grew up with computers in their homes and smartphones in their pockets were better educated. But, for me, everything was pieced together after the fact.

A few years after my discharge I found a map on the Internet that listed all of the major bases and supply routes we'd traveled. College courses taught me to understand not only the geopolitical factors that led our country to war, but also how a confluence of different social identities led me to war as an individual. I am only describing my own ignorance, the long road to understanding that I have traveled over the past two decades, but weaving personal, social, and political histories into a cohesive narrative is part of every veteran's homecoming process.

Describing the content of one's character is another piece of that narrative. I reference Charles Cooley's "looking glass self" concept several times in the pages that follow. Cooley claims that we see ourselves as we think others see us. For veterans, self-perception is rooted in assumptions of others' assumptions about military service. We can never quite be sure how we are perceived—how we stack up—and so part of the narrative remains unfinished. The homecoming process is repeatedly interrupted by the mystique of veteran identity, a social construct best relegated to the past. I am concerned with the veteran's future.

Veterans can only transcend stereotypical conceptions of veteran identity by telling the story of themselves. Sometimes these stories run counter to prevailing narratives of veterans as they exist in patriotic discourse and the American unconscious. Veterans are imperfect. Their stories are never rank-and-file. And if critical examinations of patriotism and mythmaking make any readers uncomfortable, I recommend skipping straight to the fourth chapter about veteran "storytellers." It is in that chapter you will see the communities that are formed and the healing that takes place in the lives of veterans who are allowed to exist beyond the "hero"/"wounded warrior" binary used to label post-9/11 veterans. From there, return to the start of the book, keeping in mind that it is necessary to continually revise *the practice* of patriotism so that veterans can keep growing after their service in uniform comes to an end.

Homecoming is a process, as opposed to an experience, because the work of self-narration never ends. Sebastian Junger, also cited throughout this book, believes that veterans struggle during homecoming due to the absence of communal or tribal bonds. Junger and authors like Karl Marlantes and Jonathan Shay claim veterans need a sense of purpose and belonging. To be viewed as exceptional is also to be viewed as different—apart from the tribe—and being viewed as victims does not help veterans conceive of their future potential. What post-9/11 veterans need more than anything is an unbiased audience. They need civilian counterparts and past generations of veterans willing to be a sounding board for the difficult work of redefining themselves after service. If we want to restore veterans' sense of community and provide them with a sense of purpose, veterans must be allowed to exist as individuals—imperfections and all.

This book is intended for both veterans and nonveterans. In particular, my hope is that younger veterans can draw on what I have learned (so far) during my homecoming process to make sense of the dissonance and competing pressures to conform to narratives other than their own. I hope to inspire at least a few veterans to undermine stereotypes, embrace symbolic authority earned through service, and piece together a narrative they are proud to share with the world. By virtue of exploring this topic of veteran identity, my nonveteran readers have already won half the battle. My hope for you is that you will continue to think consciously about public and private conceptions of veteran identity, social forces that inform those conceptions, and ways to revise them so as to encourage the most recent generation of veterans to find new tribes, embrace their individuality, and realize their full potential. We all have a lot of work to do.

Introduction

Post-9/11 Veterans in the American Unconscious

In November 2003, our convoy came to a halt in the middle of a busy intersection in Fallujah, Iraq. We'd been rerouted through the city with an escort after an IED disabled a vehicle and wounded its occupant earlier in the day. It was still sunny. Out the driver's side window I saw a bustling marketplace. A little kid jumped up and down a few feet away, trying his best to sell me a bushel of bananas. To my front was my friend Darin. He was fumbling with the feed tray of a .50-caliber machine gun mounted in the bed of a Cold War–era troop transport. He looked out of place: the tallest person in the platoon with 360 degrees of exposure.

The first explosion hit two or three trucks back. The little boy with bananas seemed sad, as if he knew what was about to happen. He glanced over his right shoulder, then accusingly back at me, darting off as I ducked down. The look in his eyes after the blast—pupils dilating, reflecting light, tears welling up—imprinted itself on my soul. I knew nothing of the boy or his past, but that look told me his entire world was about to be turned upside down.

My truck mirror vibrated from the blast; dark black smoke billowed upward and out—into the crowd. "This is it," I thought. I heard the *ping-ping-ping* sound of metal striking metal. Our trucks didn't have armor, only the flak vests we draped over the door and the sandbags we'd put on the floor. I knew AK-47 bullets would tear through the door easily, so I tried to make myself small and get my bearings.

Round after round made its way from our convoy—at least twenty trucks—from turrets, the tops of cabs, and driver's side windows—into the mud brick buildings. Each bullet kicked up dust as it found its mark. I remember thinking that the cavalry scouts escorting us were trying to saw buildings in half. I watched as Darin fired one burst, then another. His weapon jammed.

I'd gone to basic training with Luis, the soldier standing out of the hole we'd cut into the roof above the passenger's seat—a makeshift turret. He was laughing and cursing and cooking off his squad automatic weapon, walking the rounds left and right like waves. I realized the pinging sound wasn't our truck taking direct fire. Luis's brass shell casings were bouncing off the roof. Grabbing the steering wheel, I pulled myself up. I was the heaviest thing I'd ever lifted.

I scanned for targets with my M16, but I couldn't make out a threat in the confused pedestrians scrambling about in front of me. Taking aim, I fired a few rounds of suppressive fire at a rooftop that seemed a likely spot for the enemy. Then my weapon jammed. *SPORTS: Slap, pull, observe, release, tap, and shoot.* Another round found its way into the rooftop. My weapon jammed again. Every weapon I carried was spotless after that incident.

Bombed-out buildings rose above the passenger's side of our convoy. We were in a really bad situation tactically—large, hard-to-maneuver trucks stuck in the middle of a city; none of the high ground. Iraqis ran every which way to get out of the epicenter of the fighting. I noticed a few bodies motionless in my periphery as I scanned for targets. They looked so calm, almost as if they'd stopped to take a nap.

Another boom, farther back this time. I looked desperately for someone with a gun, but I found no one. "What the hell are they shooting at?" I thought. The crowd fully dispersed—except for those taking a nap—and Luis's machine gun began to taper off.

"Go! Go! Go!" he yelled at me. Whatever it was that halted our convoy was gone. The truck to my front had taken off while I was scanning for targets and was now twenty-five meters away. My stomach sank as I pressed down the gas pedal. I was a little afraid that the truck would stall. But it didn't. I fired another round into nothing, and we zipped in and out of traffic, over curbs, and the hell away from that city. It all lasted a total of five minutes.

Seventeen months later, I was twenty years old and a third of the way through my second deployment. My brother Kyle died by suicide in April, and I went home on emergency leave for two weeks. A few days before my leave ended, my mother had taken me to see my great grandmother and some distant relatives. One of them asked, "Did you ever kill anyone while you were over there?"

Not having to take a life in Iraq is the thing that I am most thankful for when I look back on my wartime experience. Many soldiers didn't have a choice. My mind went back to November 2003. I thought of the people in that marketplace who'd died. I thought of one of my friends who had been at the rear of the convoy. He shot a man who had a grenade, and the change was discernible. Most of us had enlisted to get out of poverty or bad home lives. He was the patriotic type—packed an American flag and everything. He kept to himself for weeks. His personality changed. We all saw it.

I didn't know how to react to the question. "No, I've never killed anyone." I sat for a minute, nervous about more questions. I noticed my hands were beginning to shake, either from anger or a panic attack—I usually couldn't tell the difference. I excused myself, "Grandma, it was good seeing you. Mom, I'll be in the car."

The longer I sat, the angrier the question made me. I began to ruminate: "No, I never killed anyone. I am proud of that fact. I am thankful. So many beautiful and horrible things, but the act of killing another human being is what she wants to know about. She doesn't care about IEDs we barely escaped, the mortars that exploded over our tents at night, living in filth and rat feces; none of it mattered. 'Hey, look at the soldier boy, everybody, he kills people and that makes him a man.'" I worked myself up to a frenzy.

My mother opened her door and sat down next to me. I started cursing about the woman. I think I used more profanity in thirty seconds than I had used in front of my mom my entire life. After I joined the army, she quit reacting angrily when I screwed up. Instead, she'd pause and think deeply before responding. "You're right. She's had a very easy life. And she shouldn't have asked that question. I don't know what she was thinking. She's a simple woman and hasn't seen much outside of this town. I hope you'll cut her some slack." I sat for a minute, trying to stare a hole in the car's red dashboard. I had never killed anyone, and something about the way she'd asked the question made me feel like it invalidated my service. At the same time, a part of me felt like the anger I'd displayed didn't belong to me—like I was serving as proxy for my friends living with perpetrator's guilt. One stupid question with so much spoken and unspoken meaning. Of course, my mom was right. She'd had an easy life and had no idea what she'd asked.

Who Is a Veteran?

Count the number of veterans' license plates during your next trip to the supermarket. See how many World War II, Korean War, or Vietnam War ball caps you can spot at an outdoor event. Or, as subtler evidence, look for those inconspicuous individuals who salute rather than place their hands over their hearts during the national anthem. Just a few years of service in the military renders an individual a "veteran" for the rest of their life. Aside from recognition of accomplishment and sacrifice, and beyond the "support the troops" rhetoric woven into the fabric of our national defense policy, does anyone know who decided that veterans should have an identity of their own? Does anyone know why?

Don't think these veterans are alone. I received an Honorable Discharge as a sergeant in the US Army in November 2006, ending four years of service overseas, two of which were in Iraq. Today, I am a faculty member, administrator in our school's program for first-year students, and founding director of the Kentucky Center for Veterans Studies. A lifelong learner, I have been continuously enrolled as a student in college courses (with only a brief pause after completing my doctorate) since 2007. Outside of higher education, I founded and led the therapeutic and creative arts nonprofit Military Experience & the Arts for nearly five years. I would go as far as to say that I have accomplished more as a student, educator, administrator, and nonprofit leader than I did as an army sergeant. Four years isn't a lot in the grand scheme of things. Yet, when I reflect on the life I've lived and my place in society, veteran status is what I identify with most.

"Veteran identity" is not a way of describing "the affectations and attitudes particular to those who have served in the military." Each branch of service and military occupational specialty has different affectations. Veterans of each era hold different attitudes. There are hierarchical classifications among veteran cultures that are unfamiliar to civilian audiences and that change over time. Intersections between veteran identity and other social identities—race, class, gender, sexuality, religion, ability—mean no single definition can describe two individuals who served in the military. I tell students in my Intro to Veterans Studies class, "If you know a veteran, you know *one* veteran."

Will I *define* veteran identity in the pages that follow? No. Any definition offered would generalize veterans collectively. I will certainly *describe* the stereotypes I see passing themselves off as veteran identity. I will map the edges of the thing, discuss what it is not, and use this knowledge to comment on how the well-being of veterans, their homecoming, jobs, and relationships are impacted in real ways by collective notions of what it means to be a "veteran."

In a way, my veteran status undermines my credibility, at least in some circles. Actual veterans, I am told, don't like to talk about it. This adage is repeated in anonymous online forums, by sweet little grandmas in church pews, and by battle-hardened veterans themselves. "It," of course, refers to military service—to war. And "real" veterans are those who've seen the worst of "it." Imaginations conceive of painful secrets, shoeboxes or corners of the mind where veterans lock away dark memories. Veteran testimony is sacrosanct, despite evidence—memoirs, novels, poems, films, oral histories, artwork—to the contrary. These creative works show ordinary people surviving extraordinary circumstances. They are human beings—people with flaws whose stories instruct on the topics of friendship and sacrifice, resilience and compassion, or violence and evil. And "real" veterans tell stories all the time. The adage doesn't hold up to scrutiny, but it serves a purpose in that it helps society avoid difficult conversations about the costs associated with military service.

What is a veteran? Many Americans would say, "anyone who served their country." Others define the word "veteran" according to the length of an individual's service, if it concluded honorably, or whether or not it took place during war. These same individuals carry mental images of "the veteran": usually white and male, a survivor of war, combat, and all the associated traumas. In fact, minorities represent 23 percent of the veteran population.[1] Women comprise about 10 percent.[2] Only 36 percent of living veterans have served in a combat zone, and of these veterans, about half claim to have suffered from post-traumatic stress.[3] There's no monolithic veteran identity, culture, *or* experience. Veteran identity is a social construct. Subjectivity—our personal and collective decisions about *who is a veteran* and *who is not*—shifts according to needs and cultural norms.

Because of subjective definitions and preconceived notions, many veterans worry, "Do I measure up? Am I a veteran?" I once had a friend—a mentor, in fact—who retired with twenty-plus years of military service. He told me casually one day that because he had not earned a combat patch, he felt unfulfilled. Media portrayals of veterans strengthen these feelings of inadequacy, amplifying the "1 percent sheer terror" commonly associated with military service, rarely touching on the more common "99 percent boredom." I remember feeling sadness for my mentor. He had devoted most of his life to service, and because of arbitrary definitions of what it means to be a "real veteran," he concluded that he did not measure up.

My mentor, along with many veterans, look back on their service and wish they'd had the opportunity to do heroic deeds. More accurately, they wish that they had been given the opportunity to demonstrate the valor they believe they possess. Yet, recent history teaches society that valor is a tangible thing that can be stolen. The crowds that stormed the US Capitol in 2021 were disproportionately comprised of veterans.[4] They thought themselves patriots. Others thought them traitors and asked if they could be stripped of their VA benefits. Is valor, and to a greater extent, veteran identity, something that can be stolen, rebuked, or forsaken?

In 2014, the *Washington Post* found that three-quarters of Iraq and Afghanistan War veterans felt *appreciated* for their service. However, only 52 percent felt comfortable *discussing* that service. The Pew Research Center in 2019 found that among post-9/11 veterans 32 percent found it "somewhat difficult" to adjust to civilian life. Sixteen percent said it was "very difficult." Interestingly, the survey found that pre-9/11 veterans were more likely to be "proud" of their service, attributable no doubt to the shift in public sentiments toward veterans since the Vietnam War. Post-9/11 veterans are certainly not met with open hostility. But they are met with an aggressive form of superficiality. And this treatment has impacted my generation in its own way.

Vietnam veterans *were* met with hostility. Some still are. I remember, at a family barbecue a few years ago, a Korean War veteran said, "Don't thank him for anything, they lost their war." He was referring to another veteran who had served in Vietnam. And I got the impression he was being serious. When veterans of the Vietnam generation returned home, their relationship with veteran identity was complicated due to the unpopularity of their war and how that war contrasted with the "just" wars that had preceded it. Perhaps the biggest contribution the post-9/11 generation can make is to subvert this hierarchy and speak openly—through testimony, creative works, and volunteering—about how war and military service changed them.

Charles Cooley, a sociologist who conceived of the concept of the looking glass self, famously said, "I am who I think you think I am."

Today's veterans are caught between stereotypes, dueling narratives of "heroes" and "wounded warriors." They return home carrying what I like to refer to as a mixed bag of skills and scars. Both are forms of cultural capital, evidence of service that can open doors, grant benefits, and bestow privileges unavailable to civilians. However, when depictions of veterans' skills portray them as hyper-violent or emotionally stunted, a stereotype emerges. Likewise, another stereotype emerges when veterans' scars are conceived of as uncurable, unique, and unspeakable. Stereotypes are not identities. They are the path of least resistance for today's veterans returning to the "civilian sector."

The Veterans & Media Lab at the University of Alabama examines how the media shapes perceptions of veterans. In 2020, one study they produced found a direct correlation between media narratives and civilians' perceptions of veterans. Participants who read victimization narratives overestimated the prevalence of post-traumatic stress disorder (PTSD) among veterans, and those who read media "in which veterans challenged their traditional representations" displayed "pro-social" behaviors.[5] In other words, they were more prone to develop relationships with veterans who do not allow themselves to be defined by others. Veterans, as seen through Cooley's looking glass, not only perceive themselves stereotypically; they are impacted by those perceptions in tangible ways. What's more, civilians who are exposed to stories of veterans who do not fit into stereotypes are more inclined to seek out genuine interactions and conversations about service. A two-way street of authenticity and humility can bridge the divide between military and civilian cultures.

Most always, when a civilian walks up to a veteran and says the words "thank you for your service" they mean to convey sincerity, gratitude, and respect. For veterans of the post-9/11 generation the encounter is ubiquitous. They are likely to have any number of friends, family, colleagues, and strangers display gratitude in this manner. I do not mean to accuse my civilian readers of disregarding the reality of veterans' experiences. Rather, I want to suggest that the phrase "thank you for your service" stops authentic communication between veterans and nonveterans before it has a chance to start. It does not give the veteran a chance to speak, and so a more appropriate greeting might be "Tell me about your service." We thank our heroes, but we do not know the specific deeds for which they deserve thanks. We show deep concern for their wounds and struggles, but we are too afraid of embarrassing or upsetting a veteran to inquire about how it is we can help. Yet, my concerns have less to do with these individual interactions than their cumulative effect.

Where are the positive examples of veteran identity? Where are the role models? Who teaches veterans the art of self-narration so that they might conceive of themselves as resilient and capable after service? These veteran "storytellers" exist, but they are often drowned out by stereotypes and well-meaning rituals. Veterans—returning home transformed by the often-harsh realities of military training and service, having seen humanity at its extremes, and interacting with a society apathetic toward their experiences—*should* engage in the act of storytelling. This act of sharing experiences and crafting self subverts stereotypes. Storytelling, whether in a book read by millions, or in a single conversation with a close family member, *should* instruct civilians on the topic of human resiliency; it *should* instruct veterans on the topic of homecoming. But typically, veterans do not tell stories. Barriers exist to storytelling in the form of hollow platitudes—"thank you for your service" or "I can never understand what you've been through"—disconnected from the meaning of military service itself.

So, many veterans have chosen conformity and silence, adopting in place of an identity one of two stereotypes available to them: the forever pitied "wounded warrior" or the superficially praised "hero." These identities are not complete. They're not even identities as much as they are collections of rumors, misrepresentations, and expectations of conformity. Once an individual veteran begins unconsciously performing the "wounded warrior" or "hero" character, the number of potential outcomes available in that individual's life is severely diminished. My argument is not that some veterans are "heroes," some are "wounded warriors," and others are "storytellers." Quite the contrary; all veterans are storytellers, but some haven't embraced their right to self-definition.

Public discourse reinforces a feeling among veterans that they are "different." This shared experience has resulted in commiseration, camaraderie, and the proliferation of new veteran organizations like Team Rubicon, whose motto "built to serve" helps organize veterans in response to natural disasters; or Team Red, White, and Blue, a community dedicated to healthy living. Efforts to work through the dissonance associated with their homecoming has also led to the growth of veterans' creative communities. And I will draw heavily on my experience leading one of these organizations, Military Experience & the Arts, in the chapters that follow. Both service and art are ways of telling stories. As storytellers, some veterans are restoring meaning to veteran-civilian discourse by privileging the nuanced experiences of the individual over stereotypes and emotionless rhetoric. They are humanizing the topics of war and homecoming, producing fictional and nonfictional representations of the veteran *capable* of competing with stereotypes, *capable* of reassimilation.

Plenty of authors have discussed these phenomena. Tim O'Brien transcends genre and taps into lived experience to discuss how wartime memories are shaped by the act of storytelling. In *The Things They Carried* (1990) he addresses the taboo that says veterans shouldn't talk about war: "All you can do is tell it one more time, patiently, adding and subtracting, making up a few things to get at the real truth."[6] He does not claim to solve the problem of war through the act of storytelling. But his voice registers as one of the loudest of the Vietnam War veteran generation because he defies a cultural norm that shrouds war in a veil of secrecy.

Another Vietnam veteran, Karl Marlantes, focuses on moral and spiritual injuries in *What It Is Like to Go to War* (2011). Marlantes believes that the civilian predilection for silence on the topic of war is a recent invention, one attached to masculinity and a desire to create "clubs" in which power is tied to secrecy—to taboo. In this scenario, silence is a form of camouflage, a disguise that allows veterans to exist outside the spotlight so that patriotic conceptions of veteran identity might take their place. Just as the civilian practice of patriotism should be altered to allow for authentic dialogue, veterans must reciprocate. It has been a tendency in the twentieth- and twenty-first centuries for veterans to join in solidarity as members of closed groups. There's this notion that military service is somehow beyond the comprehension of civilians, and therefore discussions of it are best had among veterans themselves. How does this predilection serve the veteran community in any meaningful way? It is one thing to speak about traumas and hardships among groups of peers. This phenomenon is hardly unique to veterans. But it is another thing to not share the lessons in resilience and humanity gained through military service with the rest of the society. The military instills in troops of all ranks the ability to teach and train others. Veterans need to use these skills after their service in uniform comes to an end.

Marlantes believes better preparation can lessen the damage of war on the veteran's mind and soul. He writes with conviction and affection for young veterans. He accurately points out that silence is tied to pain, saying, "Society itself would rather forget as well, and so not only colludes in this but actually enforces it with its own codes of behavior."[7] Veterans of the recent wars in Iraq and Afghanistan have written about superficiality. The codes of behavior that silence them are phrases like "thank you for your service" that preempt meaningful conversations. They are refusals couched in sympathy: "I can never understand what you've been through." How much closer would the distance between veterans and civilians be if civilians genuinely tried to understand their veteran counterparts? Many want to understand, but they're afraid of asking the wrong questions.

Of course, veterans themselves play a part in maintaining silence. Some veterans likely found out that I was an army truck driver—not a Navy SEAL, an Army Ranger, or even an infantryman—and dismissed this book outright. The military creates hierarchies in which credibility and the authority to comment on military service belongs primarily to those who are "at the tip of the spear." Naturally, those who have experienced combat are going to have more to say about it. But not every "combat arms" veteran experiences battle. And not every POG (Person Other than Grunt) survives war. Front lines are a thing of the past. No veteran is without insights on issues impacting the military community. In fact, it is the veteran's civic duty to be concerned with these issues.

Paul Fussell, a World War II veteran who earned two Purple Hearts, exposes the dangers of idealistic notions of combat in *The Great War and Modern Memory* (1975). Fussell sees "irony" as the golden thread holding narratives of war together. Deeply inspired by the works of the Great War poets—Siegfried Sassoon, Wilfred Owen, Robert Graves—Fussell argues that war occurs cyclically because "irony engenders worse irony."[8] We need veterans to discuss their wartime experiences to ensure that the decision to go to war takes their perspectives into account.

Sebastian Junger is not a veteran, yet he has experienced more combat than most. His documentaries *Restrepo* (2010) and *Korengal* (2014) placed him in some of the most intense situations Afghanistan had to offer. In *Tribe: On Homecoming and Belonging* (2016), Junger writes eloquently from a civilian perspective, reflecting on communities forged during war and how the absence of those communal bonds causes many veterans to struggle in adapting to civilian life. Junger acknowledges that war exists as an initiation rite permitting admission into adulthood. Though it is not necessarily proximity to death or dying that fulfills the obligations of this rite, these experiences are certainly held in high esteem in military communities. Look no further than the ribbons and medals adorning a soldier's chest for proof.

One of the central tenets in *Tribe* is that veterans engaged in military and wartime service form close, tribal relationships with their fellow service members. Usually, these relationships are lost after deployments end. Junger claims, similarly to Marlantes, that in tribal cultures there were rituals and rites for welcoming home veterans of war that focused on healing and purification. American society has outsourced healing to mental health workers and spouses. Furthermore, tribal cultures had stated roles for returning veterans; they emphasized storytelling because those who did not fight directly played a role in helping veterans heal. They did not simply pay taxes and thank veterans for their service. The costs of war were shared.

A cursory Internet search confirms that O'Brien, Marlantes, Fussell, Junger, and I are not alone in our defiance of cultural taboos. Numerous memoirs about military service have skyrocketed in tandem with the growth of self-publishing and presses catering to audiences hungry for first-hand accounts of the wars in the Middle East. In a conversation in an anonymous online forum for veterans, someone said, "The veterans who do the most talk about it the least." I then brought up a running joke in the forum: "Operators" writing books about their military service in droves. "What about those guys?" I asked. Surely, members of the military viewed as the most lethal and experienced writing about war undermined the group's conventional wisdom. At first, I got downvoted and heard nothing in reply for hours. The vets were not happy that I had challenged the status quo. Later, I told them that I was a veteran and that I taught college courses about veterans. Then, a more nuanced conversation emerged. They concluded that "talking about it" was only problematic when an individual coopted veteran identity for individual gain. This problem becomes cringeworthy (an online neologism referring to when you experience shame vicariously for another person) and, according to the collective decision of the group, warrants ridicule if the veteran has little or no experience in combat. Interestingly, the anonymity provided by the forum granted more veterans a voice than the hierarchy described above.

The first chapter of this book explains its theoretical approach and sets the parameters for a close examination of veteran identity. Literary and social theorists apply interdisciplinary concepts to a text. In this book, the text that needs to be examined in order to better understand veteran identity is the

American unconscious. Humans see themselves as they believe others see them; veterans are no exception. To understand veterans' homecoming experiences, it is necessary to explore the undercurrent of mythmaking that takes place in patriotic discourse. How do veterans see themselves through the eyes of others? How do these perceptions impact their well-being and social status in tangible ways? The symbolic functions of veterans within larger national narratives can be rewarding, but they can also be limiting. Specifically, this theory of veteran identity argues that returning veterans are presented with two stereotypes to perform in place of authentic, individualized forms of identity: the superficially praised "hero" and the peculiarly pitied "wounded warrior." Fortunately, veteran storytellers are working through this problem. They harness their symbolic authority, develop individualized versions of veteran identity for others to model, and define what it means to be a "veteran" in literature, artwork, and service to their home communities.

Chapter 2 examines heroism and the historical link between war and agency. Three types of heroism are identified, including a new type that has allowed for veterans of the post-9/11 generation to be referred to collectively (and stereotypically) as "heroes." Close analyses of the rhetoric used in military training and indoctrination, Medal of Honor award citations, and films such as *All Quiet on the Western Front* (1930), *Heroes for Sale* (1933), *Sergeant York* (1941), and *Top Gun* (1986) distinguish between authentic feats of heroism and the blanket use of the "hero" title. Young people view war as a proving ground, a chance to tap into the heroism residing within them; service is often a great source of upward mobility. Referring to all returning veterans as "Our Nation's Heroes" provides them with a symbolic function in the American unconscious, one with benefits. However, conforming to the "hero" stereotype requires veterans to perform identity in such a way that limits their growth and individualization.

Chapter 3 examines the "wounded warrior" stereotype that treats post-9/11 veterans as members of a victim class. The chapter employs Eva Illouz's commentary on America's "therapeutic culture" to explore the cultural capital veterans gain through embracing narratives of veteran identity centered on trauma. Likewise, an application of Judith Butler's work explains how veterans lose their right to self-definition by conforming to those narratives. "Wounded warriors" remain silent because their wounds often do not fit neatly into popular conceptions of veteran woundedness. The chapter traces the evolution of the "wounded warrior" stereotype, first in a close reading of Stephen Crane's *The Red Badge of Courage* (1895), then in examples of denigration experienced by veterans of the First World War who were afflicted with shell shock, and later in a narrative structure that makes trauma central to the identity of the protagonist in Kevin Powers's Iraq War novel, *The Yellow Birds* (2012). Veterans have the power to challenge deficit-based narratives, but like their "hero" counterparts, "wounded warriors" face ongoing pressure to remain silent and to conform to stereotypes. This chapter argues that traumas experienced in uniform are not always central to veteran identity, and that veteran testimony—talking with veterans about their experiences—is not *necessarily* psychologically damaging.

Chapter 4 draws on creative works from the nonprofit Military Experience & the Arts, an organization that provides workshops, writing consultation, and publishing venues to veterans and their families. Veteran storytellers harness their symbolic authority, demonstrate awareness of stereotypes, and develop individualized versions of veteran identity. Examples discussed in the chapter include a marine who tells stories of homecoming through interpretive dance, an army veteran who teaches veterans how to transform old uniforms into art, an author and an artist forcing audiences to face the realities of military sexual trauma (MST), and a continual return to the theme of veterans and civilians talking over each other. These veteran storytellers escape the silencing pressures and conformity experienced by "heroes" and "wounded warriors," and they provide other veterans with examples of resilience and post-traumatic growth to model during homecoming.

1

A Theory of Veteran Identity

Generally, but not as a rule, I decline the offer to stand and receive applause when musicians or speakers recognize veterans at events. Although not intended as such, I've discovered that those aware of my veteran identity often take such refusals as political statements. The best way to describe the look I've grown accustomed to receiving is to liken it to the one a person might get after disrespecting the American flag. To some, by refusing to stand I am refusing the patriotic gesture offered and claiming that it is insufficient. To others, I am behaving in a way that is controversial, even anti-American. It's as though veterans occupy the same symbolic space as the National Anthem or Pledge of Allegiance. No one insists I stand. It doesn't cause conflict. But it does result in some uncomfortable conversations.

Personally, I refuse to stand for several reasons, some more reasonable than others. Firstly, I don't enjoy praise when a speaker attempts to levy it on me for the sake of others in the crowd. Is patriotism a chore? Admittedly, and this hearkens back to my experiences in Iraq, I refuse to stand because there's a paranoid recess in my mind that tells me I shouldn't make myself a target. Mostly, however, I despise the three to five seconds of being gawked at and analyzed by those sitting in my vicinity. I've watched as their eyes go up and down and side to side—an objectifying gaze, not one cast in judgment, but in genuine attempts to discern exactly what a "veteran" looks like. After standing as the recipient of some cheap applause, I've found that the discomfort persists throughout the remainder of the event. And it shouldn't come as a surprise: the ritual results in no longer being a part of the crowd. To be recognized as *exceptional* is still to be recognized as *different.*

In its less savory form, patriotism is scripted by social architects. An example is the "halftime tributes" common at NFL football games: "Between 2011 and 2014, the Department of Defense paid 14 NFL teams a total of $5.4 million and the National Guard paid $5.3 million to 11 teams to 'honor America's heroes' before games and during halftime shows."[1] I doubt such deceptions were what President Abraham Lincoln had in mind at his second inaugural address when he said, "Let us strive on to finish the work we are in, to bind up the nation's wounds, to care for him who shall have borne the battle and for his widow, and his orphan, to do all which may achieve and cherish a just and lasting peace among ourselves and with all nations."[2] These words were delivered near the end of the American Civil War. Hundreds of thousands of veterans died in that war and those since. Still, our sixteenth president had never seen a halftime show. Those flyovers are pretty spectacular.

Patriotism can be viewed as an exchange. But it is not as simple as gain or loss. Accepting patriotic gratitude carries implicit expectations: conforming to those narratives of war endorsed by the state, condoning *all* actions of the military—past and present, privileging one's veteran identity over all other aspects of identity. These expectations are what I refuse when asked to stand for applause at public events. My *personal* brand of patriotism, informed deeply by my experiences in the military, demands that I hold my country accountable. It demands that I advocate on behalf of veterans in *real* ways. Rituals, memorials, parades, and halftime shows often do more for civilians than they do for veterans. If the people in those crowds really want to help, they should talk to veterans, get to know them, find out about the issues that impact their lives, and research ways to create change. Then we could all stand for applause, pat ourselves on the back, and tell ourselves we did something patriotic. Performative rituals are often placeholders for authentic attempts to show gratitude to service members.

It is my hope that this theory of veteran identity will help those who want to interact with Iraq and Afghanistan War veterans authentically. I also hope these words will help some of my fellow veterans better understand their place in the world. This book is not a complete historical narrative of veterans' return home experiences. Such a task is best left to historians. And while the contributions and strains placed on society by veterans are relevant, sociological perspectives play only a supporting role in the pages that follow. Nor will I diagnose the psychological ailments of a few veterans and create a mold that fits them all; that sort of stereotyping has been used, for generations, to vilify or glorify veterans according to the politics of time and place. Historical commentary about returning veterans is common. Sociological research is conflicting. And psychological theories change almost as quickly as they're developed.

Instead, the pages that follow apply an interdisciplinary approach to veteran identity best described as a combination of social and literary theory. Terry Eagleton defines "literary theory" as "a kind of meta-discourse."[3] Literary theorists examine conscious and unconscious systems of thought by applying interdisciplinary frameworks to texts. The text examined here is the American unconscious. Individual performances of veteran identity; existing historical, sociological, and psychological scholarship about veterans; and cultural representations of veterans are equal parts of that text. The chapters in this book examine discursive and ritualistic practices that impede veterans' attempts to rejoin society, namely stereotyping and mythmaking, but especially the performance of veteran identity itself.

Dennis Sobolev discusses the difficulty of examining an unconscious, concluding that it is not a byproduct of culture, but rather "the essence of that invisible collective cosmos which forms the existential and experiential world of the empirical subject."[4] The existence of veterans in the real world is impacted greatly by how they exist symbolically in the American unconscious. Veteran identity is intricately woven into the fabric of our competing national narratives. To be a veteran is to stand for something greater than oneself. But that greatness is not singular; it is myriad. No single notion of "the veteran" exists because no single story of our nation exists.

As a result, those who interact with veterans project their worldview on them, influencing their experiences, interactions, and collective sense of identity. My discomfort at music and sporting events emerges because I know those well-meaning, patriotic Americans in the crowd likely see me as something I am not. As Robert C. Fuller explains in *Americans and the Unconscious* (1986), even if an individual or cultural unconscious cannot be observed, its effects can. We can circle what we *perceive* to be the American unconscious, using conscious descriptions of veterans' experiences (like the one I provide above) to better approximate their place within it.[5] To conceive of new ways to support veterans, it is necessary to isolate their symbolic function within a larger system of patriotic discourse. The roles veterans play in that story can be rewarding, but they can also be limiting.

Exceptional Examples versus Exceptional Individuals

Regarding patriotism, the concept of "American exceptionalism" dates back to Alexis de Tocqueville's nineteenth-century work *Democracy in America* (1835). Seymour Martin Lipset's reading of Tocqueville explains that the author never intended to convey that America was superior. Lipset notes that "Exceptionalism is a double-edged concept," and scholars have used the phrase to convey that America is "different," a definition connoting both the achievements and the problems of the emerging nation state, not its superiority.[6] As *exceptional* examples of American identity, post-9/11 veterans should be treated as individuals, each one *different.* However, they've largely been placed in a *superior* symbolic position, on a pedestal and regarded with reverence. Oppositely, Vietnam-era veterans were *exceptional* examples, but they were denigrated and assigned a symbolic position that approximated national guilt. The "Greatest Generation" of the Second World War and the "Forgotten Generation" of the Korean War are monolithic portrayals of veterans in the American unconscious that deny the individuality of each veteran. Whether superficial praise or misguided scorn, these stereotypes rob veterans of their exceptionalism—their *difference,* and also of their right to self-definition.

"Semiotics," or the science of signs and how they function, emerges as one tool capable of separating symbols from the meanings they convey. A sign is a thing that conveys meaning beyond its obvious form. For example, a *symptom* is a sign of a *medical condition.* Standing for applause when asked is a sign of veteran status, but it is also a tacit endorsement of the person or power orchestrating the ritual. Arthur Asa Berger describes language as a "social institution" or a "system of signs that express[es] ideas."[7] Veterans function as symbols, a "subcategory of a sign" within the language Americans use to describe themselves, or at least how they perceive themselves.[8] Again, not all members of society agree on a shared national narrative, and often for good reason. So, the power to define the word "veteran" or to appropriate veteran identity can privilege one narrative or group over another.

Leaders recognize that the "distinction between war and peace and thus between civil and military life is established and guaranteed by the proper conduct of soldiers."[9] One way to guarantee the proper conduct of soldiers is to depict them as superior examples. Such depictions abound in military recruitment campaigns, in low-angle shots of gruff warfighters on posters, in the special rites performed at their funerals, in prayers that elevate them based on the dangers they face, in medical and educational benefits unavailable to nonveterans. However, "the example," according to Italian philosopher Giorgio Agamben, "is characterized by the fact that it holds for all cases of the same type . . . and serves them all."[10] Traditionally, heroes engage in some act of valor. However, in modern mythmaking, *all* post-9/11 veterans are regarded collectively as heroes, as *superior.* As such, they must live up to these expectations.

Veterans must perform identity in a way that does not conflict with flattering narratives, such that it feels like one is under a constant state of surveillance. It is one thing when a veteran *earns* the title of hero and uses it to lend credibility to a cause. It is another thing when groups, governments, and other stakeholders use blanket stereotypes to define entire generations of veterans. It is *easy* for a musician or speaker to ask veterans to stand in a crowd for applause. However, it is *difficult* for many veterans to bury the ensuing feelings of inadequacy, the pains of moral and spiritual injuries, or the guilt from perpetrating violence or surviving when others did not. A better approach to honoring veterans in public spaces would be to provide them with the opportunity and agency to define themselves as exceptional individuals.

Of course, this sort of thing happens all the time—at ballgames, graduations, and inaugurations. So long as the veteran plays their role in these rituals, they convey a sense of unity and acceptance to those watching. There are tangible and intangible benefits for conformity. A problem emerges, however, when the narrative that the veteran is asked to support impedes on their continued growth. Veterans' accomplishments in uniform, no matter how profound, will always be a part of their identity. But these things cannot represent a whole person or a veteran's future potential. Homecoming is impossible for veterans when their symbolic position relegates them to existing in the past.

The Veteran's Symbolic Authority

It was April 2005. I'd had two hours of sleep when I woke up to my platoon sergeant standing over my cot. He asked me to go with him outside of the tent where we could talk in private. Initially, I thought I was in trouble, that I'd left some sensitive item in the Humvee following the previous night's mission. But that wasn't the case. As we exited the tent, entering into the sunlight beaming down on that patch of desert just north of Najaf, Iraq, I recognized our platoon leader standing next to a stranger.

"Specialist Martin of Somerset, Kentucky?" asked the man that I did not know.

"Yes, sir."

"When was the last time you talked to your family?"

"I don't know, a month or so ago, sir."

My platoon sergeant asked, "Do you have a brother?"

"Yes."

I looked up at the stranger to see a cross on his lapel. He was a chaplain. I knew immediately that something was wrong back home. I didn't have time to guess what it could be.

"Your brother is dead, son." The words were followed by what felt like a physical punch in the gut. It took three helicopter rides and an airplane to get me out of Iraq. In twenty-four hours, I set foot on three continents and still missed the funeral. And that's what it is like to get a Red Cross message while at war.

I tell this story because it put me in a rare position. I was yanked out of war and sent home with no preparation. I was not wounded, nor had I completed my four years of "honorable service." And when I changed out of my uniform, soiled with sand and sweat from weeks in the field—or, more accurately, the desert—I looked and sounded like everyone else. Still, I was *different.* And it was at this point in my life, based on the way I was treated, that I first recognized that difference.

Everywhere I went, war was all anyone wanted to talk about. They'd bring up stories heard on the news, and I would respond with either clarification or affirmation, but I soon found they preferred the latter. "Do you think it is worth it?" friends would ask. Acquaintances would inquire if I knew *so-and-so*, as though everyone in the military is on a first-name basis. A distant relative once asked if I had ever killed anyone, making me so angry that I could barely speak; I could only excuse myself and mutter obscenities in the driveway. It became the first instance of the same question repeated by those who gleaned their understanding of war from movies like *Full Metal Jacket* (1987).[11] I was more forgiving when kids would ask the question. But *adults*? I thought it plainly offensive.

Perhaps strangest of all, amid the grief inflicted on me and my family by my brother's death, I received displays of patriotism in place of the type of sympathy commonly shown to those who've lost immediate family members. After sorting through my brother's belongings because my parents were unable, I'd hear "thank you for your service." Even at my brother's memorial service, held at the church a few days after his funeral, people went out of their way to tell me how proud they were of me. I didn't want to be the center of attention. I didn't want to spend my leave walking on eggshells, afraid to break with others' conceptions of veterans. I wanted to be left alone to grieve. I felt like my veteran identity was hurtful to my family—that the focus should have been on my dead brother. Then, after two surreal weeks of performance, I returned to Iraq, where no one wanted to talk about war or the military.

My feeling of difference continued in the years immediately following my discharge. I'd spent four years overseas, learning to spot threats and to maintain an aggressive demeanor. I learned to associate dead animals on the side of the road with bombs. Angry looks or aggressive posturing predicted an ambush. We drove with guns pointed out of our windows and mounted on the tops of our trucks. On the back of each vehicle was a sign: "Stay Clear 50m. Deadly Force Authorized." Even among friends, because of the hyper-masculine nature of the military, I learned to expect daily fistfights. In my 2003 deployment, "beat downs," in which one endures an onslaught of fists and boots from ten to fifteen platoon mates, served as sanctioned rites of passage for the newly promoted, birthday gifts, or off-the-record punishments.

Veterans often return home having spent years on edge, honing the hypervigilance attributed to post-traumatic stress disorder (PTSD) as a means of survival. They come home and find dad wants to arm wrestle. Coworkers code-switch, speaking what they think is a military dialect by raising their voices and puffing up their muscles. Teachers tiptoe around the topic of war in the classroom, or they defer to the token veteran's opinion, as though every GI Bill-toting private is an expert strategist or general. The religious tell them to "pray harder" when violent thoughts feel like sins. Veterans try to explain to their loved ones the pains of being different. They confess what must be dirty, violent thoughts and attribute them to the past. But the only advice they're given is to "forget about all that and start living in the present." So, they try. And they soon find that people won't let them forget, that they'll forever be reminded of a past that indicates their difference. Within the American unconscious there is a script to which veterans must adhere.

Civilians are genuinely looking for ways to help. In the private sector, the 2013 "Sea of Goodwill" report by the Joint Chiefs of Staff listed "more than 400,000 resource organizations operating to bridge the gaps and improve the outcomes of soldiers . . . transitioning to civilian lives."[12] Roughly 2.7 million individuals have served in Iraq, Afghanistan, or both. That amounts to one "resource organization" for every six Iraq or Afghanistan War veterans! The media streams reports of veterans overcoming their wounds, and society seems more invested in the reassimilation of veterans than ever. Nonetheless, veterans continue to struggle. Reassimilation may be possible, but not until veterans are permitted to exist outside of a "ticking time bomb"/"Christ figure" binary.

Veterans' identities convey a wealth of information about war, military service, and the compassion of the nation that welcomes them home; seldom do veterans recognize the implicit demands and expectations of conformity placed on them. Belief in national superiority is a great way to keep the populace invested in American democracy. But can patriotism work better? Can *the practice of patriotism* change to better accommodate veterans and their perspectives? To declare a veteran a "hero" places that individual in a new symbolic position, one with discernible privileges, but also one with responsibilities.

A hero has the power to inspire others, to represent communities, to denounce war or justify it. Smedley D. Butler, a retired Marine Corps general and two-time Medal of Honor recipient, declared war "a racket" in his aptly titled short book, *War Is a Racket* (1935).[13] Similarly, Civil War general William Tecumseh Sherman asserted: "I am tired and sick of war. Its glory is all moonshine. It is only those who have neither fired a shot nor heard the shrieks and groans of the wounded who cry aloud for blood, for vengeance, for desolation. War is hell."[14] Few question these men because of their heroic feats. Now, *all* veterans are "heroes," undermining both authentic heroism and those honorable veterans who receive the label unconditionally, anonymously, insultingly—like participation trophies at a child's sporting event. When everyone is a hero, no one is.

In basic training, the new recruit is told that the last name worn on their chest is evidence they're representing family honor while abroad. Such rhetoric inspires recruits even as it surveils their behavior. I, for example, feel surveilled when honored for military service by individuals who have no knowledge of what I actually did in uniform. Society protects the *symbolic position* of the "hero" more than any *individual* who carries the title. Furthermore, certain patriotic gestures are stigmatizing, even damaging to veterans casually referred to as part of a victim class, or as "wounded warriors." The symbolic positions occupied by "heroes" and "wounded warriors" are not easily vacated, forcing some veterans to hide their wounds and perspectives out of shame, or out of fear that they can't live up to others' expectations. They remain silent because it is the path of least resistance. However, stereotyped veterans do not self-narrate; they do not develop the individuality or well-roundedness that lends itself to a successful homecoming. Instead, "our nation's heroes" fall into a trap that robs them of agency.

Returning veterans need to tell stories. They should define who they are *intentionally* in writing, on stages and canvases, and in how they conduct themselves in interactions with nonveterans after service. Harnessing their symbolic authority is equal parts growth and self-preservation. However, there is great pressure to conform to prevailing stereotypes—to remain silent. I am perplexed at how the perspectives of service members are whitewashed out of history books, mass media, and the academy. My forays into twentieth-century American war literature yield example after example of veterans like Butler and Sherman decrying war, begging those in power to come up with alternatives. Rarely are these views taught in our public schools; espousing them openly can even lead to denigration within communities of veterans. Many college students I encounter avoid conversations with veterans, afraid that by asking a mundane question like "What was your job in the military?" they will somehow damage the veteran psychologically. Sometimes, uncomfortable conversations are the most important.

Some veteran is reading this and thinking, "I could make these points better." They likely could. Why don't *all* veterans have the authority granted to me as an academic? How many years does a member of the military have to spend in combat before they are deserving of the same privilege I have to see my words in print? Where do veterans go when they want to be taken seriously? There are platforms, institutions, and government dollars invested in distributing works of scholarship such as this one. Beyond the free market, no such parallels exist for members of military communities. There are arts- and therapy-based programs working incongruently to solve the problem. Some efforts can be found among "public historians" who lend academic talents to preserving the histories of local communities. But American culture has no public institution or mandate dedicated to educating the civilian public about the impact of military service. Defining one's sense of self in a holistic sense should be as important as crafting a resume in military transition programs. Otherwise, our veterans remain silent, and our wars leave behind no witnesses.

War recreates itself with each generation, first by enticing youths into military service with myths of heroism, and later by appropriating the symbolic authority granted to them as "veterans." As stereotypes, veterans cannot challenge these myths. Worse, despite centuries of literary and artistic depictions of veterans, contemporary representations of post-9/11 veterans provide only two stereotypes to model: the "hero" and the "wounded warrior." This binary fails to account for the unique obstacles faced in each veteran's attempt to rejoin society. And veterans who allow themselves to be stereotyped struggle in the absence of authentic, individualized identities. They do not find outlets for the altruism and desire to grow into leaders instilled in military service. They occupy symbolic positions created to sustain war or someone else's narratives, never their own. They're asked to live in the past. Stereotyping and placating veterans—the "thank you for your service" urge of the twenty-first century—harms veterans in real ways.

Competing Stereotypes: Veterans as Criminals

I wasn't overly shocked when a former professor told me, "I would never let *my* child join the army." It can be a dangerous occupation. Parents are naturally protective. I *was* shocked, however, when they said, "Most of us assume people join the military because they can't hack it in the real world—that they're *losers*." The words sort of lingered in the air, as if the professor were letting me in on some deep secret. I knew there were people who felt that way. But my professor gave me the impression that it was a valid point of view, something I should consider. We were discussing a paper I had written, one in which I began playing with the idea of a "hero"/"wounded warrior" binary. Then, after reading through the pages, my professor set them down and said, "Yeah, but do you *really* believe all of this? I mean, look at the country we live in. Look at all of the freedoms we enjoy. All of this stuff about appropriating veterans' narratives and perpetual war seems so . . . *pessimistic.*" I didn't know how to respond. I sat quietly for a moment, took notes, and eventually the meeting ended.

I left puzzled. How could we both be scholars of war and veterans' lives and see the world so differently? At the very least, I figured each of us could understand *why* the other subscribed to their chosen narrative. Later that day, my partner, knowing I'd been nervous about the meeting, asked how it went. I said, "I got a lecture about how great America was." I kept ruminating over the words, "can't hack it," and it occurred to me that military service was *beneath* my professor and their family. They stated this fact plainly at the start of our conversation. It was also insinuated that people who join the military are fundamentally flawed. Had I been stereotyped in the midst of a conversation about veteran stereotypes?

I wondered if I was upset because the words hit close to home. After all, I'd enlisted largely for socioeconomic reasons. I didn't have a lot of options. The adults in my life didn't have high expectations. And I wanted to do something honorable, to cultivate the discipline and self-respect needed to succeed. *It worked.* I'd come from a single-parent home, graduated as a first-generation college student, and was having nuanced conversations about the world with professors trained in the Ivy League. I walked into that professor's office feeling as though we were equals. And when I left feeling invalidated, the power differential didn't sit right. I respected the professor's research and expertise, but that respect didn't feel like a two-way street. My views had simply been shrugged off. My professor had *the privilege* to shrug off a veteran's point of view, the same privilege that ensured their children would never sully themselves with military service. My views and experience seemed *beneath* them.

When I use the word "identity," I am not referring to a prepackaged or complete set of character traits. I hold "identity" to be a lifelong project—the "totality of subjective experience."[15] Identity formation is not just a phenomenon located in the lives of veterans. Paul John Eakin, a scholar of autobiographical identity formation, examines the work of "crafting self" in children to better understand memoirists' attempts at self-representation. As children, Eakin argues, "we learn to tell stories about ourselves, and this training proves to be crucial to the success of our lives as adults, for our recognition by others as normal individuals depends on our ability to perform the work of self-narration."[16] As I have described, returning veterans find themselves subjected to a confluence of negative and positive stereotypes. These stereotypes position veterans strategically within competing narratives of American identity. However, and as Eakin suggests, the act of self-narration and performance of self are necessary prerequisites to a healthy existence.

Veteran testimony can be a subversive act. But it is always a *necessary* one. For example, Sheldon Rampton and John Stauber interviewed Cecilia

Bohard to better understand why the *New York Times* shied away from images of dead soldiers and civilians in the early days of the Iraq War. Simply put, readers reacted angrily and in such large numbers that the publication became fearful of the backlash. Another interviewee, a chief neurosurgeon at Landstuhl's Army Medical Center, called US media coverage "disgustingly sanitized," lamenting the lack of public awareness about veterans forever debilitated by war.[17] The authors concluded that Americans saw a very different version of the war than did the rest of the world.

Conveying the experiences, emotions, and lessons learned during military service—beautiful, horrific, everything in between—should be as normal as standing for the National Anthem. Veterans and civilians have reciprocal roles to play in this ritual. I imagine self-definition as an *explicit* part of the return home process. I don't know what my fellow veterans will say if they're given such an opportunity. Many of us will likely disagree. But the act of testimony will most certainly complicate and allow for the emergence of new forms of veteran identity. These definitions of the word "veteran" would be personalized; they could serve as examples for subsequent generations of veterans to follow as they figure themselves out after exiting military service. Importantly, they could ensure that the perspectives of war veterans are considered when our country decides to wage future conflicts. Veteran testimony can also dispel stereotypes.

In films, veterans tend to be liabilities, basket cases, or antiheroes pitted against the state. These caricatures are recreated in the wake of each major conflict. *The Manchurian Candidate* (1962) portrays a Korean War veteran as a ticking time bomb, suggesting that former prisoners of war (POWs) are lying in wait to do violence on behalf of America's communist foes. *First Blood* (1982) features a Special Forces veteran of the Vietnam War so afflicted with PTSD that he turns his military skills against a local sheriff, ending the film surrounded by police, in tears, and with the now-famous monologue: "Nothing is over! Nothing! You just don't turn it off! It wasn't my war. You asked me. I didn't ask you. And I did what I had to do to win, but somebody wouldn't let us win. Then I come back to the world, and I see all those maggots at the airport protesting me. Spitting. Calling me baby killer and all kinds of vile crap. Who are they to protest me?" These iconic words, along with Rambo's terrifying flashback in an American jail cell, imprinted themselves on the American unconscious. They showed children who would later join the military what they could expect to become as veterans.

The Punisher (2017), a television show about a Marine Special Operations veteran, is filled with death, mayhem, and senseless violence. The plot of the series revolves around the protagonist, Frank Castle, killing criminals and government officials responsible for his family's murder. Veteran side characters sit in group therapy sessions held by one of Castle's surviving comrades, a medic and amputee who tries to push the unstable veterans down a path of enlightenment. The show ends where those sessions take place, with the unarmed antagonist—Billy, another veteran from the unit—shot in cold blood by Castle after two seasons of veterans committing larceny, assaulting police officers, waging war, and participating in outright acts of terrorism in New York City. It's not uncommon to see *The Punisher* skull logo on the backs of people's cars, a statement of solidarity with all those who feel downtrodden or oppressed by the state. These individuals share a narrative in which veteran violence is a potential key to liberty.

Even the lighthearted comedy *Tank* (1984) features a veteran turning against corrupt local law enforcement. James Garner's character easily rolls over police cars and barricades in his personally owned, World War II-era tank. Likewise, *Taxi Driver* (1976) features the mentally ill Vietnam veteran Travis Bickle. Bickle, a stalker and pornography addict, ends the film as a hero after shooting and killing a pimp to save a twelve-year-old girl from prostitution. Much of the film features the veteran protagonist plotting to kill a US senator. These are only a few examples, but they are enough to establish at least *a few* perceptions of veterans: they are violent, they are unstable, and it is only a matter of time before they turn their military skills against the country they once served. There is a constant return to this fear throughout our history.

In 1983, sometime after the Vietnam War and its veterans' tumultuous return home, President Ronald Reagan gave a televised address about national defense. In it, he directly addressed negative stereotypes surrounding military service at the time. He described a lack of mission readiness due to poor equipment, low morale, difficulty recruiting new members, and low retention rates. Yet, he also explained that with bipartisan support they were able to improve in all areas, fostering "a whole new attitude toward serving."[18] It is important for the civilian populace to have positive views of its military—to believe their veterans are not *losers*. George W. Bush understood this fact on May 1, 2003, when he staged the landing of an S-3B Viking aircraft on the USS *Abraham Lincoln*. He strutted across the flight deck and gave an impassioned (though premature) speech about the Iraq War in front of a banner that read, "Mission Accomplished." The commander in chief conveyed strength and confidence, and these things are necessary to secure public support and bring in new recruits. Meanwhile, those of us who were in Iraq were scratching our heads, wondering why nothing had changed.

Machiavelli recognized war as an extension of politics, and "the military as the site of potential political upheaval and popular revolt."[19] He reimagined the Roman "citizen-soldier" to replace the conscripted warfighters and mercenaries of Renaissance Italy, believing that a constructed, "civic-minded" veteran identity could quell populism. Similarly, America touts its "all-volunteer" force. National Guard/Reserve components, in particular, exist as civilian-soldier hybrids with a mission more closely aligned with public service than active duty. Volunteerism and willingness to serve without coercion adds to the veteran's symbolic value. And veterans who remain "civic-minded" after service set examples for the masses. Displays of yellow ribbon bumper stickers by those who "support the troops" send a message about national unity. However, the *Punisher* logo is also associated with veteran identity, and it sends a very different message. In many ways, the yellow ribbon and the skull logo illustrate the binary of the "hero" and the "wounded warrior" described throughout this book. Both stereotypes are commodified and sold as ornaments. And civilians can choose whichever stereotype aligns with their worldview. These displays have little to do with veterans in the real world.

War controls the movements of many bodies, resulting in a single, destructive energy. After war, veterans possess the same potential, causing some leaders to perceive them as threats. This fact is why extremist groups work hard to recruit from veteran communities. They want to take advantage of the veteran's desire for a sense of purpose and belonging in order to appropriate their skills and symbolic authority. Fear of this very thing was echoed in 2009. A Department of Homeland Security report entitled *Right-wing Extremism: Current Economic and Political Climate Fueling Resurgence in Radicalization and Recruitment* described veterans as a potential source of political upheaval. The report suggested that extremists with right-leaning political views could recruit veterans to their cause. Defenders of the report cite Timothy McVeigh, the Gulf War veteran who bombed the Alfred P. Murrah Federal Building in Oklahoma City in 1995, as an example of its veracity.[20]

In another report from 2021 entitled "This Is War: Examining Military Experience Among the Capitol Hill Siege Participants," Daniel Milton and Andrew Mines explored data that emerged after a regretful rally held by President Donald Trump. Following Trump's directions, a group of supporters stormed the US Capitol, resulting in at least two deaths during the event. Several died after, including police who continue to die by suicide. Milton and Mines found that 12 percent of individuals charged in federal court for their role had military experience. The length of time spent in uniform for these veterans ranged from nine to twenty-five years. Roughly half had deployed, and half had been out of the service for more than a decade. More alarming, perhaps, is that 37 percent of the veterans had ties with extremist organizations.[21] Fortunately, the government was not overthrown, a fact that led some politicians to claim the so-called rioters had only been misguided "tourists."

Veterans are reminded again and again of their potential for violence. Willard Walter Waller, the sociologist author of *The Veteran Comes Back* (1944), viewed as one of the few texts in the twentieth century to treat veteran identity seriously, repeatedly bashed veterans service organizations and accused large swaths of the veteran population of malingering. He also echoed fears of veteran violence: "The veteran is politically dangerous because he has a great deal of hatred to work off. By making him into a soldier, we have carefully cultivated his sadistic-aggressive impulses, taught him to fight and kill without mercy, and then done him a series of injustices—should we then be surprised when he fights back?"[22] Waller's work, *not written ironically*, repeatedly echoes these stereotypes: "Perhaps he comes to enjoy killing. Military experience also weakens the taboos which protect property and hedge about sexual indulgence. . . . [N]early all veterans have suffered from some loss of the mental disciplines which go with civilian industry. . . . For these reasons, many veterans become criminals."[23] Waller writes in earnest to support the veteran cause, yet the narrative to which he ascribes depicts veterans as broken, unstable, victimized, aimless caricatures.

Waller fails to consider if his narrative perpetuates the "veteran problem" he wants to address. His book was wildly successful in its time: "The success of this book brought Waller not only fame but also an increasingly heavy involvement in lecturing, writing, and public affairs, which led him to exhaustion and premature death at the age of 46."[24] In fact, the work was resurrected for a 2021 panel discussion entitled "Waller's *The Veteran*

Comes Back at 77."[25] The panelists seemed at pains to separate Waller's insulting words from his historical contributions, such that several veteran-academics in attendance (myself included) responded with condemnation during the question and answer portion of the presentation. It is the responsibility of scholar-activists and others with the privilege to speak openly to not perpetuate veteran stereotypes. We should avoid positioning a text like Waller's at the forefront of the discussion. He should be a footnote, one regarded as an example of veterans' problems rather than a solution.

There are nearly 18 million veterans in the United States at the time of this writing. The 2021 statistics pertaining to the Capitol Hill riot are based on the characteristics of just *forty-three individuals.* McVeigh was *one* veteran. As Michael Robinson and Kori Schake eloquently put it in an op-ed for the *New York Times*, "Americans in military service and veterans aren't some sealed-off segment of the population; they are us. And like other Americans, they are yearning for the connectedness of community and a sense of belonging. . . . Remember that veterans stood among the heroes on Jan. 6, too."[26] There's no doubt that extremist organizations target veterans as recruits. However, I have yet to find a convincing argument that demonstrates how military service radicalizes veterans or predicts violent behavior absent the factors that cause violence among the general population.

To be sure, military service equips veterans with greater lethality. Every recruit, from the navy medic to the army grunt, is taught, in some manner or another, how to inflict violence on others. But characteristics *preceding* service or conditions experienced *after* service are more likely to breed criminality. At the same time, the media exaggerate the threat veterans represent, pretending other members of society are incapable of such violence, reinforcing the separateness of a veteran culture. Hyper-violent, almost pornographic representations of war produced by Hollywood are the greatest sources of this exaggeration. In these films, year-long deployments of killing and being killed get distilled into a few hours of scopophilic pleasure for audiences, making it appear as though survivors of war are superhuman. The only veterans I've known to enjoy such films are those who experience memories of war trauma on repeat in their minds. They seek out external stimuli that correspond with their inner turmoil. For nonveterans, such films are voyeuristic pleasure, a way to experience war without enduring the costs.

About 8 percent of Americans in jail or on probation are veterans.[27] However, studies have shown that deployed and nondeployed soldiers are equally likely to commit crimes.[28] And, according to the National Center for PTSD, when "risk and protective factors are considered, the association between PTSD and violence diminishes."[29] The broad brush used to paint veterans—*especially those with mental illness*—as recidivist criminals fails to consider their intersectional identities. Gender, socioeconomic status, substance abuse, and educational backgrounds are all stronger predictors of crime than military service. In fact, many of these factors are emblematic of the lives many veterans seek to escape by enlisting. Violent crime is a symptom of a society that has yet to solve the problems of inequality, disease, and prejudice. Veterans are just one social group among many impacted by these ills.

Veteran identity begins forming in childhood, long before the decision to enlist. Many of the children watching Reagan's address in 1988 would be of fighting age at the start of the Iraq and Afghanistan wars. Reagan's speech refers to a generation of veterans willing to serve in unsatisfactory conditions, in unpopular wars, and for a country that allowed the military to deteriorate. They did so despite rumors of soldiers being poorly equipped and despite the views of many members of society who felt that military service was evidence of inferiority. They continued to enlist after being maligned as potential terrorists in 2009, and young people are joining the ranks today despite the dishonor forty-three individual veterans brought on themselves in January 2021. On one hand, veterans are regarded superficially with reverence as "heroes," and on the other hand they are portrayed as a victim class. Most enlistees and newly commissioned officers have a desire to do something honorable. They want to improve their station and hopefully the lives of others. They're willing to risk their lives to do it. Courage does not make veterans perfect. But even imperfect veterans deserve the right to self-definition.

Tribalism in Veteran Culture

During the initial weeks of basic training, when our cohort of mostly eighteen- to twenty-five-year-old recruits were learning to speak across the racial, gendered, and socioeconomic divides we learned as civilians, a drill sergeant said to us, "In the United States Army there's only one color: *green*." I heard that axiom repeated no less than a dozen times during my four-year enlistment. I took comfort in knowing that I'd entered into an allegiance with the individuals standing to my left and right. I was comforted to know they'd protect me, that we'd somehow transcended the petty squabbles of our former lives. Now, I wonder if that drill sergeant was telling a story or if it is possible for an institution to fundamentally alter the identities of its recruits? Did taking an oath of enlistment somehow transform me into a member of a new culture, one less defined by skin color or socioeconomic background than by the habituations common to those who've endured military service? Were we all, in fact, *green*? And if I *was* green, what am I *now*?

"Camaraderie" is the word used to describe the intimate relationships that members of the military forge during service. These relationships are rooted in shared experiences, overcoming obstacles, and commiseration. Pain and rewards are shared in equal measure, and all members of the collective carry some important piece of information learned through sacrifice. The private works to become a sergeant. The lieutenant works to become a captain. Eventually, enlisted leaders and officers learn to "function in tight-knit groups, and those emotional bonds become incredibly important."[30] These soldiers gain power and respect by taking on subordinates, younger soldiers with their own ambitions, and leaders advance in rank based on how well they lead and educate troops. In the civilian workforce there are also leaders, managers, and educators. In the military, an individual occupies all of these positions at once. Military identity is defined by strengths and knowledge—a soldier's future potential. Their day-to-day life is always in service of that potential: training, exercises, leadership development.

In contrast, returning veterans find themselves in an individualistic society rooted in personal gain. Veteran identity in the civilian world, not surprisingly, revolves around past accomplishments, and the veteran's difference can be perceived as a liability. By contrast, past generations of Native Americans returning from war experienced a much different sort of homecoming. Sebastian Junger explains that "cohesive and egalitarian tribal societies" excelled at dealing with trauma, while mainstream, contemporary US culture tends to be more individualistic and hierarchical.[31] Such individualism can be alienating once one becomes accustomed to a communal culture. In communal cultures, healing is possible because the perspective and wisdom of the person healing has value.

Most Americans expect returning veterans to use newfound skills and earned benefits to advance themselves. It is an individualistic notion rooted in the myth of meritocracy, or the belief that upward mobility is possible no matter the uniqueness of an individual's position. Talent, ambition, and hard work—the myth holds—are coequal with wealth, lineage, and opportunity. And it is a notion that contrasts strongly with the collectivist sensibilities taught in the military and described by Junger. Therefore, calls for veterans to "reassimilate" imply that veterans should end the period of disassimilation they experienced as members of a collectivist society and embrace more self-serving notions. I am not making a moral argument. Rather, I hope to point out that embedded in the notion of reassimilation is also a call to regress. And regression implies undoing much of the growth that came about *because* of military service. Veterans are told, "Translate your skills for the civilian workforce." Meanwhile, Waller and others of like mind warn that "veterans will descend upon us with frightening suddenness . . . resentful and explosive . . . strangely naïve and unsophisticated; expecting jobs and good jobs too but lacking the skills or the stability to hold them."[32] Tax dollars pour into campaigns designed to help veterans find employment, such that hiring a veteran is now considered a charitable act. The inherent value of the veteran's resilience, leadership experience, and ability to educate others is accepted more as a sales pitch than truth.

In *Odysseus in America* (2002) Jonathan Shay distinguishes between civilian perceptions of those actively serving in war and of veterans who've returned home: "What in wartime is a heroic amphibious landing, is in peacetime a criminal pirate raid. What in war is bold and courageous, in peace is reckless and irresponsible; in wartime resourceful, in peace lawless."[33] Shay, drawing on Homer, distinguishes between feelings of the "heart" and those of the "belly," explaining that civilians take pride in their soldiers' abilities. They know that soldiers keep them safe. However, once unseen enemies fade into history, the veteran remains as an ever-present danger. The solution to this fear, Shay believes, is to give veterans a voice.[34]

It has to be a two-way street: "When trauma survivors hear that enough of their truth has been understood, remembered, and retold . . . then the circle of communalization is complete."[35] The problem with this solution is that it requires a civilian audience to be knowledgeable of veteran culture, dismissive of veteran stereotypes, and willing to listen. The prevailing stereotypes of post-9/11 veterans stand in the way of all three of these needs. "Thank you for your service" ends conversations that bestow knowledge. Stereotypes are manipulated to support narratives and groups that are far more influential than any veteran willing to talk or any civilian willing to listen. Our individualistic culture and the veteran's symbolic role within it are designed in such ways that reassimilation is always out of reach. The veteran's past is more valuable to society's narrative than their future.

"Industrial societies," Eric Leed argues, "define war as an abnormal state of emergency and presume that war and peace are distinct and separate realms of existence; those who adapt to these contexts are presumed to have changed identities, and are required to forget, again and again."[36] Stories about the Afghanistan and Iraq wars dominated the news in 2001 and 2003. However, as these wars waned in popularity, the news shrank to a growing body count that scrolled casually across the bottom of television screens. Many veterans watched this body count grow—as coverage of their actions dissipated—even as they completed multiple deployments, spending years in hostile environments. In time, not even the body count remained, and millions of veterans returned from war to find that their sacrifices were something that society would prefer to forget, an unfortunate accident of history.

Amid such dissonance, Junger believes *missing* war is a "healthy response" to homecoming.[37] Junger's examination of Iroquois tribal culture describes war as something experienced by every member of society, not just combatants. Welcoming veterans home was a process, not an event. Homecoming *continued* as veterans healed; it was the responsibility of the collective to provide aid.[38] Veterans didn't just reassimilate and try to forget the past. The tribe assimilated their knowledge. Their trauma was a wound, but it had instructional value.[39] As a result, Iroquois warriors used their knowledge, collective desire to share lessons, and the spirit of camaraderie to help their tribes rebuild themselves after conflicts.

These outcomes are supported by the research of Matthew Zefferman and Sarah Mathew, who compared PTSD among veterans in industrialized nations to what veterans experience in small-scale societies. Zefferman and Mathew distinguished between "learning-and-reacting" symptoms and depressive symptoms, finding Turkana warriors tend to experience fewer depressive symptoms due to a lack of "moral disapproval" from nonwarrior counterparts.[40] Zefferman and Mathew explain, "By contrast, in the United States and other industrialized nation states, support for war and those who participate in war is often far from universal. . . . [A] soldier's duty in combat can violate the prevailing moral norms within the soldier's society."[41] After the Vietnam War, 37 percent of veterans expressed a desire to live in a country other than the United States.[42] That generation's veterans continue to die by suicide in the greatest numbers (38 percent more than any other age group).[43] Junger, Zefferman, and Mathew show that one explanation could be the symbolic function those veterans were assigned during homecoming, one representing American guilt and "moral disapproval." Importantly, homecoming is a process, not an event. Things can change.

Waller describes veterans as "resentful" of fellow citizens who did not experience war.[44] Junger believes veterans simply "need to feel that they're just as necessary and productive back in society as they were on the battlefield."[45] Combat and different forms of military trauma plant the seeds of illness and disillusionment, but it is the alienation veterans feel in relation to larger society that creates the conditions for those seeds to germinate. Junger suggests that the inequity in our society—unequal access to health care and education, for example—indicates a lack of resilience on a societal level. Veterans' stories contain lessons in resilience, and dialogue between veterans and civilians spreads those examples to the masses. As educators, veterans have the power to help improve society by sharing lessons of survival, the values of collective existence, and perspectives bought through sacrifice.

Veteran Self-Actualization

A marine veteran, social worker, and fellow scholar of veteran identity named Steve Wahle once invited me to a panel, "PhDs Who Can Win a Bar Fight." It was specifically for veteran-academics, and though the title harnessed one stereotype to get a laugh, the speakers shattered many others. Wahle, in particular, provided me with a lot of insights I hadn't considered. He explained that many of the older veterans service organizations—the American Legion, Veterans of Foreign Wars, Disabled American Veterans—have struggled to recruit members from the post-9/11 generation.[46] Instead, these members are coming together in new ways. In their attempts to rewrite the cultural script of veteran identity, many veterans are naturally drawn to groups and activities that recreate the altruistic and tribal aspects of military service.

For example, more than a thousand veterans traveled to Standing Rock, North Dakota, to aid Native Americans threatened by the installment of an oil pipeline near precious water resources in 2016 and 2017. Opponents on social media argued that veterans coopted the protests, placing their own distrust or disdain for the government above the intent of the Native Americans. However, when interviewed by *The Guardian*, veterans told a different story: "We are prepared to put our bodies between Native elders and a privatized military force. . . . We've stood in the face of fire before. We feel a responsibility to use the skills we have," said Elizabeth Williams, a US Air Force veteran.[47] Jake Pogue, a Marine Corps veteran, claimed, "We're not coming as fighters, but as protectors. . . . Our role in that situation would be to simply form a barrier between water protectors and the police force and try to take some of that abuse for them."[48] In these brief interviews, veterans justify their actions, demonstrating an awareness of how others perceive them. Williams deems it important to emphasize veterans' skills. Pogue underscores that veterans have experienced the type of violence faced by the nonveteran protestors.

Sam Levin, the journalist who wrote the *Guardian* article, draws parallels between veterans' mental health problems and reports of trauma emerging among tribal protestors who were psychologically and physically injured by police and government officials: "At Standing Rock, indigenous activists say the mass arrests and police violence have led many of them to develop PTSD, suffering symptoms that many veterans understand well."[49] The stated intent of the veterans indicates altruism and, specifically, a willingness to experience violence for the sake of others: "I don't want to see a twentysomething, thirtysomething untrained person killed by the United States government," claimed Vietnam veteran Dan Luker. In traveling to Standing Rock, these veterans battled the stereotypes of fellow Americans who vilified them because they disagreed with their politics.

Aubree Peckham, a member of the Mescalero Apache tribe who protested at Standing Rock, claimed, "We don't know how to protect ourselves against the tactical weapons they are using. . . . [The veterans] are getting us better prepared. . . . We are able to talk about PTSD. And they finally feel like they are understood."[50] The veterans were simply looking for a way to serve—for community. If anything, the veterans proved willing to suffer bodily injury for the sake of others. They also shared their knowledge and used lessons learned from surviving trauma to make their chosen community more resilient.

Iraq and Afghanistan War veterans are increasingly drawn to veterans service organizations that give them a mission. Team Red, White, and

Blue, for example, defines itself using "The Eagle Ethos," which consists of just six words: "passion, people, positivity, commitment, camaraderie, and community."[51] The group, founded in 2010, is dedicated to helping veterans stay physically active and socially engaged. They are inclusive of both veterans and civilians, a policy that 87 percent of veteran members claim allows them to demonstrate the strengths veterans possess. Likewise, 75 percent of the civilian members claim that membership provides them with a deeper understanding of veterans in the local community.[52]

Team Rubicon, started in 2010 by post-9/11 veterans, was founded by two marines to provide aid in Haiti following a devastating earthquake. The group claims that in "applying medical and leadership skills honed by years of service in the military, Team Rubicon provided aid to thousands of survivors of the Haiti earthquake. From this initial operation, a larger organization grew, one committed to helping underserved communities impacted by disasters."[53] In contrast to portrayals of veterans as superficial heroes, members of a victim class, or dangerous criminals, Team Rubicon emerges in a time of need, tapping into military skills and an innate desire to serve and make a difference.

There are other examples. VETPAW is a group of post-9/11 veterans dedicated to training park rangers, protecting endangered species from poachers, and educating the community about conservation efforts.[54] Student Veterans of America advocates for veterans in higher education, and they were instrumental in the fight to protect veterans from predatory schools.[55] Wahle's theory presupposes that veterans of the post-9/11 generation are wary of groups that focus on the past. And Jennifer Steinhauer, who writes about veterans' organizations for the *New York Times*, says that "contrasts between the groups is stark. Many of the old V.F.W. halls remain outposts of fellowship over beer, while younger veterans prefer community centers with healthier and more practical assets, like Wi-Fi, childcare and yoga classes. In many cases, social media has replaced physical spaces as a place where veterans congregate."[56] Older veterans worry that the outward focus of these groups will backfire, that the immeasurable work they carried on for decades—advocating for the equal treatment of veterans, securing veterans' benefits—will be lost. However, groups like Iraq and Afghanistan Veterans of America and the Wounded Warrior Project appear poised to fill voids left in legislative chambers.

Consumer culture emphasizes the many benefits available to returning veterans, legislating disability compensation, paying for them to go to college, pressuring each returning veteran to enroll in therapy. But veterans themselves are increasingly in search of authentic interactions and opportunities to serve. Emphasis on extrinsic rewards and well-being is the cause of much isolation. As an alternative, veterans tell the story of themselves—engage in the act of self-definition—by using their knowledge and skills to address social inequality at places like Standing Rock. They're building bridges between veterans and nonveterans in groups like Team Red, White, and Blue. Or they're engaging in humanitarian outreach with groups like Team Rubicon. Veterans begin their lives as members of disparate tribes, each with its preferred narrative. Military service does not remove that aspect of the veteran's identity. That said, the military *does* teach service members to live and work alongside people from other cultures—to function as a collective. Veterans return home with knowledge, skills, and insights about our common humanity. When given the opportunity, they can share lessons about collectivist existence. What if veteran testimony has the ability to bring our disparate tribes together?

2

Our Nation's Heroes

Somewhere today, a veteran walked into a college classroom. Something made them immediately recognizable as a veteran to the other students. Maybe it was their haircut, or a patch sewn onto their book bag. It could have been something more obvious, a hat reading "Veteran of the ________ War." Maybe they were on active duty, attending night classes near base, still wearing a uniform.

There's a lot more going on in this moment than most people realize. Once a veteran signifies veteran status, the minds of others come alive with theories, expectations, notions of what, exactly, it *means* to be a veteran. In return, the veteran anticipates these unspoken beliefs. In the scenario above, nonveteran students attribute subtle behaviors, appearances, and gestures to imagined scenarios, to hypothetical situations the veteran knows nothing about. Likewise, the veteran anticipates some of their presumptions, adjusting their behavior to conform or contrast with others' preconceived notions. It all happens in an instant. From the time the student veteran walks from the doorway to their desk, an entire set of conscious and unconscious exchanges takes place. Assumptions are made. Theories are confirmed or adjusted based on the available evidence. Then, the veteran takes a seat, having played a localized yet pivotal role in maintaining a larger cultural narrative about their country, its beliefs, and fellow veterans. Not a word has been spoken.

Erving Goffman's *The Presentation of Self in Everyday Life* (1959) uses the language of theater and stage directing to discuss these sorts of human social interactions.[1] Goffman claims that we all play a variety of roles in our daily lives. Veterans are no exception. The stage is a classroom, a sports stadium, a church. It's any place or situation involving a group of people in which the veteran is considered the "other." The topic of the play taking place upon that stage is American nationalism. Its grand themes are patriotism, history, and foreign policy. But it's also about humanity, resiliency, and compassion. The veteran, as character and plot device, serves as a mirror through which larger society sees itself reflected. In most circles, all the veteran has to do is remain silent in order to be considered an exceptional example. Granted, there have been periods in American history when veterans have not been held in such high regard. But, for the most part, veterans of the post-9/11 generation enjoy, at least superficially, a sort of "hero treatment"—the opposite of what Vietnam veterans experienced.

Unsurprisingly, being a plot device requires a great deal of what Goffman calls "impression management," subtle variations in a person's demeanor—methods of storytelling. Impression management fills in blanks for others. Over time, and if the veteran doesn't go against the grain of what others hold to be true, it produces a degree of trust and acceptance. Civilians come to believe that they understand not only the veteran standing in front of them, but *all* veterans. For some veterans, this brand of acceptance is enough. It is all they need to feel as though they are part of society. However, Goffman explains that "no amount of such past evidence can entirely obviate the necessity of acting on the basis of inferences."[2] The work of impression management never ends. Each veteran will be scrutinized, judged, and held to account for their performance. To exist symbolically as a veteran requires being "on" all the time.

Veterans praised or elevated through patriotic discourse implicitly agree to certain levels of conformity. They must follow Goffman's script, hiding such things as mental illness or disillusionment, invisible scars that depart from a story in which the veteran is a "hero." The "hero" character is an archetype; it portrays a specific form of military masculinity, which is strong, dutiful, and courageous. Veterans feel an unspoken pressure to conform in their day-to-day lives. Prevailing societal narratives suggest *any* veteran can be the *ideal* veteran. In a way, civilians who perpetuate such stories claim, "You're all heroes. Let us prove it," even when the hero in their story of salvation is clearly not the veteran.

I use quotation marks around the word "hero," in modified states (e.g., "heroism," "heroics"), and in accompanying phrases (e.g., "heroic moment," "heroic narrative," "the hero treatment") to distinguish between heroes or veterans who personally commit some act of valor, and "heroes," a word recently diluted in colloquial usage to mean "any veteran." I will provide examples of authentic heroes: Medal of Honor recipients. Their experiences show that there are two types of heroes in war: the *sacrificing hero* who gives of themselves to save others, and the *attacking hero* who displays valor offensively. Among post-9/11 veterans there is a third type of hero: the *enduring hero*, or a veteran who is treated as a "hero" simply for serving honorably. This "hero" stereotype achieves silence among former service members by harnessing feelings of inadequacy among those who have not personally performed some act of valor.

Altruism often precedes and informs the recruit's decision to join the military. For many, the decision to enlist or accept a commission is an automatic qualifier for "hero" status. However, altruism does not equate to heroism, at least not in all cases, and stereotyping all veterans as "heroes" does little to improve public perceptions of veterans. In fact, labeling all veterans "heroes" devalues military service, replacing genuine reverence with a wink and a nod, appropriating honorable service so that it might be understood more generally, generically, and with little care for the individual veteran's accomplishments or values.

Authentic heroism is a rare confluence of chance and ability. It is a thing that happens, an opportunity seized. It is one individual's display of courage in the real world. Heroism is not a story. But there are many "heroes" who serve as characters in our nation's patriotic narrative. Mostly, military heroism exists in the minds of nonveterans as an abstraction, a product of superficial patriotic discourse, a mass application of the titles "Our Nation's Heroes" or "Our Brave Young Men and Women in Uniform." These abstractions are packaged and sold by recruiters, politicians, and history books to young people seeking social status, respect, or merely an escape from a tumultuous upbringing or an unpromising future.

The Pursuit of Heroism

Joining the military is no easy task. If fortunate enough to meet the physical, mental, and educational requirements, a recruit can expect drug tests, criminal background checks, as well as regular appointments and exams leading up to the day they ship off to basic training. Failure to maintain these standards—even *prior* to military service—can lead to setbacks or changes to a recruit's contract. This newfound responsibility accompanies an overwhelming sense of awe. For teenagers especially, the military ushers in a new chapter in their lives, one in which the boundaries of the world extend beyond the walls of high school classrooms, and self-actualization is just a matter of time.

Suddenly, a college education seems attainable. Distant lands seem reachable. Recruits are told that they will have everything they need to succeed in their new lives: training and education, pay and benefits, camaraderie, and a chance to prove themselves. Even better, the skills and experience earned in uniform translate to the "civilian sector," should they choose not to make a career of the military. Twenty years. Four years. One weekend a month and two weeks a year. "The length of service does not matter," recruiters tell young listeners. "It is *the courage to serve* which sets you apart from your peers."

If it is courage that drives young people to service, then it is *blind* courage. Most young adults view "the military" as a *single* entity, or as a *single* transformative experience. They fail to realize that soldiers, sailors, airmen, and marines lead very different lives. Each branch of service has its own language, history, and values. I teach these topics in my Veterans Studies courses at Eastern Kentucky University because veterans tend to be understood monolithically. The day-to-day grind of the drone pilot could not be more different than that of the grunt patrolling the mountains of Afghanistan. At the same time, exposure to fellow soldiers from diverse cultures and with intersectional identities is among the most valuable experiences a recruit can expect to receive in uniform. Each veteran's individuality matters.

Recruits, who begin as civilians, aren't fully aware of what military service entails. For example, I struggled to grasp the difference between enlisted soldiers and officers. At eighteen, while digging a hole or performing some other menial task, I perceived officers as a group of well-groomed twenty-somethings who held a considerable amount of power for no other reason than because they possessed college degrees. I called them "Sir" or "Ma'am," ever aware of the likeness these practices shared with antiquated notions of gentility. I remained silent because the mission was more important, but also because I had no choice. Unlike rank or title in a civilian job, military rank gives individuals the power to punish soldiers mentally and physically, through embarrassing, demeaning forms of hazing known as "corrective training." Usually, it wasn't the officers themselves who oversaw these punishments. Rather, the responsibility fell on the shoulders of senior enlisted troops. In that way, the military hierarchy displaces the resentment inspired by hazing by making the perpetrator "one of your own." Of course, many veterans will laugh and question my loyalty just for saying these things. We all volunteered. And there were ways to report abuse, but not without incurring social and professional exclusion.

As someone who grew up in a Kentucky "holler" entrenched in antiauthoritarian sentiments, it wasn't easy to submit to such power or understand why the highest-ranking enlisted person yielded authority to the lowest-ranking commissioned officer. Over time, it became clear that commissioned officers were responsible for executing the orders of the president, whereas enlisted leaders were responsible for the care and training of those soldiers tasked with carrying out officers' orders. Enlisted troops filled sandbags, repaired vehicles, and burned feces. In fact, I did a lot of the latter because of my constant (yet sincere) questioning of the system. High-ranking officers, on the other hand, did paperwork, attended briefings, and gave orders. Junior officers existed somewhere in between, learning how the army worked from noncommissioned officers so that they could someday be effective leaders in tune with the needs and capabilities of their troops.

The scenario I am describing certainly isn't universal, but I never lost sight of the fact that a college degree, privilege preceding military service, and socioeconomic class were often the things that separated enlisted troops and officers, at least initially. Given these conditions, it came as no surprise when my younger brother, Josh, asked if he could simply "sign up" to become an officer and a pilot in the navy.

"You'll never be Tom Cruise," I told him. "You'll be Goose."

Little Brothers, Ghosts, and Top Guns

Tom Cruise and Goose, an actor and a character, respectively, are of course featured in Tony Scott's 1986 blockbuster, *Top Gun.*[3] Tom Cruise is the "hero," and Goose, played by Anthony Edwards, dies a tragic death. My joke—my attempt to confront Josh with an uncomfortable truth so that he would laugh rather than take offense—was this: You *think* you're going to become a *hero*, but you're more likely to end up *dead* and no one is going to remember your name. Crass, I know. True, too many veterans know. I wanted to make sure my younger brother was aware of *all* the potential outcomes that can arise as a result of military service, including less savory ones. Josh wanted to escape poverty and get an education without accruing tens of thousands of dollars in debt. He wanted to see the world. Mostly, I think he wanted to become a "man." Why wouldn't he want to be an officer? Why wouldn't he want to be Tom Cruise in *Top Gun?*

Top Gun illustrates many common tropes in both veteran literature and veterans' experiences. The film also stars Val Kilmer, Tim Robbins, and Kelly McGillis. It is the story of "Maverick" (Cruise), a daring American fighter pilot whose mettle is first tested by MiG fighter jets in the Indian Ocean. Maverick's cockiness quickly catches up with him. After the incident with the MiGs leads to the resignation of one of his peers, Maverick is sent to Top Gun, the Navy Fighter Weapons School, for advanced training. Maverick's mystique as a boyish (sometimes shirtless) wunderkind follows him to Top Gun. There, he forms a rivalry with "The Iceman" (Val Kilmer), learning the value of a "wingman" and relying on others for survival.

Top Gun continues in the tradition of films that first featured war pilots. In the twentieth century, films such as *Wings* (1927)[4] and *The Right Stuff* (1983)[5] presented the valor of combat without the muck and interpersonal gore commonly attributed to war. Linda R. Robertson's *The Dream of Civilized Warfare* (2003) explores the iconography of World War I aerial combat.[6] The author explains that imagery of the combat pilot contrasted "the carnage and stalemate of ground war."[7] Robertson suggests aerial combat revived notions of chivalric combat and the belief that heroism could be achieved by all ranks of society. This illusion of chivalry had been shattered through the mechanization of war that occurred in the nineteenth and twentieth centuries. Any hero daring to charge enemy lines and "win the day" would simply be mowed down by a machine gun. The promise of a chance at glory inspires youths to go to war. The invention of aerial combat restored that promise.

Kevin L. Ferguson claims that movies about military pilots send a "contradictory" message, one that presents wartime service as part of an "ideological narrative" that holds war as "thrilling" and, at times, "comedic."[8] The danger of death is downplayed by appealing to young viewers who believe proximity to death brings them closer to perceived notions of military masculinity. In other words, aerial combat is still a dangerous, deadly affair. But at least there's a chance of survival.

In the early days of the Iraq and Afghanistan wars, children saw patterns throughout mass media of veterans becoming men through brushes with death. For example, the popular music video for "The Ghost of You," a song written and performed by the band My Chemical Romance in 2004, begins with the band's performance at a military "send-off" event. Nothing in the lyrics indicates that the song is about war. In the video, however, the men are clad in World War II-era dress uniforms, the young women wear their finest dresses, and the age-old story of "loss of innocence" is told through lyrics and imagery depicting a group of friends traumatized by war. In the scenes that follow, some of these friends are lost to extreme violence in the invasion of Normandy.[9]

The soldiers depicted in the video could just as easily have been dressed in desert fatigues. The send-off party at the beginning connotes a sense of dread because, collectively, society has not forgotten the bloody sacrifices that took place in World War II. American fans of My Chemical Romance were feeling the effects of the war at home at about the time they heard "The Ghost of You." Civilians began to dread the possible outcomes of the Iraq and Afghanistan wars as their brothers, sisters, mothers, and fathers were whisked away to foreign lands in increasing numbers. The song's radio release was in 2005. By then, the Afghanistan War had been raging for three years, and the start of the Iraq War preceded the video version of "The Ghost of You" by about three years. The combined number of troops with "boots on the ground" in Afghanistan and Iraq rose from 5,200 in 2002 to a peak of 187,900 in 2008. With little knowledge of what was taking place, family members of deployed soldiers were caught in a continual state of fear and apprehension, as news from the front lines featured violent imagery of improvised explosive devices and an ever-increasing body count scrolling across the bottom of the screen. At the same time, this violence was sanitized and made suitable for public television, such that the "horrors of war" were limited only by the viewer's imagination.

"The Ghost of You" captures those worst fears. In the battle scenes, the band members play the roles of soldiers. One scene depicts the death of the band's bassist, Mikey Way, as the lead vocalist, Gerard Way (Mikey's brother in real life), attempts to save him. Mikey dies, and later, at a bar, Gerard laments the loss of his brother as he grows more intoxicated and more unstable with each painfully delivered lyric. The characters in the video do not find glory. Instead, they find death and a compulsion to stay ahead of memories of their wartime service. The video begins with members of the band saying goodbye to their sweethearts. Later, as scenes of war coincide with the lyrics about never returning home and outrunning ghosts, the illusion of military heroism fades, giving way to war trauma and regret: lost friends, lost loves, lost innocence.[10] Ironically, the music video addresses the "old Lie" written about in Wilfred Owen's Great War poem "Dulce et Decorum Est."

Owen, one of the "Great War poets" of World War I, describes the horrors of a gas attack and tossing the bodies of fallen comrades into the back of a wagon. The speaker admonishes the reader:

> If you could hear, at every jolt, the blood
> Come gargling from the froth-corrupted lungs,
> Obscene as cancer, bitter as the cud
> Of vile, incurable sores on innocent tongues,—
> My friend, you would not tell with such high zest
> To children ardent for some desperate glory,
> The old Lie: *Dulce et decorum est*
> *Pro patria mori.*[11]

The last lines translate as, "It is sweet and proper to die for one's country." Owen challenges the notion that the *action* of dying for one's country *because* it is sweet and proper imbues the act with meaning. Instead, the poem suggests, death perpetuates war, and the reason for war becomes war itself. The My Chemical Romance video engages with the "old Lie" by presenting war as a way to escape, to achieve "desperate glory," elicit sympathy, or gain respect. However, it turns that story on its head, ending with a traumatized veteran at a bar, drowning his anger and grief, and perhaps hoping for sympathy. The lyrics indicate that the speaker must stay one step ahead of war trauma, but also one step ahead of the past that precedes his wartime service—the past he shared with his brother. If these ghosts catch him, the singer is not sure he can survive it.

"The Ghost of You," at least in my reading, is not prowar. If anything, it presents war as an experience that forever scars its participants. But so does every literary and film example I examine in this book. These representations of war are encountered by American youths *prior* to enlisting. Oddly, they're enticing because they equate heroism with suffering. No doubt, some recruits had lyrics about escape or dying in heroic ways in their minds even as their recruiters drove them to processing stations. My Chemical Romance's album containing "The Ghost of You," *Three Cheers for Sweet Revenge*, sold over 1 million copies in the United States. Despite the promise of trauma and beyond promises of heroism, war manages to sell itself as a way of staying ahead of the "ghosts" haunting recruits *before* they enlist.

The same attraction to danger appears in *Top Gun.* Maverick seeks out danger, finds it, and struggles to remain true to himself while living in the aftermath.[12] Ferguson explains how aviation cinema presents combatants in a space between gallantry and the horrors of trench warfare: "The airplane is an ungrounded space of transformation; it is always a different plane that lands, a different passenger who disembarks."[13] While Ferguson focuses on aviation cinema—films about planes and pilots, not necessarily military ones, the themes presented by the author correspond with the sorts of "transformation" sought by military recruits. Movies such as *Top Gun* are a particular subset of war cinema, one which provides examples of the "rites of passage" offered to recruits, but in a way that suggests that pilots, unlike their comrades on the ground, can emerge from such a transformation unscathed. Of course, examples of pilots shot down and captured like John McCain and Fred Cherry easily undermine this myth.

Ferguson recognizes *Top Gun* as the "most famous" example of aviation cinema, and although it came out shortly after my birth and more than a decade before my brother's birth, it has clearly positioned itself symbolically in American culture alongside music videos such as "The Ghost of You." These examples present war as a form of escape, a way of transcending a society that young adults perceive as limiting.[14] Innocence is exchanged for emotional capital, sometimes in the form of wartime trauma, that grants survivors the agency needed to escape circumstances ranging from childhood abuse to unrequited love, socioeconomic disadvantage, or simple teenage angst. "If you're lucky enough to encounter death and survive it," the myth goes, "you'll return home with status and respect unavailable to you in your present form." Children listen to these songs before war, during it, and after. But the lyrics shift in meaning over time.

Agency, Illusions, and "Letting Go"

Both *Top Gun* and Tom Cruise's "Maverick" are illusions. Amy Nicholson explains, "*Top Gun* gets dismissed as a popcorn blockbuster about a pompous son-of-a-bitch. That's wrong—and worse, that's exactly the movie Cruise worked so hard not to make. We remember the highlights—the volleyball, the thumbs-up, the bitchin' Kenny Loggins soundtrack—but the real movie is darker and more complicated."[15] During his training at the US Navy's Fighter Weapons School in Miramar, California, Maverick tries to win a school contest. In one scene, Maverick's fighter jet gets too close to that of his rival, Iceman, and as a result Maverick loses control, crashing into the ocean. Maverick escapes. His radar intercept officer (RIO), Goose, crashes into the canopy of the aircraft after activating his emergency ejection system and dies; his lifeless body parachutes slowly to the water below. The scene ends with Maverick, floating in the ocean, holding onto his friend's body as a helicopter rescue crewman says, "You've got to let him go, sir."[16]

Much of the remaining film is about Maverick "letting go." Later, he and Charlotte Blackwood (Kelly McGillis), his aviation instructor turned lover, sit in a car, reminiscing. Maverick says, "I think maybe it was my fault. I don't know what the hell went wrong." Charlotte offers to help, but Maverick walks away, and in the next scene he confides in Goose's widow, Carole (Meg Ryan). Carole tries to encourage Maverick by assuaging some of his guilt: "He'd have flown anyway, without you. He would have hated it. But he would have done it." Subsequently, Maverick is assigned to the USS *Enterprise.* Along with Iceman and his new RIO, "Merlin" (Tim Robbins), the characters move from simulations to actual combat operations.[17]

Indeed, the internal conflict in *Top Gun* is complex. Nicholson explains that "Maverick's dad, a pilot himself, disappeared in Vietnam and now the son must restore the family's pride. That's the key to the whole film: Maverick is insecure. He's not a cocky asshole—he's just pretending to be one."[18] First, Maverick is compelled to reclaim his family's name, and this compulsion results in reckless flying and, at least in Maverick's mind, Goose's death. Cruise's character faces the choice of giving up on his dream or pushing forward despite his grief.

In combat, the trauma of Goose's death recreates itself when Maverick gets caught in the exhaust of an enemy jet. Maverick flashes back to Goose's death, which in turn forces him to briefly retreat from battle. The climax of the story involves Maverick overcoming his shame, guilt, and fear. When he returns to battle alongside Iceman, they destroy several MiG fighter planes and force the remaining aircraft to retreat. In the end, Maverick overcomes his past, becomes a flight instructor, and at the end of the film throws Goose's dog tags into the ocean, signifying that he has found peace.

Like many others, my younger brother, Josh, wanted to be a fighter pilot. And the most popular example of a fighter pilot available to him before his enlistment was Tom Cruise's Maverick. However, as Nicholson shows, Josh's perception of veteran fighter pilots was based on an illusion, one carefully constructed to produce a character who masks shame and guilt with bravado and cockiness.[19] As a result, Maverick ignores the reality of war to his own detriment and to the detriment of those with whom he serves. Iceman says as much in one scene, "You're everyone's problem. That's because every time you go up in the air, you're unsafe. I don't like you because you're dangerous."[20] So, when I made my joke, "You'll never be Tom Cruise. You'll be Goose," I was fully aware of the irony of the situation: A potential recruit—my brother—wanted to be a fighter pilot, even when his conception of fighter pilots was based on "romantic" notions of aerial combat and a movie that is really about an insecure, irresponsible kid trying desperately to prove himself as a man.

Patchwork Masculinity

Perhaps it wasn't the allure of combat that Josh found so attractive. Maybe because of the options available to him, the military was the best "rite of passage" he could find. Maybe he listened to songs like "The Ghost of You" and concluded that the risks inherent in war, including death, were preferable to his life as a recent high school graduate in a socioeconomically depressed area.[21] Teens fed elaborate fictions about military service as children bring many assumptions with them to the recruiter's office. Many of their fantasies disappear as they weigh the harsh realities of basic training and wartime service against the many benefits promised by recruiters. For others, the opposite is true: the exhilaration and camaraderie found in combat are the most enticing enlistment incentives of all. Combat is the surest way to become a "hero," and becoming a "hero" is the surest way to become a "man."

I remember talking to my friend Scott about these issues while we were in Iraq. We spent days at a time occupying the same vehicle—me as the gunner, Scott as the driver. One day I told him, "Most of my high school friends are now drug addicts or criminals. At least if we die here they'll remember us as 'heroes.' No one back home gives a shit if people like us die otherwise." This conversation took place not long after my older brother back home died by suicide. Josh, who was less than ten years old at the time, had to endure this loss up close and personal while I was off in some remote desert. I was feeling pretty cynical when I made my comment in that Humvee. But I still agree with the assessment.

War gave soldiers like us a way of staying ahead of the ghosts that *preceded* our decision to enlist. It gave us a feeling of self-worth after society wrote us off as losers, delinquents, future addicts, or statistics. My little brother saw my emotional and physical distance as a form of privilege. But he didn't know (and neither did I) that my identity was largely a social construct. G. Thomas Couser describes "the self" as a "quilt patched together," the "product of internal autobiography."[22] Social constructionists claim self and identity are social projects that are never really fragmented; they appear that way only because of the shortcomings of autobiographical narratives. Veterans' narratives are personal, but they are also defined by their intersectional identities—race, gender, age, socioeconomic status, ability. Viewing identity as a system in which individuals are subjected to alternating forms of privilege and oppression is an approach rooted in gender and cultural theory. Veterans are forever patching together a quilt, weaving veteran identity into a larger set of social identities so that they might accurately perform the version of themselves that grants them agency. Naturally, my brother, with whom I share many social categorizations and experiences, would pick up keenly on how military service set us apart.

I do not intend to go into details about our brother's death, other than to say that there were things that could have been avoided had we come from a family with access to more privilege. Regardless, Josh did not begin an internal debate about intersectionality and privilege when he died. He'd never heard the words. Instead, he unconsciously began to compare my situation to his own. He began to believe in the patriotic rhetoric that paints veterans as exceptional examples. Indeed, it was likely my own impression management—my willingness to conform to society's unspoken script—that convinced Josh of the value of military service. At some point, Josh decided that he would join the military like his brother. He would become a "military man." He would find a way to either let go or stay one step ahead of the ghosts from his past. It was a perfectly valid decision. In fact, I drove him to the recruiter's office.

The Military Man

The pinnacle of *military* masculinity—the identity that confers the most agency and the most power—is the "hero." Military heroes represent a model of masculinity almost as old as violence itself. In *From Chivalry to Terrorism* (2003), Leo Braudy argues that a fundamental difference, historically, in the lives of men and women has been male freedom to "escape from (or to express) biology, often in elaborate rituals of competition—for women, for possessions, for position."[23] As Ferguson's research suggests, Tom Cruise wanted to make *Top Gun* "more about competition than war."[24] However, war encompasses competition, makes it violent, and leaves few survivors feeling like winners. Any portrayal of war that describes it as a "competition" is misleading. To kill others or to die during war are just two forms of loss.

Not surprisingly, the military "hero" is an identity that is at war with itself. Victoria L. Bromley lists some characteristics of hypermasculinity associated with military service: "aggressive, physically strong, dominant, authoritative, independent, detached, rational, objective, reasonable, and sexually proficient. . . . Boys and men learn to conform to these stereotypical ideals."[25] Not all of these descriptors are pejoratives. They are traits that grant their performers access to power, to a place where they fit within a patriarchal society. They are different ways of looking at a single veteran, suggesting that the benefits outweigh the consequences of military service, positing military masculinity as something that cannot be achieved without dying first, or encountering death and overcoming it through masculine mettle.

One example of how military masculinity transforms civilian identity occurs in the ways in which Braudy's "rituals" are becoming more inclusive. If anything, twenty-first-century warfare and the increasing presence of women and nonbinary individuals on the front lines only reinforce the separation between sex and gender. Jack Halberstam, whose *Female Masculinity* (1998) articulates an impressive number of alternative gender roles, warns readers against reducing masculinity "to the male body and its effects."[26] Nor do the claims made about military masculinity in this chapter apply only to men. The proliferation of "versions of masculinity that we enjoy and trust," specifically, the "heroic masculinities" sold to recruits, "depend[s] absolutely on the subordination of alternative masculinities."[27]

Brenda M. Boyle explores the gender-based performances of veterans in *Blackhawk Down* (2001) and *Rescue Dawn* (2006): "The captivity and rescue trope reveals how the urgency to perform masculinity ironically can result in the performance of femininity, it clarifies the precarious and mutable nature of masculinity even under war conditions."[28] Again, war is held as a source of agency. Experiencing war violence is one way to achieve the status of "military hero." However, the difference between a POW and someone who single-handedly takes an enemy trench is the difference between surviving and perpetrating violence.

Of course, the military privileges one form of military masculinity above all others: the hero. To leave the military as anything less than a hero connotes inferiority. Veterans' feelings of inferiority are reinforced when authentic communication is replaced with well-meaning patriotic gestures. After all, inferior versions of military masculinity have no place among the superior examples of veteran identity portrayed in patriotic rhetoric. Non-heroes are not the characters found in unspoken performances; they're not the goal of veterans' attempts at impression management. Indeed, veteran identity exists in a peculiar hierarchy created and maintained in both civilian and veteran communities, one in which the content of the veteran's character corresponds to their proximity to death—to killing or dying.

Veteran identity is a historically informed label that institutionalizes war violence as a means by which certain—usually socioeconomically disadvantaged—youths might attain agency through brushes with death. An extreme example occurs in the stories of former slaves who fought for the Union army in the American Civil War. In *Standing Soldiers, Kneeling Slaves* (1997) Kirk Savage explains, "To be a soldier in battle was the ultimate test of manhood, because men battled men and battled to the death. For the male slave the test was even more profound since his masculinity had been denied from the outset."[29] Of course, economic disadvantages do not equate to the experience of slavery. It is an entirely different thing to be viewed as property than to be viewed as a failed member of a capitalist society. However, war, its horrors, and the pursuit of agency through feats of heroism are present in both examples.

On one hand, "heroism" is imbued with high notions such as honor and courage. On the other hand, it is intertwined with violence and victimization. Because one qualifier of "hero" status is proximity to death, it should come as no surprise that veteran identity is intrinsically woven into public narratives about PTSD. Annessa Stagner argues that during and after World War I, shell shock was characterized as a short-term illness. Stagner explains that because women were essential to male recovery, the emergence of shell shock further "delineated male and female gender roles, and advanced often unrealistic social and cultural expectations for both men and women."[30] In this scenario, veterans' wounds are appropriated to maintain established gender roles. "Heroes" with wounds are able to exist as such, but only because their wounds serve a purpose.

Stagner believes that early treatments for shell shock "symbolized optimism not just about the recovery of the soldier, but the recovery of masculinity, of scientific certainty, and ultimately the recovery of the nation."[31] However, this view of shell shock—what we now call PTSD—ignores the longevity of the condition. It does little to comfort warfighters who struggle decades after their wars end. In fact, it alienates them.

Within a matter of weeks, Maverick loses his best friend, graduates from Top Gun, and returns to the Indian Ocean to become a hero. He has not processed his trauma. And in *Top Gun*, young viewers are led to believe Maverick's trauma is so easily curable that it can be solved by throwing a pair of dog tags into the ocean. Charlotte and Carole—the women characters in *Top Gun*—are essential to Maverick's recovery. And Maverick begins his journey with the unrealistic cultural expectation that he has to restore his family's name.[32] In many ways, the scene in "The Ghost of You" in which the lead singer laments the death of his brother at a bar is a more accurate portrayal of military service than what *Top Gun* presents.[33] In *Top Gun*'s bar scene, which takes place *before* Goose's death, the pilots are immaculately dressed in white uniforms, singing "You've Lost That Loving Feeling" to Maverick's love interest. They're not haunted by trauma because they have not yet experienced it.[34] The two bar scenes depict the different perceptions of veterans outlined in this book's introduction: one is about a perpetually broken veteran; the other is about a veteran put on a pedestal. Both are fictions, so potential recruits feel as though they have a *choice.* Surviving war without some sort of physical or psychological wound is rarely a matter of choice.

Halberstam believes "heroes" claim a "'dominant masculinity' [that] appears to be a naturalized relation between maleness and power."[35] Indeed, becoming a "hero" is the most straightforward path to becoming a "man"; at least, that's the belief driving teenagers to join. However, as women and nonbinary individuals have shown in their desire to participate in every facet of military service, becoming a "military man" has less to do with *maleness* than it does with *agency.* We're not as far removed from Braudy's "elaborate rituals of competition" as we would like to think.[36] If anything, contemporary branding of the "hero"—by a media in need of ratings, a government in need of warriors, and a military desperate to prove that not all recruits come home mangled or in body bags—has made masculine ritual *more* compelling and masculine competition *more* rewarding.

Instead of a competition, war should be viewed as a methodical extermination of human life meant to achieve political aims. This unfortunate truth is where a patriotic narrative emerges, once again, as a tool used to mediate veteran testimony as well as civilian perceptions of veterans and their wounds. Calling all veterans "heroes" marginalizes those veterans whose experiences run counter to public conceptions of military masculinity. Alternative narratives of wartime experience that accentuate death and carnage are devalued as inferior. Veterans conform to this script through impression management, or they risk giving up the authority given to them along with the "hero" stereotype. What these veterans fail to realize is that living their life in service of that stereotypical role limits their continued growth as civilians.

Ambivalence

I edited more than five hundred works of veteran prose, poetry, artwork, and scholarship as editor-in-chief of Military Experience & the Arts. My philosophy, which I am expanding on here, held that we could harness patriotic rhetoric and false perceptions of veterans long enough to get the attention of civilians. Once they were willing to listen, we yanked down the curtain, exposing our readers to uncensored, often graphic representations of war that our editorial board felt was a closer approximation of the real thing. Ironically, we never felt it was gore and violence that was missing from popular representations of war. It was humanity that had gone missing in action. We provided a platform from which veterans could share alternative worldviews. Our storytellers transformed themselves from silent stereotypes into educators, destabilizing the symbolic function of the veteran and claiming their own version of veteran identity.

Brian Mockenhaupt, a former infantryman and combat correspondent who serves as the nonfiction editor for Military Experience & the Arts, writes about the exhilaration of combat in "I Miss Iraq. I Miss My Gun. I Miss My War," published in *Esquire* in 2007:

> I've been home from Iraq for more than a year, long enough for my time there to become a memory best forgotten for those who worried every day that I was gone. I could see their relief when I returned. Life could continue, with futures not so uncertain. But in quiet moments, their relief brought me guilt. Maybe they assume I was as overjoyed to be home as they were to have me home. Maybe they assume if I could do it over, I never would have gone. And maybe I wouldn't have. But I miss

> Iraq. I miss the war. I miss war. And I have a very hard time understanding why.[37]

Mockenhaupt's ambivalence toward military service is plainly stated: he loathes war; he misses war. And he doesn't know how these two feelings can coexist. Perhaps Mockenhaupt's reflections are a product of the emphasis placed on mental health in the twenty-first century. More likely, he's exploring the very same antiwar sentiments expressed by war authors and veterans throughout this book. He continues, "[W]ar twists and shifts the landmarks by which we navigate our lives, casting light on darkened areas that for many people remain forever unexplored. And once those darkened spaces are lit, they become part of us."[38] Specifically, Mockenhaupt refers to violence, to owning power unavailable to him as a civilian.

War changes those who experience it, Mockenhaupt claims, exposing once-innocent recruits to inhumanity—to the innate inhumanity residing within us all. Mockenhaupt recognizes how war recreates itself with each generation: "That men are drawn to war is no surprise. How old are boys before they turn a finger and thumb into a pistol? Long before they love girls, they love war, at least everything they imagine war to be: guns and explosions and manliness and courage."[39] In many ways, military service is a disavowal of childhood. It is a source of upward mobility. But many recruits, like Maverick in *Top Gun*, use military service to do battle with inner demons. My brother, *Top Gun*, and Mockenhaupt all show that veteran identity begins forming in childhood. It is something recruits seek to cultivate purposefully, unaware of the true nature of war or the changes it will cause inside of them.

Mockenhaupt describes himself as being caught between two poles, expressing the shame he feels on realizing that he misses war:

> For those who know, this is the open secret: War is exciting. Sometimes I was in awe of this, and sometimes I felt low and mean for loving it, but I loved it still. Even in its quiet moments, war is brighter, louder, brasher, more fun, more tragic, more wasteful. More. More of everything. And even then I knew I would someday miss it, this life so strange. Today the war has distilled to moments and feelings, and somewhere in these memories is the reason for the wistfulness.[40]

After war, he reflects on the friends and colleagues he lost, concluding, "I felt disgusted with myself for missing the war and wondered if I was alone in this . . . I don't think I am."[41] Perhaps the excitement of war is something only a child can experience. Perhaps the growth promised to those who agree to fight wars is something that exists in the moment just prior to realizing the value of human life and how quickly it can be extinguished. Wartime experience, then, paradoxically results in forms of trauma that young recruits can comprehend only *belatedly.*

In *Unclaimed Experience: Trauma, Narrative, and History* (1996), Cathy Caruth explains, "Trauma . . . is always the story of a wound that cries out, that addresses us in the attempt to tell us of a reality or truth that is not otherwise available. This truth, in its delayed appearance and its belated address, cannot be linked only to what is known, but also to what remains unknown in our very actions and our language."[42] Caruth's view of trauma is that it is an experience that cannot be fully understood in the moment it occurs. Instead, parts (if not all) of the traumatic experience are repressed. I'm not referring only to chronological memory, but also to the emotional experience, to fear, shame, and guilt. Rather than experiencing all of these things at once, and especially because of the psychological conditioning received by soldiers, many returning veterans feel the experience of combat *over time.* It can be found in the symptoms of PTSD. It can be found in the types of veteran characters they perform. Overcoming survivor's guilt and moral injury is not as simple for veterans like Mockenhaupt; he can't just throw a buddy's dog tags into the ocean like a hero in an action film.

Military masculinity, as a gender-based performance, exists on a scale in which privilege corresponds with maleness and oppression corresponds with femininity. As a form of oppression, trauma connotes femininity—weakness. So, veterans' attempts at impression management involve hiding the invisible wounds of war in order to avoid the sense that others view them as weak. Importantly, in the next chapter's discussion of "wounded warriors" I will argue that another reason to hide war's invisible wounds is to elicit sympathy by allowing those wounds to be limited only by the civilian imagination for what horrors occur during war. They conform to the civilian assumption that all veterans are psychologically damaged. The "hero" and "wounded warrior" stereotypes are two sides of the same coin, one designed to silence veteran testimony.

Braudy refers to "heroism" as part of a "masculine myth" corrupted by nationalism. He describes governments wise to the needs of masculinity and their efforts to redirect its competitive urges into violence, which then reshapes societies and political landscapes. "[W]ar," Braudy claims, "is a purifying crucible that melts away the false and corrupt manners of a bourgeois society to display the basic masculine mettle beneath the dross."[43] This assessment insinuates that there is a truer, more essential identity available to men that cannot be explored outside of war's context. It reflects the desires of recruits seeking agency, but also a desire to achieve a form of "manhood" that is superior to the gender-based performances of civilians. Cyclically, war relies on masculinity for its violent energies, and masculinity relies on war for its purifying effects.

The Army Values

The army requires its recruits to memorize and live "The Army Values." Loyalty, Duty, Respect, Selfless-Service, Honor, Integrity, and Personal Courage form the acronym "LDRSHIP."[44] As "leaders of men," soldiers learn and carry such high ideals with them into battle. The soldier's actions, if honorable, reflect their commitment to "The Army Values." Dishonor is synonymous with cowardice, with not having the courage to overcome one's fear when the moment of truth arises. I remember worrying about how I would react when faced with combat during the initial months of my first deployment. How does a person know if they are a coward until tried in combat?

"War and war leaders," Braudy argues, "had always been crucial factors in the history of public celebrity, with its Roman bias toward rooting personal honor in military and political action."[45] Later, when these "war leaders" wrote histories of their wars, they imbued the narratives with "positive warrior traits—honor, integrity, self-sacrifice, camaraderie, openness . . . while purging negative ones."[46] Obviously, these "positive warrior traits" are still present in military cultures, with "The Army Values" cited above being one example. Leaders wrote histories of war that bestowed intangible rewards like honor, integrity, or glory on those who survived. Dead men tell no tales. Our histories—or, more accurately, our carefully constructed myths—are written by those who survived and those who could write, both forms of privilege.

Anthony Swofford, a Gulf War veteran and the author of *Jarhead* (2003), writes of a "moral high ground" when discussing his role in a combat arms unit. He suggests that there is something superior about the combat arms soldier, something more "heroic" about perpetrating violence.[47] A Harvard University study conducted in 2005 entitled "Ninety Percent of U.S. Wounded Survive: In Iraq, Firepower Increases, Deaths Decrease" found that "Better, faster medical care has reduced deaths from the more than 10,000 war injuries in Iraq and Afghanistan to the lowest percentage of any war in American history. In World War II, 30 percent of US soldiers died from wounds received in combat; in Vietnam, 24 percent of the wounded died. In Iraq and Afghanistan, despite the horrific increase in the destructibility of weapons, mortality has dropped to 10 percent."[48] Swofford's "moral high ground" has gained in prestige due to the relative scarcity of death. It is possible among post-9/11 veterans to inch ever closer to the precipice of death that confers manhood and live to tell the tale.

Generation after generation, veterans write about the horror and the futility of war to no avail. And while popular cinema perpetuates violent war narratives as rites of passage, there are plenty of examples that run contrary to this trend. For example, in *All Quiet on the Western Front* (1930), the protagonist, Paul, walks down streets featured in the opening scenes of the film, streets that appear deserted in the absence of soldiers marching happily off to the First World War. He sees the schoolroom window he looked out of as a child, hearing the same nationalist rhetoric falling on the ears of the newest crop of students. Paul stops. There's no mistaking it: the look on his face is one of anger and conviction. To emphasize this point, the camera pans left as Paul exits the scene to the right.[49] By moving the focus upon the classroom, the subject becomes the children and their instructor. Paul's anger drives him in their direction, but they sit unaware that he is storming toward them, that their worldview is about to be challenged.

The teacher continues his speech and Paul enters the room. The instructor says, "You must speak to them. You must tell them what it means to serve your fatherland." Paul holds back his anger. He looks on the students with pity. He doesn't know if he should expose his true feelings. He doesn't know if he should engage in impression management and conform to the script. He says, "I can't tell you anything you don't know. We live in the trenches out there. We fight. We try not to be killed. Sometimes we are. That's all." Since this description is devoid of propaganda, the teacher attempts to get more out of Paul. Once again, the pressure builds until the war veteran bursts with conviction. Paul turns toward the teacher and exclaims:

> I've been there! I know what it's like. . . . You still think it's beautiful and sweet to die for your country don't you? Well, we used to think you knew. The first bombardment taught us better. It's dirty and painful to die for your country. When it comes to dying for your country, it's better not to die at all. There are millions out there dying for their countries and what good is it?

The words "beautiful and sweet" are a reference to Owen's poem, one which references the *Odes* of Horace ironically. The children become audibly concerned at this point; one calls him a coward. Paul replies that it is much easier to say "go and die" than to "watch it happen," exiting the room, claiming he will go back to the front "tomorrow" because "he can't stand it" in his hometown.[50] Despite his disdain for war and his belief in its futility, Paul prefers life in the trenches to having to conform to someone else's script.

Because of his imminent death, Paul speaks from the vantage of a ghost, representing all of those who died in the First World War. As a ghost, his proximity to death and combat cannot be questioned. After all, it is proximity to death that transforms service members into "heroes." This vantage enables Paul to break down barriers to the narrative-making process: accusations of cowardice, stigma, and other resistances. Paul lays claim to the symbolic authority granted to him by military service. He does not have to prove himself through impression management, or by overcoming the symptoms of shell shock so as to appear more resilient. He channels the voice of those who perished, encouraging those who will listen to learn from those who survived. In place of gallantry, power, and agency, World War I was only death (millions dead on both sides), the mechanization of death (technology replaces battlefield prowess), and new ways of experiencing death (poison gas, barbed wire, and tracer rounds, to name a few), which robbed the individual soldier of the ability to achieve heroic status.

And for the disillusioned veterans who returned home, as well as for the civilians who interacted with them, cared for them, and tried to understand their wounds, war began to lose the appeal it held in Ancient Rome: "The old catchwords—freedom, dignity, justice—simply rang hollow. Even arguments relating to what had been averted by the war, as opposed to what had been achieved, offered little sustenance in relation to the sacrifice. Best not to ask such questions. Commemorate, yes; think, no."[51] This description from Modris Eksteins's *Rites of Spring: The Great War and the Birth of the Modern Age* (2000) is markedly different from Braudy's description of warfare in ancient Greece. Specifically, war is less "a purifying crucible" than a carefully orchestrated scam, a cull perpetrated against the poor and disenfranchised.[52] And so Eksteins describes a common refrain, a society that glorifies war despite a lack of veterans willing to attest to the glory that can be found there. In the end, there's but one way to keep the war industry booming: call *all* veterans "heroes," thank them for "their service," and ensure their continued silence.

Ironically, Lew Ayres, the actor who portrays Paul in *All Quiet on the Western Front*, a character distinguished by his innate sensitivity and abhorrence of war, became a notable antiwar figure after appearing in the film. Lesley L. Coffin's *Lew Ayres: Hollywood's Conscientious Objector* (2012) references newspapers circulated around the start of World War II, which claimed "that it was the experience of making this film that led [Ayres] to oppose all forms of violence and particularly war."[53] After serving in a labor camp, Ayres spent three and a half years as a noncombatant in the Medical Corps. He became a chaplain's assistant, "a jack of all trades, and available to the men to simply talk, listen, and help them both medically and emotionally."[54] In 1942, he served in a relief hospital, treating children with "bullet holes in them."[55] News of Ayres's service in New Guinea connected his actual wartime duties with Paul's character, and when victory was declared in Japan, "Lew finally returned home, a war hero."[56]

Memory Is a Booming Industry

Jay Winter argues that twentieth-century warfare altered collective notions of memory. Describing "memory booms" in *Remembering War* (2006), Winter explains, "For some the memory boom is nostalgic, a yearning for a vanished or rapidly vanishing world. For others it is a language of protest, seeking out solidarities based on common narratives and traditions to resist the pressures and seductions of globalization."[57] Authors such as Winter see a fundamental shift in the way the world came to understand war. The twentieth-century's "memory booms" revolved around new forms of media and access to knowledge about war, and subsequently a desire to remember and commemorate warfighters.

War changed the nature of memory, such that a collective focus on war and its consequences emerged in cinematography. The hyper-violent caricatures I have described could almost be viewed as an effort to work through societal trauma. This working through can be found in memorials, in our language, in our basic ways of relating from one human to another and every sector of capitalist society. However, it is most viscerally experienced in cinema.

If war results in societal trauma, theorists like Caruth would explain memory booms as our inability to experience trauma in the moment it occurs.[58] To take this line of logic a step further, collective trauma suggests a "working through" in the American unconscious. In the unconscious, things can be represented by their opposites. Veterans are no exception. As Peter Karsten's *Encyclopedia of War and American Society* (2005) explains,

> The intensity of war itself produces changes in language. Militaries use euphemisms to cover the true horror of war. Thus a man accidently killed by a comrade is a victim of friendly fire. Civilians accidentally killed are collateral damage. Dead soldiers are wasted or lost. In cases where language offers no terms at all to describe new phenomena, soldiers invent them. The intentional killing of one's own officers in Vietnam came to be known as fragging, a reference to the fragmentation grenades used in such incidents. Soldiers also use language to reveal their own image of themselves. Soldiers have often described themselves in animalistic terms, reflecting their close-to-nature existences and the general indifference with which they often feel civilians treat them. Thus soldiers call themselves "grunts" or "dog faces" and they wear "dog tags." They eat "slop" in a "mess hall" and, when not in a "fox hole," they sleep in a "pup tent."[59]

Notably, the examples provided by Karsten describe soldiers in "animalistic," dominated ways. Children learn a language in which soldiers are subjugated by design. In fact, their subjugation becomes a source of pride, and later, a narrative that leads to agency. I will show a similar phenomenon among the "wounded warriors" who function within a twenty-first century "therapeutic culture" in the next chapter. Military service offers young adults the opportunity to reverse meanings, to turn past oppression into new forms of privilege. Pain becomes evidence of resilience.

Extreme Heroism: Medal of Honor Recipients

According to the Congressional Medal of Honor Society, "The Medal of Honor is the highest award for valor in action against an enemy force which can be bestowed upon an individual serving in the Armed Services of the United States."[60] Medal of Honor recipients' actions clearly indicate superior moral courage. These examples are exceptional because their courage is superior. Yet, awarding any medal for valor seems a subjective decision. Otherwise, lesser awards—Silver Stars, Bronze Stars, or ribbons that connote valor—would not exist. After all, some heroes are more heroic than others. And when dealing with the most recent generation of veterans returning from Iraq and Afghanistan, some "heroes" never do anything heroic at all.

The phrases "Support the Troops" and "Our Nation's Heroes" are politicized attempts to quell public dissent to war. Popular memory holds that an antiwar media directed attacks on Vietnam veterans. Moreover, in the decades preceding the Gulf War, the American public saw the suffering of Vietnam veterans and experienced guilt for how it treated them. In "Who Supports the Troops? Vietnam, the Gulf War, and the Making of Collective Memory," Thomas D. Beamish, Harvey Molotch, and Richard Flacks discuss media coverage of the Vietnam War. They found that much criticism was directed at politicians and policy-makers even as viewers were educated about ways to support deployed and returning veterans. Still, memories and anecdotes of veterans being spat upon stuck with the American public, and by the end of the Gulf War an intentional media campaign ensured that veterans would be heralded as "heroes" in public discourse.[61]

By definition, a hero is a "man (or occas. a woman) of superhuman strength, courage, or ability, favoured by the gods; esp. one regarded as semi-divine and immortal."[62] Heroes physically, mentally, and morally transcend human limitations in their "heroic moments." The duration of a "heroic moment" corresponds to the duration of a threat. Afterward, an official account, or "heroic narrative," emerges from the tales of those who witnessed the hero's feat. This narrative may highlight one instance or the cumulative effects of many instances of heroism to tell a single story.

Sergeant Alvin C. York is probably the most famous Medal of Honor recipient. He was born in 1887 in Pall Mall, Tennessee, and drafted into the army, where he served with the 82nd Infantry Division in World War I.[63] The film detailing his exploits, *Sergeant York* (1941), stars Gary Cooper, Walter Brennan, and Joan Leslie.[64] As David D. Lee explains in *Sergeant York: An American Hero* (1985), it is York's humility, his "fundamentalist piety" that endears him to audiences of the film.[65] York's socioeconomic class, Appalachian roots, and religion are primary components of his intersectional identity. He eschews military masculinity, which ingratiates him with audiences of military veterans and nonveterans alike, emphasizing their common humanity. Described as "the big lanky fellow, fourth from the end" among a trench of enlisted troops digging a ditch early in the film, York is reported to his commanding officer as a "conscientious objector." This information worries his leaders, at least until a later scene in which he displays his prowess with a rifle.[66]

York's marksmanship is put to the test. With bullseye after bullseye at the firing range, he impresses his instructors. York comments, "I reckon that there gun shoots a mite to the right," even as he excels at the task. "Where'd you learn to shoot, York?" another soldier asks. "I ain't never learned, Sergeant. Folks back home used to say I could shoot before I was weaned. But they was exaggerating some," York explains to laughter. York is presented as humble, exceptionally talented, and unassuming. I've described military masculinity as a gender-based performance, but York doesn't perform. He *is* the military man, and as the movie progresses, others begin to mimic York's behavior and look up to him for reasons other than rank.[67]

In the next scene, York moves from trainee to trainer, teaching those in his unit how to pick out a target among "a flock of wild turkeys." It doesn't take long for the audience to realize that York's demeanor—his accent, lack of knowledge about lands existing beyond the hills of Tennessee, his humility—is not, in fact, a sign of simplicity or ignorance, but rather evidence of forgotten knowledge that is quintessentially American. Later in the film, when York famously captures a German trench, he does it without displaying fear, explaining to his superior officer, "You done give me command," as he climbs over cowering and dead soldiers to make his advance.[68] His Medal of Honor Award citation explains:

> After his platoon had suffered heavy casualties and 3 other noncommissioned officers had become casualties, Cpl. York assumed command. Fearlessly leading 7 men, he charged with great daring a machinegun nest which was pouring deadly and incessant fire upon his platoon. In this heroic feat the machinegun nest was taken, together with 4 officers and 128 men and several guns.[69]

In many ways, York's simplicity is his greatest source of strength. His unwillingness to perform a hyper-masculine character allows him to account for the unexpected, for the realities of war not discussed in patriotic discourse.

For example, in the film, York uses a turkey call to distract the Germans closing in on him. One by one, as York kills German soldiers, he says, "Just like a flock of turkeys." It's an almost comical scene until the moral implications of his actions arise. Soldiers certainly dehumanize their enemies in order to kill them. But the film appears almost propagandistic in its tone when one considers that the titular hero began as a conscientious objector. At the end of the scene, the Germans raise a white flag, signaling their surrender, and York emerges as one of the war's greatest heroes.[70]

"Heroic moments," like the one explained above, are a prerequisite to two of three types of heroism. The first, the *sacrificing hero*, is an individual who may not display superhuman abilities like York, but one with a willingness to give their life for others, a trait indicative of superior moral courage. A popular conception of the *sacrificing hero* is a scene often repeated as a trope in both cinema and actual combat: a hidden enemy throws a grenade into a patrol of five soldiers, and four of the five soldiers are paralyzed by fear; the remaining soldier sees the threat, makes a conscious decision, and throws themself onto the grenade, blunting the impact of the blast and saving their friends. A recent example of this sort of action can be found in *Captain America: The First Avenger* (2011). In the film, a "skinny" Steve Rogers participates in a group exercise at a training site before he acquires superpowers. A superior officer, played by Tommy Lee Jones, compares Rogers negatively to a larger, more accomplished soldier, saying, "You win wars with guts," and tosses a fake grenade into the group of soldiers. Every other soldier runs. But Rogers, jumping on the grenade, yells, "Get away!" Indeed, a recurring theme in the *Captain America* films is Rogers's innate morality, his willingness to sacrifice. His superpowers come second to these traits.[71]

Sacrificing heroes risk death even when they know the odds of survival are low. Kyle Carpenter might have watched films or heard stories about *sacrificing heroes* growing up. In 2010, on a rooftop in Afghanistan, he threw himself on a grenade to save a friend. Among his wounds were a fractured skull, shattered bones in his right arm, a perforated lung, two ruptured eardrums, loss of use of his right eye, shrapnel in his lower legs, and the loss of most of his bottom teeth. Since then, he has undergone dozens of surgeries. And, almost four years after his "heroic moment," he became the nation's youngest living recipient of the Medal of Honor. "I'm totally fine knowing that I gave part of myself to a bigger purpose and a bigger cause, to not only serve my country but try to make a better way of life for other people and much less fortunate people," Carpenter later told reporters.[72]

Later, as a college student, he was known for competing in grueling endurance challenges—even skydiving into sporting events. The wonders of medical science have repaired many of the physical wounds caused by the grenade incident. In fact, Carpenter demonstrates how heroes must *sublimate* woundedness in order to maintain the appearance of "heroism" in their postwar lives. It's no surprise that Carpenter announced the release of his first book in 2019. The title is *Are You Worth It: Building a Life Worth Fighting For*, and the publisher describes it as a self-help guide and memoir meant to "show that big battles are accomplished by small victories."[73] Carpenter's story shows how his trauma and woundedness were not enough to keep him down. It never was. Something about his character prevented it.

Any veteran called a "hero"—regardless of whether or not that title is earned—exists at the center of a war of appropriation waged by military and civilian cultures. According to Mark Straw, "Scripts of American national identity therefore . . . give rise to mythical constructions of Americanness. This mythical construction of American national identity is strongly constituted on performances and ideas of masculinity."[74] Carpenter, as a hero, becomes a construction of Americanness through the appropriation of his story. His skydiving into sporting events speaks to American grit. His recovery boasts of the strength of our science. And photos of Carpenter competing in marathons camouflage his visible and invisible wounds. Constantly reminding heroes of what was likely the most traumatic period of their lives certainly contradicts calls for "reassimilation." In place of reassimilation, for veterans like Kyle Carpenter, a "bigger purpose and a bigger cause" is readily available. For *famous* heroes, the script isn't unspoken. It is imposed on them. And it could be that heroes seek out the appropriating effects of a spotlight because it is preferable to suffering alone in obscurity.

In *Sergeant York*, it is York's innate qualities, the derivatives of his life in the hills of Tennessee, even his instinctual aversion to war that underscores his heroic qualities.[75] Straw, however, believes that the myth of innate heroism is a "raced, gendered and sexualized form of hegemonic power in contemporary American culture [that] attempts to project the idea of itself as a victim, when the truth of the matter is that it is a victimizer par excellence."[76] Straw's premise would charge that the character of Sergeant Alvin C. York is portrayed as simple only to deemphasize his prowess as a killer. This myth of innate heroism is seldom challenged. And York's likening German soldiers to turkeys certainly supports Straw's argument. However, cultural examples of military heroes distributed for political reasons do not explain the motivations of heroes like York and Carpenter. It is only after their narratives are appropriated that they become politicized. Attempts to connect heroic narratives to American military might are acts perpetrated by larger society, not by veterans themselves.

On closer examination, myriad factors create a "heroic moment": training, mental health, adrenaline, to name a few. The most important prerequisite for a "heroic moment," however, is *chance.* A hero cannot emerge without a friend to save or a threat to neutralize. But this fact is quickly forgotten and romantic stories about integrity and personal courage take its place. The myth of innate heroism ignores the circumstances mitigating heroic action, suggesting that heroes are born, not made. At least, that's the story told to the generation tasked with fighting the next war. Veterans, civilians, recruiters, and history books don't tell children that they can *become* heroes. They're told that they're *already* heroes; war simply allows innate heroism to rise to the surface. Maintaining this myth—Wilfred Owen's "old Lie"—is precisely the symbolic role "heroes" occupy in their postwar lives.[77] Paradoxically, real heroes are pressured to perform veteran identity in a way that conforms to the "hero" stereotype.

Some veterans never get a chance to experience appropriation. They never get a chance to suffer alone. Donald Cook is an example of a *sacrificing hero* who earned the Medal of Honor posthumously as a prisoner of war (POW). In fact, he remains the first and only marine to receive the award as a POW. His award citation tells a harrowing tale of deprivation at the hands of the Viet Cong, one in which he "establishe[s] himself as the senior prisoner" (despite not actually being the senior prisoner, suggesting that Cook's immediate superior in captivity was either unable or unwilling to lead). He gives "needy men his medicine and drug allowance," and "refuse[s] to stray even the slightest from the Code of Conduct." Cook's sacrifices eventually cost him his life. His "heroic moment" lasts the duration of his imprisonment: "31 December 1964 to 8 December, 1967."[78] But his award was not presented to his family until 1980.

Cook's Medal of Honor was likely a comfort to his family. And maybe it righted a wrong recorded in America's official history. Mostly, belated awards are given only after some racial or social injustice is highlighted as the cause of the delay. For example, in 2014 President Barack Obama awarded the Medal of Honor to "24 Army veterans, most of them Hispanic or Jewish, who were passed over for the nation's highest military award because of their race or ethnicity."[79] Despite the overture, it should be noted that these veterans were largely regarded collectively rather than for their individual feats of heroism. Their heroism is used as a salve to treat inequality in the civilian world. Their deeds, though plainly stated, are passed over in their time due to politics, and then brought back to the forefront of American consciousness when the country is ready. As Caruth would suggest, America returned belatedly to the site of trauma.

The *attacking hero* displays superhuman abilities in an *offensive* manner, saving the day. Dakota Meyer, like York, is an example. After being ambushed by "more than 50 enemy fighters," Meyer ignored incoming fire and put himself at great risk, killing some enemies "at near point blank range" on three trips that saw the rescue of two dozen Afghan soldiers. Even Meyer's wounds did not stop him from leaving the security of his gunner's hatch to "find and recover the bodies of his team members." Meyer's actions are a chance meeting of skill and opportunity. His "heroic moment" is a "6-hour battle [that] significantly disrupted the enemy's attack and inspired the members of the combined force to fight on."[80] The moral authority that *attacking heroes* yield to *sacrificing heroes*, should one fall into the trap of creating a hierarchy, is largely based on the fact that the violence perpetrated by *attacking heroes* is morally unacceptable in the civilian world.

Audie Murphy, the most decorated US soldier to serve in World War II, wrote a memoir and starred in a film adaptation of his exploits, *To Hell and Back* (1955).[81] His individual story was amplified through its recreation and distribution as cinema, and it further cemented the legacy of what would be dubbed "The Greatest Generation," or that group of "heroes" that rid the world of Nazis in World War II. Dakota Meyer, by contrast, had a ghostwriter and it was either insinuated or Meyer was directly accused of exaggeration in news outlets such as *National Public Radio*, the *Washington Post*, and the *Daily Telegraph.* The forces of appropriation move quickly on heroes. In fact, in the moment after the first telling of a hero's story, the hero and the "heroic narrative" begin to exist apart. As Meyer's individuality crept into the larger societal narrative forming around him, he became mired in controversy.

Subsequent developments in Dakota Meyer's life revealed that he struggled with PTSD, alcoholism, and suicidal ideation even during the initial fanfare surrounding his receipt of the Medal of Honor. Still, Meyer's postwar focus has been on raising awareness about these issues and helping veterans find employment, causes which may be more *heroic* than the symbolic role conferred on him. Can a veteran become a hero after war? What if they miss the chance but still possess that innate *heroic* quality? There's nothing to suggest otherwise. In fact, both Meyer's work helping veterans after leaving military service and Kyle Carpenter's self-help book are evidence of the altruistic nature I attribute to authentic veteran identity.

Enduring heroes are the third and most prolific variation on "hero" identity found in the twenty-first century. They have no need for a "heroic moment." Colloquially, and functionally, an *enduring hero* is simply a veteran. That's it. They are the individuals civilians refer to as "Our Nation's Heroes," as though every high schooler capable of etching their name onto an enlistment contract instantly transforms into the embodiment of human courage. They're the "heroes" applauded anonymously in airports. After service, only the most damning of evidence can disqualify a veteran from enjoying *enduring hero* status: a "dishonorable" discharge, crime, or particularly visible addiction. But the most peculiar thing about *enduring heroes* isn't their anonymity. The strange thing about *enduring heroes* is that they never do anything *heroic.*

I believe *enduring heroes* gain their "hero" status as a roundabout social recognition of the altruism and proclivity for leadership found among veterans. However, altruism is not synonymous with heroism. An *enduring hero*'s award citation might read something like this:

> Meritorious service while serving as a heavy wheel vehicle operator, convoy protection platform gunner, and team leader during Operation Iraqi Freedom III. Your skills and courage enabled you to contribute significantly to successful combat operations.

The above citation is from the Army Commendation Medal that I received after returning from my second deployment to Iraq in 2005. It is the sort of award referred to by veterans as a "wartime award," which is another way of saying, "This is what I got for showing up." It lists my responsibilities, attaching words like "courage" to make me sound braver than I am. Driving large trucks requires skill, a machine gunner's hatch is a dangerous place to sit, and a "team leader" must care for their soldiers. But skill, danger, and responsibility do not equal heroism. From January 15 to December 24, 2005, I never experienced a "heroic moment." I *endured* indirect gunfire and several IED blasts. But I did not sacrifice "life or limb" to save friends. I never responded offensively in any exceptional way. As the award states, I "contributed."

I am not a hero, and I am not ashamed of this fact. Never experiencing a "heroic moment" is not a detriment to a veteran's character. Being *called* a "hero" when you know you more closely resemble a "perpetrator" or "survivor" is damaging. I can't even call myself a "servant." I was paid. For me, war boiled down to *perpetrating* and *surviving* violence. Existing within closer proximity to that violence were *sacrificing* and *attacking heroes*, not those like me: those who *endured.*

In sum, there are two classic kinds of heroes: *sacrificing heroes*, like Kyle Carpenter or Donald Cook, make a conscious decision to give up personal safety and/or well-being in order to save others; *attacking heroes*, such as Alvin York or Dakota Meyer, make a difference *offensively. Enduring heroes*, like me, are far more common because the only requirement is to "contribute" to the war effort. "Heroes" in this last category never experience a "heroic moment," and because there's no proof or evidence required to achieve "hero" status in contemporary America, the "heroic narratives" of *enduring heroes* are viewed monolithically.

Veterans, as *enduring heroes*, exist unanchored from such pivotal moments and memories, from the past as well as the present. Any trouble with reassimilation experienced by *enduring heroes*—troubles I have heard referred to as "the growing divide between military and civilian cultures"—may be caused, in part, by the "hero's" inability to recall personal acts of heroism. In short, *enduring heroes* must remain silent in order to perform their roles in the unspoken script, the prevailing patriotic narrative of the nation state. Silence is just another form of impression management. Civilians claim that veterans "don't like to talk about it." They tell veterans, "I can never understand what you've been through." But symbolically, they *need* veterans to remain silent. They need for military service to remain a mystery. Otherwise, the veteran would cease to function as a plot device. The individualized and often uneventful narratives of their service would destabilize the war effort.

Any veteran can exist as a "hero" in the American unconscious if they are willing to remain silent. But this stereotyping leads to a feeling that authentic heroes do not exist. For years after my discharge, I dealt with this "hero treatment" in one of two ways:

1. I passively accepted the title of "hero" and became complicit in the denigration of *authentic* heroes, regarding my lived experience superficially so that it could exist in the imaginations of others as something that conformed to their prescribed narratives; or,
2. I existed in a state of constant conflict, personally rebuking civilian attempts to confer "hero" status on myself and others. For example, after hearing the words "Thank you for your service," I often chose to reply, "You're welcome," "No problem," or "Any time" to emphasize the irony of the situation. More often, I interrogated the person's definition of the word "hero."

These situations were ironic because those praising me knew nothing about what I did in uniform. To be called a "hero" is to feel like the opposite. But the problem wasn't *only* what I perceived. If *any* of my guilt was deserved, then *all* of my anger was warranted. Civilians implicitly devalue the service of veterans they arbitrarily label as "heroes." The act ignores the individual. It suggests that the veteran's memories and experiences are not sufficient for the public narrative. It's insulting.

Heroes. For Sale?

By its very nature, the "heroic narrative" can exist only if memories of the "heroic moment" are shared by others. It is at this juncture—during the first telling of the hero's story—where appropriation begins. Eventually, inaccuracies seep in and outside forces twist the narrative to suit their purposes. Creative nonfiction replaces lived experience. A "heroic narrative" replaces memory.

The Depression-era film *Heroes for Sale* (1933) explores the consequences of separating heroes from their heroism. Tom Holmes, played by Richard Barthelmess, the protagonist of the William A. Wellman film, resembles the "wounded warrior" discussed elsewhere in this book. He returns home from World War I perpetually broken, battling the pain of physical and psychological wounds. With the help of a friend, Tom manages to be hired at a bank, but he loses the job as a result of a morphine addiction. Destitute, he is carried away to an asylum, all while holding on to a secret with the power to restore him to a station of privilege and respect. A central theme within the film is "misidentification." Like many who struggle with addiction, Tom was first prescribed his drug by a doctor while convalescing from an injury in the war. However, moral judgment is passed, and he is treated as though he is a criminal and a communist during different stages of his homecoming.[82]

Tom's secret? He is very much a hero—an *attacking hero*, to be precise. He didn't sustain those physical and psychological wounds while suffering passively. Quite the opposite; Tom is wounded while heroically and single-handedly capturing an enemy position, similar to the titular character in *Sergeant York*, and it is a feat rendered even more gallant by Wellman's juxtaposition of Roger Winston, played by Gordon Westcott, cowering in an adjacent trench. Tom becomes an "addict" in a German hospital bed; he is presumed dead while his friend is falsely celebrated for his heroism. It is Roger who receives credit for Tom's "heroic moment." It is Roger who bribes Tom into silence with a job at his father's bank. Tom may appear perpetually broken, propped up by the pity of others, and *silent.* But *Heroes for Sale* shows how, in the case of war heroes, appearances can be deceiving.[83]

To survive, Tom must recognize the unseen forces shaping others' perceptions. He must engage in impression management. In one scene, Roger's father berates Tom about his morphine addiction: "I wonder if you realize what this does to my standing in the community. After 25 years of public confidence, I find myself with a drug addict in my employ. A drug addict handling the depositors' money. An employee of mine with this loathsome, cowardly habit. I can't understand it." Tom's addiction is not the result of some "loathsome" or "cowardly" habit. It is a wound inflicted on him and one kept in the shadows for the sake of the banker's son.

Tom sits angrily wringing a rag, clutching the arms of his chair, scowling at the floor. Irony permeates the scene. The truth of Tom's actions during the war would alter meaning, transforming his addiction into *just* another wound—his *wounds* into badges of courage. Tom, not unlike a *sacrificing hero*, just not in a combat situation, protects his friend's honor. However, he recognizes for the first time exactly what Roger stole.[84] In many ways, Roger is an early example of the "stolen valor" that many veterans hold in contempt.

In the office scene with Roger's father, Tom is expected to sit idly by as his war narrative is written for him. Out of options, despised by one man in the room, and harboring a terrible secret about the other, Tom can either conform or challenge the narratives that he didn't write. His testimony can transform the situation. However, and despite the truth of his wartime heroism, Tom turns to a victimization narrative to save face:

> Whoa, wait a minute. How do you think I started taking that stuff? For fun or pleasure? Well, I'll tell you how. They gave it to me in a German hospital to keep me from going mad with pain. Pain. Agony. Continuing torture, day after day like a million ants eating me alive. Do you know what that means? No, you don't. Because when I was being blown to bits you were sitting here safe and comfortable. And you're still sitting here, in judgment.[85]

Tom, unable to draw on his "heroic narrative," paints himself as something more closely resembling the "wounded warrior." By occupying this privileged role of suffering, Tom places himself beyond the reproach of Roger's father, a man who did not serve in World War I. And in doing so he protects his friend. Superficial understandings of war wounds and heroism enable Tom to exist in a liminal state between these two narratives. It is an example of a veteran trying to maximize his agency.

The scene in the banker's office manipulates an impulse, an urge to draw back the curtain and assert, finally, and for all to hear, "This man is a hero! Treat him accordingly." If this discussion switches the tone of this chapter to something more spiritual, then it is by design. There's an almost sacred obligation to recognize heroes. I say that this duty is *sacred*, as opposed to *civic*—like jury duty, voting, or picking up litter—because failure to recognize Tom as a hero says something about the character of the individual who remains silent. Roger paces nervously in his father's office because he, too, feels the call of his sacred obligation. Roger's failure reflects the audience's own. He may have cowered nearby while Tom became a hero, but, in Roger's mind, civilians didn't fight at all. They cowered on the other side of an ocean. At least, this is the lie Roger tells himself to justify his actions.

Of course, the "heroic narrative" Roger steals is a fiction. Wellman's movie about hope does not rely on patriotic constructs. Instead, in the wake of the Great Depression, Wellman portrays veterans such as Tom Holmes as one source of salvation: honest, battle-tested, socially conscientious men who, despite the hardships imposed on them, have not lost their faith in humanity.

To be sure, much of Tom's development as a character depends on Wellman's needs as a director. Further, much of Wellman's directorial decisions were determined by regional attitudes toward veterans and addiction. A series of letters between Warner Bros. executives and the Association of Motion Picture Producers (which preceded the Association of Motion Picture and Television Producers) reveals the work of censors in every stage of creating *Heroes for Sale.* In a March 1933 letter from James Wingate, director of studio relations for the MPAA, to Darryl Zanuck, the Warner Bros. producer at "the center of the studio system" who sent him the script, the primary concerns about the film were its depictions of drug use. Wingate suggested cutting a scene in which "Tom tries to buy dope from a peddler." Likewise, Wingate suggested, "It would be advisable never to mention the actual drug 'morphine,' as several censor boards are pretty consistent in deleting any such reference." These references remain in the film, though it is not clear if they made it into the copies that were distributed regionally.[86]

In a complex movie about returning veterans' struggles with addiction and misidentification, the primary concern of producers and censors was producing a socially acceptable film in as many regions as possible. Economic considerations were more important than telling stories about veterans. Tom is a fictional character, but I have shown examples of real veterans undergoing the same sort of manipulation: war stories stripped of their gore, war wounds made temporary, mental illness cured through school or the free market. Censor boards didn't always get their way, but the practice of censorship exists today in various forms.

In May 1933, Wingate wrote J. L. Warner to express that the film was "satisfactory under the Code." However, he anticipated concerns would arise from the various censorship boards overseeing the North American distribution of the film, asking that Warner "trim the scenes in which the police are shown as overly officious and unfair" and "shorten" the scene "between Tom and the dope peddler outside the bank."[87] References to Communism, police brutality, profanity, a nude drawing, and a lack of patriotic zeal are among the concerns raised by censorship boards in the New York, Pennsylvania, Ontario, Alberta, and Australia territories. Just because political boards objected to scenes did not mean that those scenes were automatically cut. In the version that exists today, the film's riot scene includes absolute chaos: protestors hurling rocks at police; police firing into crowds; Tom's wife struck in the head as police restrain him. In the next scene, Tom's child is taken away as police officers linger in the doorway. Afterward, Tom is sentenced to five years of "hard labor in a state penitentiary." Different regions would have received variations of the same film. In all versions, however, Tom Holmes remains pitted against the state, against decency, and for no fault of his own.[88] The concerns expressed in the studio's correspondence indicate a united preference for patriotic constructions of veteran identity over the nuanced example of Tom Holmes.

Six months later, in October 1933, the MPAA board in Quebec, Canada, officially objected to the last six words of one revealing statement: "Tom, that was a terrible thing that I, the way I—the way the old man and I made you suffer. And all because of a medal and a couple of lousy ribbons."[89] In the end, this line also survives. It is problematic because it devalues military awards, suggesting that they're not worth the horrors one must endure to earn them. It departs from patriotic rhetoric, reflecting the disillusionment with the Great War felt by American society as a whole. Importantly, Tom retains the right to decide on the meaning of his awards, his wounds, and his role in postwar society. But the audience—not the other characters or the country that Tom defended—permits this right to self-definition. Even fictional veterans are subject to appropriation.

Tom discovers anger, as opposed to conviction or guilt, because the scene with Roger's father finally causes him to realize what he has lost along with his "heroic narrative." Tom doesn't understand that his story was appropriated by the same military that left him for dead. Roger can't give it back. It's too late for recompense at the end of the film, when both Tom and Roger are destitute long after the war has ended, and after a series of deleterious life events and crimes. And there are more than a few clues—discomfort accepting credit for Tom's actions, pacing nervously in his father's office—that suggest Roger might not have accepted credit for Tom's "heroic moment" if it had not been forced on him. Roger is more of a foil than an antagonist. Any anger directed at Roger by his former friend would be fruitless. Roger is but a cog in a propaganda machine in need of "heroes." Because of his addiction, Tom could never have served as a superior example.

Heroes for Sale is relevant to a theory of veteran identity because it exposes heroism's precariousness. Not only is Tom's heroism something he can lose, but it is also something Roger appropriates to elevate himself within the eyes of the military, his father, and the larger community. In the hierarchy of military masculinity recognized in the preceding sections, Roger would have been elevated above his friend, claiming heroic feats in order to sit at that hierarchy's pinnacle as a "hero." But Roger is not a real hero. In fact, his actions are dishonorable, not unlike his rich father's actions: financial crimes that leave Roger and his family destitute later in the film. Roger and his father merely occupy a symbolic role, and so it is fitting that they lose everything by the end of the film: poetic justice.

If heroism resembles American "grit" or "spirit" in *Heroes for Sale*, it is only because Wellman appropriates the trait for the needs of his civilian audience, and to the chagrin of veterans watching silently. Wellman's heroism is uniquely "American." He draws on a myth of innate heroism, or the belief in the lie told to recruits, "it is the courage to serve which sets you apart from your peers." These myths endear Tom Holmes to his audience. From there, the director paints a ravaged society, introducing Tom Holmes not as a hero or even a stereotype, but as a pure soul used by a calloused society. The film makes a simple argument: Tom Holmes is no different from the millions of Americans who lost their jobs and savings in an economic collapse. His devastation is their devastation. His appropriation is their appropriation. They all share the disadvantage of class.

In a society devastated by economic collapse, Tom Holmes models heroic qualities that cinema scholar Philip Hanson recognizes as part of a search through "thirties global and national politics . . . [for] persons and strategies on which to model a response to the Depression."[90] In the film, Wellman chooses the American World War I veteran as his response. The film ends with no less than a recitation of portions of Franklin D. Roosevelt's inaugural address. In the scene, Tom preaches a uniquely American prosperity gospel, appearing to others as eccentric or perhaps in denial about his circumstances. But to the viewers, those who witnessed Tom's "heroic moment," it is a message delivered by a Christ figure. It is innate goodness that propels Tom forward.[91]

He and Roger find themselves living side by side in a hobo village at the end of the film. Tom has given up all worldly possessions; his wife is dead; he has given up his child. Even without a grand speech, the audience knows that Roger will continue on a dark path downward into despair and Tom—no matter his disability, poverty, or secrecy—will emerge as the hero he was always destined to become. As a stereotypical "hero," Tom could barely function. The reality of his addiction, Roger's appropriation of his "heroic narrative," and a social climate that treats addicts as inferior all combine to set the protagonist at odds with the society to which he returns. Today, as fewer and fewer "attacking" and "surviving" heroes return home from war, a product of decreased mortality rates, decreased numbers of troops mobilized, and the disappearance of the "front lines" in combat, "heroes" are taking their place. Wellman tried to warn about the dangers of misidentifying heroes and cowards. Now, society ignores such warnings, up to and including those provided by veterans themselves.

The veteran's experience has value to a society closed off from war, one in need of inspiration and instruction on the topic of human resilience. Veterans are ideal instructors on this topic. But not everyone agrees. In 1936, W. B. Yeats refused to include the works of the trench poets in the *Oxford Book of Modern Verse*.[92] "He objected not to method but to subject," claiming, "passive suffering is not a theme for poetry," Fred Crawford observes in *British Poets of the Great War*.[93] I include that information here because of the symbolic exchange it represents. British Great War poets such as Wilfred Owen, Siegfried Sassoon, and Robert Graves were veterans who chose to use their respective platforms to register protests against war. However, when it came time for their works to be considered alongside literature not devoted to the topic of war, W. B. Yeats refused on grounds of sophistication, reducing the experience of war to mere "passive suffering," implying that war writers are somehow deficient, that the experience of war is not a means through which true knowledge can be attained.

Yeats wasn't the only one to discriminate against veterans after World War I. As discussed earlier, to return home wounded was to appear effeminate, or weak. Caroline Cox argues that early clinical descriptions of war neuroses were influenced by the invisible hands of sexuality and gender. Cox reveals that shell shock's definitions were largely derived from researchers interested in women and hysteria, as the condition was understood in Sigmund Freud's work.[94] *Heroes for Sale*'s Tom Holmes would have returned home to an environment hostile toward "broken" or "damaged" veterans. In many ways, he experiences discrimination based on his gender, his inability to perform military masculinity, and because his knowledge is derived from experience.

Recruiters and Skull Tattoos

Gone were the days of enlistment bonuses, guaranteed duty stations, and picking your job when I took Josh to the recruitment station. Those benefits were commonplace when I enlisted, as the Afghanistan War heated up and talk was leading to an invasion of Iraq. Josh turned eighteen and sought out the military at a time when massive cuts to the number of active service members were already underway. "The military is only taking the best and the brightest these days," one recruiter told us. What did that make the people I'd served with? Fortunately, there were a number of subpar jobs with no incentives that needed filling. Maybe, if Josh were lucky, he could scrape by.

I'd talked Josh out of becoming a fighter pilot. In fact, he'd all but settled on the navy when I took him to see the army recruiter. "Never hurts to explore your options," I told him. The recruiter we met was a staff sergeant. His uniform told me he'd deployed multiple times, earned multiple awards, and performed in such a way that the army thought it befitting to assign him to the public sphere. From his high and tight haircut to his perfectly creased uniform and massive stack of ribbons, the staff sergeant appeared the consummate soldier. But one thing was off: his short sleeves. Specifically, the tattooed lines of skulls wrapping around his arms didn't fit the usual recruiter's office decor of flags, motivational posters, tracking boards, and pictures of local high school legends living exciting lives in exotic locations on the government's dime.

Skulls. Death. Pain. That's what I read on his arms. His black metal bracelet told the rest of the story. It was an item that became popular just as I was leaving active duty: A simple tin or aluminum bracelet bent around the wrist, painted black and engraved with the names of friends lost in battle. Looking a little closer, I could see inscriptions near the skulls tattooed on his arm. I couldn't read them. But there were other things to read. "Red eyes. Messy hair. But his uniform is so perfect," I thought to myself. It felt like the crisp and clean image of the soldier perpetuated by the military uniform was doing battle with a veteran who knew better. He spoke the words of a recruiter. But the sum of the message he delivered painted a more nuanced story of military life.

I was probably the only one in the room who recognized the irony of the situation: a teenage boy who wanted nothing more than to be Tom Cruise in *Top Gun* sitting across from an obviously war-weary soldier who likely dreamed of the type of service depicted in those Hollywood films. I wondered why his superiors let him wear short sleeves. Maybe the issue had been contested behind closed doors. Maybe the staff sergeant with skulls on his arm didn't realize he was *actively* performing veteran identity. Maybe his form of impression management was intentional.

His tattoos were fine art. His bracelet was a label explaining it. And when juxtaposed alongside a pressed, polished army dress uniform, one weighed down at the chest by medals and other accolades, the recruiter's art registered as a political statement. He was not a "wounded warrior." Nor was he a "hero." He was an individual. And though his pitch didn't dissuade my brother from joining the navy, I respected his honesty, and I appreciate the complexity that his every encounter adds to civilians' understandings of military service.

A conscious, active performance of veteran identity is one that uses subtle actions and demeanors as much as stories of service to fill the void created by civilians' lack of military knowledge. Active performances of veteran identity work against stereotypes. Active performers see through vague representations of veteran identity like "wounded warriors" or "heroes." Civilians already have a "veteran" character—forged from education, films, and superficial interactions with veterans—in their minds. Active performers of veteran identity disrupt those narratives.

In the next chapter, I'll tell more of my brother's story and examine the "wounded warrior," another version of veteran identity modeled by contemporary veterans. While both "wounded warriors" and "heroes" are defined by a proximity to death, the "wounded warrior" stereotype requires a victimization narrative (or, more accurately, evidence that will *imply* a victimization narrative). Veterans who play this role through impression management will comb the past for brushes with death—with *almost* dying. Those memories serve the needs of the "wounded warrior's" audience: civilians eager to dispense pity. This phenomenon occurs among those veterans who are disabled, who object to war, or who do not fit neatly within patriotic rhetoric as exceptional examples. In the end, and like "heroes," "wounded warriors" sacrifice agency and the right to self-definition, the very things they thought military service would provide.

3

Our Wounded Warriors

The phrase "wounded warrior" was made popular by the US Army's Wounded Warrior Program, but even more by the Wounded Warrior Project (WWP), a Florida-based nonprofit organization. The latter has raised millions of dollars for veterans' assistance initiatives—among them, one that used to send me a free hat, water bottle, or magazine each year. The emblem of WWP, a silhouette of a soldier carrying a wounded comrade to safety, is always at the forefront. The vulnerability of the wounded veteran (the soldier being carried), when depicted alongside the glorification of charitable aid (the soldier who is carrying), draws on notions of camaraderie and sacrifice common among veterans. It also draws on a civilian desire to shape the destiny of veterans they deem "wounded warriors."

WWP's donors are mostly civilians, suggesting that the nonprofit organization has succeeded in marketing camaraderie—the feeling of carrying a wounded comrade to safety—to the masses. By donating just a few dollars, civilians can play the role of the rescuer. In 2014 alone the organization received more than $300 million in charitable donations.[1] WWP advertisements have been featured during the Super Bowl, and there are few Americans who would fail to recognize the organization's name. In the wake of the Iraq and Afghanistan wars, WWP emerged as the preeminent nonprofit organization combating "the invisible wounds of war": PTSD and traumatic brain injury. The organization's influence is such that the words "wounded warrior," I would argue, have come to represent *all* veterans dealing with war-related disabilities.

I first encountered WWP when an employee asked to give a presentation to my class of student veterans in 2012. He listed the organization's initiatives, some very impressive, including a desire to see WWP branches at every college. He brought professionally made brochures. And he spoke about WWP from the perspective of a veteran whose life they'd saved. To paraphrase his story, "I was on the verge of suicide when WWP showed up at my doorstep and gave me a new purpose in life." It was a wonderful story. At least, it was wonderful until I started encountering it again and again, in region after region that I visited while building my own veterans' nonprofit organization and presenting research on veterans' issues. At each college or event, in a booth or as a featured speaker, WWP had stationed members of its "Warriors Speak" initiative.[2]

"Warriors Speak" teaches a veteran how to self-narrate. But the narratives produced are skewed by the motivations of a nonprofit organization in need of donations. Essentially, WWP helps participants craft victimization narratives that are then appropriated to solicit those donations. I am not making a value judgment, simply stating the function of identity in this particular scenario. Judith Butler, an American philosopher and gender theorist, describes this sort of appropriation as one in which a person loses their identity in order to explain who they are to others.[3] Again, the symbolic positions of "hero" and "wounded warrior" are stereotypes, not complete, healthy identities. When veterans mirror one of these stereotypes, they give up the agency available to veterans who choose to continue learning and growing after service. WWP knows every veteran who speaks publicly about their wounds represents twenty or thirty who cannot. "Warriors Speak" lifts the veil separating veterans from civilians just long enough to fill in the blanks about veteran identity with tales of veterans in need of civilian saviors.

WWP gets its donations, and they do some remarkable work, but at what cost? I imagined the "Warriors Speak" representatives I saw as disproportionately healthy when compared to those representatives I could not see. The statistics cited by their speakers about veteran PTSD and suicide rates painted a picture in which the speaker was but one in a growing cast of severely disabled veterans. "Who will question the veteran missing an arm or a leg when that person says the Wounded Warrior Project saved their life?" I often wondered. For many years, the answer was "no one."

It all seemed a little too good to be true. The free hats, water bottles, expensive brochures, and salaries paid to their public speakers always struck me as lavish. In January 2016, CBS News reported that WWP's spending on conferences and meetings rose from $1.7 million to $26 million from 2010 to 2014.[4] Apparently, only 60 percent of the money raised by WWP was going to veterans, a number at odds, the report found, with comparable organizations, such as the Disabled American Veterans Charitable Service Trust and Fisher House, whose rankings were in the 90 percentile range during the same year.[5] It didn't take long for one of WWP's public speakers to change his mind about how his identity was being marshalled: "You're using our injuries, our darkest days, our hardships, to make money. So you can have these big parties," said Erick Millette, a former army staff sergeant who received both the Purple Heart and the Bronze Star in Iraq.[6] I found myself wondering how Millette would cope with this betrayal. He had fashioned an entire identity around this new mission.

I am interested in individual stories like those of Erick Millette. He lent his veteran identity to the cause only to retract it once the cause did not match his personal code of ethics. When Millette reclaimed his agency and started telling his own story, he harnessed his symbolic authority as a veteran. He defined himself as a veteran through his actions, as much as any author or artist. Veterans alter meaning when they tell their stories. They revise collective narratives of service and homecoming to accommodate lived experience. Silent veterans do not engage in such discourse. They let others develop myths of heroism and woundedness that result in comfortable symbolic positions—nooks and crannies in silent corners of the American unconscious. Where should returning veterans look for healthy models of veteran identity when examples like Millette are few, and when stereotypes of commodified, broken veterans are perpetuated by massive organizations?

"I'll be damned if you're gonna take hard working Americans' money and drink it and waste it," said Millette.[7] Supposedly, the allegations of misappropriated funds were debunked by forensic accountants within the organization and the Better Business Bureau. But negative perceptions of the organization remain, such that it is hard to learn about WWP without sifting through stories of litigation, management shake-ups, and public image. According to more recent estimates by Charity Navigator, 71.5 percent of WWP's finances go toward programming.[8] Certainly, any charity bringing in roughly $300 million a year is doing something right, but I am more concerned with the means to these ends. How did this heavily commodified conception of veteran woundedness emerge? How did we get here?

The Historical Treatment of Military Veterans in America

In *The Wages of War* (1989) Richard Severo and Lewis Milford examine how veterans were treated after each of America's major conflicts. The authors describe repeated instances of the government seeking to "limit its financial liability" and a society that often regards returning veterans as mercenaries for seeking out the benefits owed to them.[9] Severo and Milford reveal a bait and switch: encouraging military service with promises of upward mobility, denying veterans access to these forms of agency, and inexplicably shifting the blame for this denial on veterans themselves. Stereotyping has always been a major tool used to manipulate public perceptions of veteran identity. It morphed and took different forms in the wake of each major conflict of the twentieth century.

Veterans found it increasingly difficult to prove their heroism with the use of machine guns and chemical weapons in World War I. Vincent Sherry describes World War I as a war "where any single man's strength is subordinate to the power of the new weaponry, and where individual martial prowess, which offers the source of the distinctive heroic action, is subordinate to the co-ordinate force of massed infantry."[10] Machine guns and gas attacks exposed heroism as something attributable as much to luck as character. These extermination methods and growing interest in psychology resulted in a focus on veterans' psychological wounds. Prior to World War I, understandings of war neuroses were influenced by gender stereotypes and "associations of the condition[s] with hereditary or moral weakness."[11] In particular, veterans' psychological wounds were likened to "hysteria," a stereotypically female condition. And it caused much concern for social architects and families seeking to preserve war as a male "arena of instinctual liberation."[12] Veterans groups like the American Legion fought against military establishments in the United States and Britain that "saw a blurred line between shellshock and cowardice."[13]

After World War II, fewer images of unstable, violent veterans emerged, and the sacrifices of World War II became synonymous with economic prosperity and American exceptionalism. However, the term "Greatest Generation" wasn't coined until the 1990s, when Tom Brokaw wrote, "I think this is the greatest generation any society has ever produced."[14] Cultural memory seems to indicate that World War II veterans always held this exalted position. In many ways, World War II veterans, unlike veterans who came before and after, successfully functioned as the superior examples of veteran identity found in patriotic rhetoric. This generation set the bar at an unreachable height for subsequent generations. It's impossible to live up to a myth.

McCarthyism and "Red Scare" campaigns treated Korean War POWs as "cowards" for reasons such as accepting food and shelter. Severo and Milford explain that speakers on the national circuit used these POWs as their primary sources—a kind of victim shaming—when describing a lack of fortitude in America's youth: "From the Army's point of view, the Americans who had been held prisoner had exhibited a weakness that was nothing short of psychopathological."[15] Prisoners of war on the Korean peninsula—some veterans of World War II, others who joined because they'd been too young to fight in that war—were being pointed to as examples of male infirmity even as they endured imprisonment. Their generation of warfighters quickly earned the moniker of the "Forgotten Generation" due to the lack of tangible and emotional involvement required of the larger American public in the conflict. In fact, this theme of detachment emerged in every American war that followed World War II. Veterans and civilians became increasingly estranged.

The mistreatment of Vietnam-era veterans was much more explicit. The massacre of My Lai and other atrocities resulted in a generation of veterans held in contempt and feared as murderers. Kendrick Oliver argues that the story of the massacre gradually grew from one about the perpetrators to one about "the ranks of those who managed war, and horizontally across American society as a whole."[16] Oliver's research, in fact, is emblematic of a type of memory, one predicated on shame and guilt, feelings so prevalent in the wake of the Vietnam War that the sufferings of Americans and Vietnamese could not occur simultaneously in the American unconscious. Oliver believes "most young Americans who fought in the conflict were probably conscientious and humane . . . [but] establishing the body count as the central index of operational success . . . created incentives toward the killing of anyone whose corpse might subsequently be reported as that of any enemy soldier."[17] The author points to futile efforts on the part of historians seeking to "rehabilitate the war as a necessary and noble cause" even as they struggle to denounce inhumane tactics such as targeting the homes of South Vietnamese civilians. In short, the symbolic function of the silenced Vietnam-era veteran was to embody American guilt.

In the second half of the twentieth century, the emphasis placed on PTSD and other wounds of the mind shifted from a problem of gender to a problem of psychology. Meanwhile, for larger society, Eva Illouz argues that traumatic narratives became sources of power.[18] The author recognizes a "therapeutic culture" in which testimony now holds potential for individual and collective healing. Freud, as read by Illouz, psychologized normality before self-help literature emerged, providing "vocabularies through which the self understands itself."[19] But psychological care largely existed in the domain of privilege until the National Mental Health Act in 1946 rebranded psychology and moved it from the upper class to the military, from the military to the workplace, and finally to the individual.[20]

Psychologists became "healers of the psyche" who instituted changes in the workplace and redefined masculinity by requiring male leaders to take on "feminine attributes—such as paying attention to emotions, controlling anger, and listening sympathetically to others."[21] In the end, Illouz claims that this shift in gender normativity "democratized the power-ridden relations between workers and managers and instilled the new belief that one's personality—independently of social status—was the key to social and managerial success."[22] This belief transcended the workplace and took root on a national level, realigning "emotional cultures" and turning empathy and introspection into valued commodities.[23] Power now comes from within. Overcoming psychological trauma is evidence of that power.

Illouz's "therapeutic culture" explains how war wounds, once viewed as shameful signs of femininity among members of hypermasculine military cultures, were ameliorated through a shift of emphasis to the psychological experience of trauma. Trauma now occurs as part of a larger "story," and in that story the traumatized veteran exists passively until a civilian savior can come along to save them. As a result, the wound possessed by the post-9/11 "wounded warrior" is a commodity, a form of cultural capital. When a veteran remains silent the value of this wound is only limited by the civilian imagination. Thus, the "wounded warrior" occupies a symbolic position not dissimilar to that of the "hero," except that the assumption about them isn't that they did something heroic, but that their ability to function despite their suffering is nothing short of miraculous.

Mostly, veteran stereotyping is a matter of convenience, a way of avoiding difficult conversations for civilians and veterans alike. Sometimes it is a way for veterans to avoid post-traumatic symptoms or the difficult work of redefining themselves after exiting the service. I am interested in the functions of these symbolic positions, not taking a stance based on their subjective value. I am describing how veterans are perceived by others who would treat them as part of a victim class. As with the "hero" identity, I use quotation marks to distinguish between wounded veterans who openly share and shape the meanings attached to their war wounds and those who perform the "wounded warrior" stereotype in ways that rob them of symbolic authority. "Wounded warriors" lay claim to woundedness as the primary source of their identities. Importantly, the wounds—psychological or physical—are purposefully undefined so as to serve the needs of civilian imaginations. Patriarchal societies have historically described wounded or disabled veterans in essentialist, gendered terms—as veterans displaying weakness, not glorified military masculinity. The "wounded warrior" stereotype is rooted in earlier conceptions of cowardice, not bravery. Specifically, the wound is a form of cultural capital that can help veterans escape the "coward" label in the absence of feats of heroism.

Stephen Crane's Lasting Depictions of Cowardice and Woundedness

In the wake of the American Civil War, "cowards," as portrayed in Stephen Crane's *The Red Badge of Courage* (1895), were described as effeminate, lacking the quintessentially *male* qualities of military heroes. Crane's novel tells the story of Private Henry Fleming, a young soldier who lives in constant fear of combat. More accurately, he is afraid he will emerge from combat as a "coward." This fear becomes a self-fulfilling prophecy, driving Henry to desert his unit during battle. As events unfold, Henry receives a wound to the head from a comrade, and he somehow shifts the meaning of this wound so that it serves as evidence that he is *not* a coward. He satisfies public expectations of veterans—that they be brave and stoic in the face of certain death. As a result, Henry enjoys the hero treatment, and his wound has tangible value.

Crane's depiction of Henry Fleming emerged as the premiere cultural representation of military service in the American Civil War, defining notions of cowardice and bravery leading into the twentieth century. Eric Solomon argues that *The Red Badge of Courage* "gave the war novel its classic form."[24] Ironically, Crane was not a war veteran. In fact, as one of fourteen children, Crane grew up the son of a Methodist Episcopal minister. He was born after the American Civil War, in 1871, and began writing in the 1890s as a freelancer. His first book, *Maggie: A Girl of the Streets* (1893), is a story about the abuse of a young girl and her eventual suicide. It was not a successful novel in its time, and *The Red Badge of Courage*, in addition to reshaping the ways in which people write about war, rescued Crane from obscurity.

So, the novel held by critics such as Solomon to be the premiere, foundational, and most enduring representation of the American Civil War is not written by a veteran, but rather a man who conceived of his protagonist through research and oral histories decades after the Civil War ended. In "A Remarkable Book," a review published a year after the publication of Crane's novel, George Wyndham wrote that Crane's depiction of war was "truer" than Tolstoy's and asserted that war can instruct on the topic of human resilience.[25] I am not trying to make an argument about the novel's inauthenticity; quite the opposite. These words are evidence that veteran identity is defined as much by civilians as it is by veterans themselves, like how Tom Brokaw labeled the "Greatest Generation" fifty years after World War II.

James Jones, drawing on his own service in World War II, includes a poignant reflection on military heroism in his novel about the Guadalcanal campaign, *The Thin Red Line* (1962). Welsh, one of the central characters, remembers interactions with veterans from previous generations:

> Welsh had never been in combat. But he had lived for a long time with a lot of men who had. And he had pretty well lost his belief in, as well as his awe of, the mystique of human combat. Old vets from the First World War, younger men who had been with the Fifteenth Infantry in China, for years he had sat around getting drunk with them and listening to their drunken stories of melancholy bravery. He had watched the stories grow with the years and the drinking sprees, and he had been able to form only one conclusion and that was that every old vet was a hero. How so many heroes survived and so many non-heroes got knocked off, Welsh could not answer. But every old vet was a hero. If you did not believe it, you had only to ask them, or better yet, get drunk and not ask them. There just wasn't any other kind.[26]

The character's critique of veteran identity runs in stark contrast to those who claim veterans "do not like to talk about it." In fact, veteran identity is in continual negotiations with historical memory. Beyond obvious acts of military heroism, the telling and retelling of stories about service are a form of bartering for status and respect. Jones's irony, of course, is that heroism is defined by its rarity. Likewise, Crane ironically presents war as a game meant to coax it out.

Henry enlists in the Union army in search of battlefield glory. However, he soon realizes that war guarantees neither glory nor survival. As the story progresses, each painful moment of waiting registers as anxiety and fear. Henry discovers a "problem" within himself, a predilection for survival, which outweighs his desire to fight and earn his manhood.[27] Henry, like subsequent generations of veterans, began as a civilian, was transformed into a warfighter, and returned home someone new. Henry's "problem"—his fear of emerging from war as a coward—is evidence of the socially constructed nature of veteran identity. The *military hero* sits atop a masculine hierarchy of veteran identities, and to leave war as anything less than a hero connotes inferiority in the minds of veterans and civilians alike. At the bottom of this hierarchy sits the "coward," colloquially understood as any person who refuses to contribute to the war effort or who puts other soldiers at risk.

An example from the Afghanistan War can be found in the story of Sergeant Bowe Bergdahl. He walked off base and deserted his unit in 2009, an act that resulted in his capture and "brutal conditions for five years, including locking him in a cage in darkness for lengthy periods."[28] Bergdahl's actions and eventual release were heavily politicized. Though designated a POW, members of his unit publicly denounced him as a deserter, expressing disdain over the subsequent missions and raids launched to retrieve him. Meanwhile, many outsiders looking in felt sympathy for the young sergeant, wondering if his imprisonment and torture were punishment enough. Though no Americans were killed during the search for Bergdahl (an allegation made early in the ensuing debates), the fact that soldiers were wounded is undeniable.[29] In fact, one soldier, Master Sergeant Mark Allen, died in 2019 from complications related to a severe head injury sustained during the search for Bergdahl. Still, I remain ambivalent about the series of events and am left wondering about the mental state of the young soldier when he felt it necessary to walk off a military base in hostile territory with the belief that he could survive. There are certainly valid arguments to be made both for and against the handling of Bergdahl's case, both by the military and the American public.

It is the fear of this sort of dishonor—of being labeled a "coward" after their service ends—that can determine a soldier's actions in combat, and an individual's playing the part of a veteran in interpersonal situations. The "coward" label is one most veterans will fight vehemently to avoid. Or they will at least attempt to live their post-service lives in a way to dispel rumors. Crane wrote an addendum to the life of Henry Fleming entitled "The Veteran" in 1896. In the story, the older Henry explains the American Civil War to those who did not experience it, noting that "their opinion of his heroism was fixed."[30] When he finally admits that he ran away from the battle, as depicted in *The Red Badge of Courage*, his grandson (named after a friend Henry had served with, Jim Conklin) "was visibly horror stricken. His hands were clasped nervously, and his eyes were wide with astonishment at this terrible scandal, his most magnificent grandfather telling such a thing."[31] The story's climax involves the protagonist trying to save animals from a barn fire, rushing into the flames repeatedly to save them. The moral seems to be that older, more experienced men are better prepared to survive dangers such as war, or that veterans are driven to avoid being labeled—by self or others—as a coward. It is also interesting to note how the grandson's identity is attached to Henry's heroism, perhaps another example of veteran identity forming long before service.

Compare the types of stories described by James Jones in *The Thin Red Line* alongside Henry's first experience with combat in the sixth chapter of Crane's novel. Henry begins in a state of exhaustion, unsure of what he is seeing due to smoke and chaos. He experiences the scene like "an onslaught of redoubtable dragons," waiting with his eyes shut "to be gobbled."[32] These descriptors underscore the childlike innocence he will undoubtedly lose. War is an abstraction until Henry makes the decision to run "like a rabbit" with "no shame in his face" because, logically, he is engaged in the biological act of self-preservation. Put this drive to survive alongside words like "the majesty of he who dares give his life" and it's hard not to discern the true power of public conceptions of veteran identity, of shame triumphing over biological imperatives.[33]

Crane's novel gained popularity during a time when memories of war were beginning to resurface in the minds of his readers. Henry Fleming, for example, would have been in his forties. Crane recreates memories, preconceived notions, and stereotypes rooted in the actual experiences of Civil War veterans. As a result, *The Red Badge of Courage* succeeds in producing a true-to-life protagonist. Veterans like Henry Fleming were still around. They were discussing their service. They were bartering for status and respect. Crane had many real sources to draw on when constructing his imaginary war veteran. The product is Henry: young, naive, afraid, and in search of some battlefield glory that will cure him of a "problem" socially constructed by others.

Henry Fleming's "Problem"

E. Anthony Rotundo, a scholar of nineteenth-century American masculinity, suggests, "Men devised experiences that helped transform the impulsive passions of the boy into the purposeful energies of the man."[34] In other words, some young soldiers view military service as a stepping stone toward careers outside of the military, or maybe just adulthood, hoping that military service will provide them with the type of masculine experience and homosocial bonding needed to attain positions of privilege in larger society. Crane's character emerges in a country ravaged by war, and apprenticeships and academies are not the most readily available sites of masculine transformation. And as Leo Braudy claims, "wars . . . require such a focus on one prime way of defining what a man is that the reaction against them is central to either the revision or the bolstering of traditional gender ideas."[35] Wartime experience permits self-definition, but only in a way that grants privilege within patriarchal power structures. As Braudy explains, stories like *The Red Badge of Courage* and the experience of war throw "the contours of masculinity . . . into high relief."[36] These contours are more clearly defined through the juxtaposition of femininity and masculinity in the novel.

Descriptions of the war reveal "The captain of the company . . . coaxed in [a] schoolmistress fashion."[37] Such associations of fear and femininity continue in their preparations for battle: "There was rustling and muttering among the men. They displayed a feverish desire to have every possible cartridge ready to their hands. The boxes were pulled around into various positions, and adjusted with great care. It was as if seven hundred new bonnets were being tried on."[38] Crane feminizes anything related to fear, or, more succinctly, not killing: "schoolmistresses," "bonnets," and a "girlish," "trembling lip," made in passing reference to another character, are all Henry's projections. After deserting, Henry finds refuge in the feminized space (or what Donald Pizer has called "the chapel") of nature.[39] Crane's treatment of "nature" as feminine sanctuary was likely informed by the Transcendentalist American authors from half a century prior.[40] In fact, Crane presents two opposite and competing spheres: The patriarchal, masculine sphere emblematized by war, or the fear that Henry wants to conquer; and the feminine sphere represented by nature, or the place where Henry finds solace and time to reflect after deserting his unit and before getting a second chance at manhood.

Ironically, Henry suffers from a defect of character when he claims—very reasonably—that "It was criminal to stay calmly in one spot and make no effort to stay destruction."[41] His "flaws" further emerge when he "regard[s] the wounded soldiers in an envious way" and when he wishes that he had "a red badge of courage."[42] The result of his failings becomes the invention of his own brand of courage, one he creates after wandering back to his unit, nursing a wound exacted on him by another Union soldier: "I got shot. In th' head. I never see sech fightin'."[43] Henry believes honor—a form of cultural capital—is legitimized by a physical wound. He is unwilling to sacrifice himself within a community of brothers. But the experience of marching toward war, running away from it, and becoming wounded educate him about what such sacrifices entail. As a result, he can concoct a story, one which allows him to commodify his wound and draw on it as cultural capital among men he feels are braver than himself. They believe his lie. And importantly, Henry believes it himself.

Henry's wound is the physical referent for the psychic wound inflicted on him as a child: debasement within the masculine hierarchy and homosocial order. This wound occurred long before Henry dreamed of going to war. His story is a cautionary tale about the "possibility of anarchy," a fear woven into performances of masculinity that scholars such as Rotundo claim is caused by men who refuse to become parts of the patriarchal order.[44] Pizer underscores the precariousness of Henry's position: "Put briefly, the riddle is the seeming disjunction between, on the one hand, a structural center of initiation, in which a young man, after at first failing, successfully meets a community standard of conduct, and is thus welcomed back into the group."[45] Indeed, he displays bravery by embracing the most visible sign of masculinity on any battlefield, a flag that was "projected, sun-touched, resplendent." Henry leaves the feminine altar of nature for the altar of masculinity, carrying the phallic guidon—the regimental colors—valiantly into battle. Henry's rhetorically constructed wound gives him courage. It is equal parts guilt, post-traumatic stress, fear, and physical distress. This constructed pain *becomes* his emblem of masculine allegiance, of his *willingness* to sacrifice and join masculine society. His red badge of courage is based on a lie, but it provides him with pain, which in this case is a commodity.

Henry's manhood is tainted by "the old Lie," the trap that Wilfred Owen warns about in "Dulce et Decorum Est": "My friend, you would not tell with such high zest / To children ardent for some desperate glory, / The old Lie: *Dulce et decorum est / Pro patria mori.*"[46] Henry never believes, even for a second, that it is fitting and proper to die for one's country. But he finds ways to circumvent his lack of belief. He transforms himself into something other than a coward by redefining the wound he receives from a fellow soldier. He begins with the psychological wound of growing up without a father, one for which he receives no sympathy in the homosocial order. He then experiences a physical wound in war that conveys respect. In this way, Henry's story is a precursor for the "wounded warrior" stereotype described in this chapter. The wound is a commodity. It is most valuable when it is a secret. And post-9/11 veterans live in a world that assumes they are all damaged.

Evolution of the "Wounded Warrior"

The "coward" of Crane's novel is not the same as the post-9/11 "wounded warrior." I'm not arguing that "wounded warriors" are deserters, malingerers, or in any way deficient in their military service. However, I am arguing that the "wounded warrior" identity is a stereotype, one that can be traced back to a need to escape the coward label, and Crane's Henry Fleming is one example of a veteran who goes to war with a desire (on some level) to be wounded because wounds can be a form of cultural capital. Another, more contemporary example, would be Gary Sinise's character "Lieutenant Dan" in *Forrest Gump* (1994), a character who is angered when he does not die in battle. It was his family's claim to honor, and the character broke with tradition. Both Henry Fleming and Lieutenant Dan view wounds as commodities that can be brokered in exchange for respect.

Following the American Civil War, public perceptions of veterans began to shift. No longer was the public as concerned about heroism or cowardice. They were concerned about the threat veterans with disabilities posed to federal tax dollars. Glenn Altschuler and Stuart Blumin's *The GI Bill: A New Deal for Veterans* (2009), includes a satirical cartoon labeled "The Insatiable Glutton." The character shown in the cartoon is a Union army veteran, with dozens of arms digging into a soup bowl labeled with the words "U.S. Treasury."[47] This caricature of Civil War pensioners as malingerers and grifters persisted into the First World War. As the American Legion fought to have shell-shocked veterans treated humanely after that war, American employers turned their backs on returning veterans in droves. Instead of commodities, the psychological wounds of these soldiers were viewed as threats to stability and safety in the American workforce. Modris Eksteins explains in *Rites of Spring* (1989), "Employers were encouraged to hire former soldiers, but many found them a poor risk. The incidence of unemployment among ex-servicemen was pitifully high."[48]

It was around this time in history that cinema emerged as a quintessential American art form. In *Reel Patriotism* (1997), an examination of war films produced in the 1920s, Leslie Midkiff DeBauche argues that films focused on "[c]elebrating the end of the war, relegating the war to the historical past, and directing attention away from its presence."[49] For the first time, the public could glimpse war from afar. It could be experienced vicariously as a source of entertainment rather than personally as a source of trauma. The profit motive changed the way audiences viewed war. Representations of it became a commodity, a product with all of the excitement and propaganda of military service but none of the sacrifice.

During World War II, the president of the University of Chicago, Robert M. Hutchins, anticipating the influx of returning veterans, warned that "colleges and universities will find themselves converted into educational hobo jungles. And veterans unable to get work and equally unable to resist putting pressure on the colleges and universities, will find themselves educational hoboes."[50] At the same time, clergy warned against the "sin" of soldiers infiltrating society, suggesting that war corrupts the souls of those who fight in them.[51] While World War I veterans were labeled as weak or cowardly for inescapable wounds like shell shock, World War II veterans had to deal with this denigration along with the view that physical wounds somehow made them deficient. They became good at staying quiet and hiding their wounds, and these secrets later led to the myth that they were made of "tougher stuff" than other generations.

Representations of war came to shape audience expectation. J. E. Smyth's *Reconstructing American Historical Cinema* (2006) argues that the nature of modern warfare, coupled with an industry keen on selling war as a source of entertainment, gradually turned the "doughboy" into "a nameless and passive American reacting to the horrors of war and the poverty of the aftermath."[52] The "wounded warrior" starts to take shape in the

American unconscious. First, mechanized warfare increasingly robbed World War I veterans of their ability to prove their heroism. Woundedness emerged as a commodity that could explain away a lack of heroism and dispel suspicions of cowardice. Then, war became a source of entertainment at the same point in history in which veterans were perceived as leeches on the federal tax system. Naturally, the American public preferred the clean narratives of heroism found in cinema and rhetoric to the real thing. Mental illness is an invisible wound, often subjectively experienced. In recent history, psychological wounds are assumed among all veterans. The "wounded warrior" simply refuses to challenge this assumption in exchange for comfortable silence.

In *Male Subjectivity at the Margins* (1992), Kaja Silverman examines post-World War II cinema in which "the 'hero' returns from war with a physical or psychic wound," arguing that such wounds imply that the veteran is "incapable of functioning smoothly in civilian life."[53] In these examples, the bodies, minds, and souls of veterans are all used as evidence in arguments *against* allowing veterans back into society. New understandings of war neuroses after World War II took that shame away from the families of soldiers, but it remained a stereotype faced by veterans themselves. Silverman elaborates, using examples from *The Best Years of Our Lives* (1946) and *It's a Wonderful Life* (1946) to discuss an "ideological fatigue" provoked by the "historical trauma of World War II and the recovery period."[54] Insecurity is at the "heart of all subjectivity."[55] Influenced by Jacques Lacan, Silverman is saying that we are all castrated, and that coherent masculinity is a fiction. War wounds, likewise, reveal the constructed nature of masculinity. This "lack" is Henry Fleming's "problem," his fear of emerging from war as a coward, as deficient.

It is the same lack experienced by veterans again and again in cinema, in examples like *Top Gun*'s Maverick or *Forrest Gump*'s Lieutenant Dan. After war and war violence destabilize the male ego, the "lack" is relocated and experienced as an obsession over not suffering enough, or not suffering in the right way. Abstract notions of woundedness contained in stereotypes such as the "wounded warrior" provide every veteran with an invisible but undeniable wound. In other words, a type of wound emerged that could be seen or felt only by veterans themselves. It was something created out of necessity. It stopped conversations about veteran identity and questions about veteran masculinity dead in their tracks simply by virtue of never being interrogated. I argue that this phenomenon can best be described as a "traumatic assumption," or society's mistaken belief that all veterans are psychologically damaged.

The inability of World War II veterans to confront the damage done to the male ego during their war is a by-product of patriotic rhetoric. Specifically, it is a product of the myth of "The Greatest Generation," which assumes that all veterans from that war came home and immediately picked up where they left off. When memories of the gruesome experience of World War II evolved into a collective memory of what is now regarded as America in its prime, veterans were assigned their symbolic function: they became repositories of memories of war, keeping the horrors of war a secret so that America might shine as an exceptional nation. The "traumatic assumption" ensured that veterans of future generations would continue to serve as repositories. Later conflicts and evidence of veteran imperfections complicated these idealistic notions of American masculinity.

World War I veterans were shamed for their psychological wounds. World War II veterans were shamed for physical ones. Korean War veterans were shamed for being captured, and Vietnam veterans were labeled as mass murderers. For veterans, it is as though the goalposts for sympathy kept getting pushed farther and farther back. So, a new form of woundedness emerged, one best described as a secret. And for post-9/11 veterans the "wounded warrior" stereotype persists so long as their wounds are never defined.

Yes, many recruits join the military for employment and benefits. But there are other jobs that offer those things. The military has the added incentive of being an honorable profession, one in which the recruit can cultivate a sense of self that ties into the larger narrative that service members are altruistic. However, instead of focusing on the altruistic nature that leads recruits to war, and instead of emphasizing the veteran's capacities as leaders or educators, those who are labeled "wounded warriors" are defined by abstract notions of woundedness.

Therapeutic Culture: The Entanglement of Veteran Identity with PTSD

The "hero"/"wounded warrior" binary strips veterans of agency, of the right to self-definition by marginalizing their stories, experiences, and lessons. "Heroes" are marginalized due to patriotic rhetoric and the state's need to showcase exceptional examples of wartime bravery. If individuals labeled as "heroes" exist openly and honestly regarding military service, they risk not being exceptional enough. On the other hand, "wounded warriors" are never considered exceptional examples; their wounds preclude it. The rhetoric that shapes their identity is not patriotic; it is "therapeutic." For "wounded warriors," the risk of engaging in testimony or self-definition is not one of failing to be exceptional. Rather, these veterans risk being perceived as not wounded enough or in the right way.

In *Rethinking Therapeutic Culture* (2015), Tim Aubry and Trysh Travis explain that perpetrators, nonconformists, and racists are all lumped together with survivors in that mental health treatment is often the prescribed course of action: "Why? Because we have made the individual psyche the primary object of our attention. We treat its improper functioning as the principal source of society's ills and see its balance and well-being as the ultimate goal of our strivings on this earth."[56] This reading states that therapists, in all of their different forms and with all of their varying degrees and qualifications, have come to replace clergy, elders, and educators as subject matter experts on the human mind, but also on the human soul. Aubry and Travis argue that "therapeutic culture is an especially American phenomenon," a "complex web of shared assumptions, behaviors, and institutions that brings individuals together and shapes their values and ideals."[57] Social theorists, both liberal and conservative, have criticized "therapeutic culture," and Aubry and Travis discuss alternative views of this phenomenon, views that indicate how such a culture "dupes, demoralizes and pacifies those it claims to help—it deepens their problems rather than resolving them."[58]

Here is an example of how "therapeutic culture" can be problematic. Payton Jones, Benjamin Bellet, and Richard McNally (2020) found that trigger warnings do very little to help survivors of trauma. In fact, they argue that the opposite could be true: when individuals in positions of authority provide such alerts, they actually elicit behaviors and reactions that make those they are trying to help see their trauma as a cornerstone of their identity.[59] "Therapeutic culture" represents a shift in emphasis. Henry Fleming, like generations of young soldiers who came before him, sought out agency and a way to define himself in battle—in the physical world. Modern Americans have the option of looking inward for a wound, or a psychological scar that can lend their lives meaning. In a "therapeutic culture" psychological wounds are commodities, but the narrative of those wounds is required in order to gain access to them. Fleming was able to build a narrative around a blow to the head perpetrated by a fellow soldier. Now, psychiatric diagnoses make pain, sadness, and despair matter to the outside world. It is unfortunate that these are the lengths veterans (or anyone) must go to in order to elicit sympathy.

Veterans are products of "therapeutic cultures," in part, because clinicians and scholars seek to make sense of their abstract wounds: "Indeed, the growth of mental health services for soldiers and veterans, especially during and after World War II, helped to destigmatize therapy, as huge numbers of purportedly normal individuals availed themselves of it."[60] Again, the "wounded warrior" label functions on the assumption of trauma. Individuals who model the "wounded warrior" stereotype remain silent, sometimes to make wounds appear less threatening, sometimes to make them appear more threatening, but usually to maintain the notion that they are "veteran enough" for their civilian audience. Indeed, "therapeutic culture" and the veteran's symbolic function seem to go hand in hand. Veterans are given a choice: remain silent about war, avoiding the triggers and memories; or speak openly about wartime experience, risking the appropriation of their stories—their *pain*—by a larger collective.

Testimonies and Shortcuts

In many cases, "wounded warriors" do experience combat. They do have wounds. And they suffer for years after their wars end. However, the way the "wounded warrior" stereotype frames war, as an experience *defined* by woundedness, deprives veterans of their symbolic authority in the same way that "therapeutic culture" has the capacity to deprive survivors of a chance to heal, especially if the therapy doesn't encourage veterans to share their story outside of the therapy setting.

Testimony is the source of power veterans relinquish when they exist *silently* as "wounded warriors." Stevan Weine defines it as an act with the "ability to 'fuse' or create a shortcut between the private and public worlds, [which] combined with its considerable redemptive promise, [has] given it a unique therapeutic and cultural power."[61] In scholarly circles, "testimony" tends to refer to individuals who speak out against atrocity, such as Holocaust survivors, people who survive traumas like rape or attempted murder, and certainly veterans and noncombatants who survive war.

Testimony has the therapeutic value of helping survivors reimagine their respective places in the world after trauma. It has the social value of reshaping collective memory. "Therapeutic culture," however, includes the confluence of *many* acts of testimony, describing a society *obsessed* with personal narratives of triumph over adversity. But not every veteran's story is one of triumph. And, sometimes, the needs of the listener do not reflect the needs of the veteran. Veterans experience this dissonance as a pressure to tell stories in which they, too, triumphed over adversity. So, narratives of "heroes" and "wounded warriors" are vague, ignoring negative aspects of military service—such as perpetrator's guilt or lifelong disabilities—so that the story might become one about healing.

The "wounded warrior" stereotype cannot function as a complete identity because it requires veterans to remain in a perpetual state of victimization. Veterans who model the "wounded warrior" stereotype unwittingly accept the privileges of conformity and the comfort of silence in exchange for individual rights to testimony. Unfortunately, remaining silent about one's past prevents veterans from developing healthy, complete identities—from continuing to evolve as individuals after military service. Humans are storytellers: Children tell stories about themselves to *conceive of* and *relate* who they are to others.[62] As adults, we all tell stories about ourselves, even if it is just talking to a romantic partner about a long day at work. Each day that story continues, allowing the teller to evolve as a character and to make sense of the ongoing experience. Veterans are pressured not to tell the whole story, and so they adopt either the "wounded warrior" or "hero" stereotype as a placeholder for identity.

Weine suggests that "investment in the personal can come at the expense of the social."[63] In other words, the act of giving testimony stakes a claim to a form of identity that may conflict with the identity others prescribe for an individual. The social aspects of testimony are often overlooked, and Weine's view is that testimony becomes public property when it is injected into social discourse. Veterans are not exempt from this kind of "therapeutic culture"; they're prime examples of its damaging effects. When they bow to pressures from third parties—governments, media, or even fellow veterans calling for a single record of events—they forfeit the rights to their narratives. Often, they experience a growing sense that they're *different*, that "the act isn't working," or that they're not meant to exist as more than victims who once wore a military uniform.

Junger's *Tribe* (2016) attempts to understand the psychological and emotional experiences of veteran homecoming. He laments the billions of dollars spent on VA health care for post-9/11 war veterans and large disparities between the percentage of veterans who've seen combat and those who have applied for PTSD compensation. Junger wonders how a fraction of veterans experience combat amid the record rates of PTSD reported: "[M]ost disability claims are for hearing loss, tinnitus, and PTSD—the latter two of which can be imagined, exaggerated, or even faked."[64] He cites evidence of veterans dropping out of treatment after receiving total disability ratings, listing off the amount of compensation these individuals receive each month, but failing to consider whether or not these "dropouts" are simply able to afford better treatment. Junger quotes angry veterans, whom he calls the "real deals" who fantasize about physically assaulting these *fakers*, but he never contemplates whether such hostility scares away other veterans who deserve treatment. Nor is there much concern for the overlap between PTSD and other disorders, or different causes of trauma, such as military sexual assault. This particular line of argument within *Tribe* seems to extend and update "The Insatiable Glutton" stereotype used against Civil War pensioners, and also the myth of "welfare queens" that was used to stigmatize poor and Black citizens in the 1970s and 1980s.

Junger may be correct that veterans risk becoming a "victim class," but that eventuality is linked to civilian perceptions of veterans, not the amount of compensation veterans receive for fighting wars.[65] More likely, veterans' struggles with reassimilation are a combination of the literal and symbolic limitations placed on them. Whereas Junger's overarching thesis about veterans searching for the comforts of tribalism in their postwar lives is a needed addition to discourse concerning veterans, his perpetuation of this particular stereotype is not. Junger is right to criticize the VA for misdiagnoses. But how does implicating veterans as a disparate group of welfare cases serve them collectively as a culture? I agree with Junger that veterans should resist victimization narratives, but his fears of rampant abuse of the VA health care system only exacerbates the guilt felt by deserving veterans who are simply unsure about how their traumas stack up. Among members of any population there will be those who abuse the system. But as one example of a veteran who used his education benefits and disability compensation to support himself while earning a Ph.D., and as an educator who has worked with dozens of veterans also seeking to better themselves, I can state for a fact that those individual *fakers* do not represent the whole or even the majority.

I know Junger means well. His service to the veteran community is immeasurable. And he articulates this particular point much better in a

TED Talk entitled "Our Lonely Society Makes It Hard to Come Home from War."[66] He acknowledges that individuals prone to long-term PTSD tend to be those who suffered traumas as children, who come from low socioeconomic backgrounds, or who present with other risk factors. Junger argues, "Maybe what determines the rate of long-term PTSD isn't what happened out there, but the kind of society you come back to."[67] And, to be fair, Junger says outright in *Tribe* that the "vast majority of traumatized veterans are not faking their symptoms."[68] Ultimately, however, his argument leaves me searching for generational or occupational norms among service members with PTSD that I doubt exist.

Veterans returning from the Vietnam War, the Gulf War, and the Global War on Terror have different rates of disability and recovery because they returned to very different countries. Junger advances this argument by describing America as a country with "low social resilience," one in which "resources are not shared equally" and veterans are offered "lifelong disability payments" when working to improve the social conditions contributing to the longevity of their PTSD would be more therapeutic.[69] Instead, veterans are counted and sorted, assigned percentages that place a monetary value on their woundedness, which inadvertently validates or invalidates their experiences. As a country, the United States needs to find ways to allow self-definition, treatment, and compensation to take place separately.

PTSD should not dominate discussions of veteran identity. Certainly, PTSD should inform those discussions, especially when it is an obvious influence in the life of an individual veteran. But discussions of PTSD, as they take place in America's "therapeutic culture," suggest every veteran should be mentally or physically handicapped. Further, "therapeutic culture" keeps veterans silent by blaming the veteran's struggle on some deficiency in the human mind, even when wars and those who start them exist as much simpler, more easily defined sources of that struggle.

Testimony versus "Get Off My Lawn"

On my way home from Iraq to attend my brother's funeral, I shared a plane with a unit returning home to Texas in 2005. I remember Vietnam and Korean War-era veterans greeting the passengers as we arrived in the Houston airport. I, too, was in uniform, so the older veterans assumed that I had completed my "tour of duty" and deserved a "hero's welcome."

Obviously, given the circumstances, I did not feel like a "hero." Nor did I feel like usurping praise meant for others on my layover. So, I avoided the scenes of heartfelt reunion and chatted with the older veterans.

"Start your claims now," one said.

"I am still waiting on mine," said another. "Don't take no for an answer, always appeal." It took me a while to figure out what they were talking about, not only because of the cloud of my immediate grief over my brother, but mostly because my understanding of the world was so very limited when I enlisted that I knew nothing about the VA health care system. When I was growing up, the nearest VA hospital was over an hour away. I'd heard a few things, all bad, and those gentlemen only made the system sound worse. More important, for me, was the fact that they were filling in blanks about what it meant to exist as a "veteran." Specifically, those first lessons taught me that I would return home (after I finished my deployment) "wounded," and that my life would revolve around proving that fact.

They weren't wrong. I've since gone through many battles for compensation related to injuries—physical and psychological—that I sustained as a result of serving in Iraq. To be sure, I've felt guilt about receiving a check. Lots of my veteran friends say the same thing. Many veterans deserving of compensation and treatment refuse to interact with the VA because they fear they will take away from others. I try to remind myself that larger society would not have made benefits available to veterans had they not wanted those benefits to be used. However, what are the cumulative effects of forcing veterans to shape stories of military service around narratives of trauma, repeatedly, and for a biased audience such as the Department of Veterans Affairs?

The word "survivor" is intentionally used when referring to "testimony" because it indicates the giver's accomplishment. To speak about atrocity, individual trauma, or war robs those experiences of their harmful power. Testimony gives that power to the individual. It is the power to reshape meaning, to redefine one's existence, to help others avoid the same. The veterans I met at that airport in Texas were using their stories of struggling with the VA to help me. They engaged in the act of testimony, and it's likely they did not realize it. The power of testimony is that it drags the unspeakable into the light of day, revealing its ugliness, describing the survivor's weakness to show how far that survivor has come. But, given the conditions I have described—"therapeutic culture," patriotic myths, and the symbolic function of veterans—is such testimony even possible?

Indeed, the stories told about veterans are often written by others, by civilians more interested in becoming saviors than in allowing veterans to reassimilate. Again, and in a return to Butler, "wounded warriors" lose their sense of self in telling the stories of themselves. I often felt like I lost the story of the growth I experienced in the military when constantly having to explain my military experience to the VA in terms of how it had damaged me. Gatekeepers of trauma and benefits will point and accuse any veteran with a complex story involving both growth and wounds of malingering or stealing valor. They point out the moment veterans fall outside the boundaries of being "wounded warrior" or "hero" stereotypes, or when a veteran shares a nuanced story. For many veterans, it is infuriating to a degree that they would rather not interact with the VA at all.

At the same time, veterans aware of the "traumatic assumption" often use it as a defense mechanism to avoid uncomfortable questions and truths. And, especially in those cases of veterans dealing with PTSD, this defense mechanism feeds the avoidance symptom, which gives the condition its staying power. I am not referring to a large-scale phenomenon, but rather local performances of victimhood by individual veterans. And it is important to know that when I say "performances of victimhood," I am not referring to malingering. More accurately, I should say that "wounded warriors" embrace the narrative of victimhood prescribed for them by others because it is the path of least resistance.

The assumptions made about veterans define the characters they perform. For instance, one assumption holds that veterans hate those with the ethnicity of the country against which they fought. Clint Eastwood's disgruntled Korean War veteran in *Gran Torino* (2008) is an example.[70] *Gran Torino* is a film about a veteran attempting to reform a teenager who tries to steal his car. A certain level of racism in Eastwood's portrayal of Walt Kowalski is accepted under the pretense that he suffered brutal trauma at the hands of enemies in the Korean War. Kowalski is acutely aware of this assumption and performs it in his interactions with the outside world. He uses the "traumatic assumption" to keep people at a distance.

At its core, *Gran Torino* is a film about letting go of anger and sadness. Its lessons and thematic elements pertain to *human* experience, not just *veteran* experience, echoing the sentiment that veterans have much to teach society as a whole. However, there are some challenges unique to veteran identity for the protagonist to overcome. Namely, Kowalski must confront the source of his racism: fear. This confrontation within the protagonist corresponds to an external conflict in the real world. In dealings with a young Hmong boy who tries to steal his car, Kowalski develops a relationship with the boy and his family. The apartness that the veteran feels in relation to civilian society fades away. Soon the reason for his loneliness—for his veteran-disgruntledness—is revealed as the performance of veteran identity. Kowalski realizes that keeping people at a distance has prevented him from experiencing the full range of human emotions.

Perhaps the most famous scene comes when Kowalski, pointing a gun at a group of young Asian gang members, utters his famous line, "Get off my lawn." The line is an homage to the lawn-obsessed "crazy veteran next door" many children encountered growing up. But it also serves as a window into that character's psyche. Soon after the iconic line, in a matter-of-fact tone, Kowalski states some context, "I blow a hole in your face and then I go in the house . . . and I sleep like a baby. You can count on that. We used to stack fucks like you five feet high in Korea . . . use ya for sandbags." The gang members accept this highly unlikely scenario as fact and retreat. And so the psychological trauma of the veteran in *Gran Torino* is ultimately a source of power. Sure, it forces a gang into retreat in the film, but what about the days, months, and years Kowalski spent performing that character? How much of his life was spent in service of that one moment of power?

Eastwood's trademark grimace perfectly complements his hard-boiled tough veteran character. In fact, it is a character so stereotypical and misunderstood, or so *exceptionally* "veteran," that pity yields to intrigue. Penetrating Kowalski's rough exterior to identify with the protagonist results in the audience's empathy. The more Kowalski reveals about his past, the more his stereotypical facade melts away. He's not "telling a story" in the literal sense. But in his interactions with those around him—especially in those instances in which the character moves beyond the limitations imposed on him by his veteran persona—Kowalski begins to self-narrate, continuing to evolve where previously his stereotypical existence prevented it. Kowalski rejoins humanity, and in the process reshapes attitudes toward veterans.

His actions employ Weine's "shortcut," erasing those boundaries that separate private suffering from public performance. Kowalski resists the appropriation of his narrative, an act common in America's "therapeutic culture," by dealing directly with the racism and violence assumed to be inextricable from his identity. In return, the characters in *Gran Torino*, its audience, and even those reading about the film through this third party must confront Kowalski's individuality. The film illustrates exactly what I mean when I say veteran storytellers do not have to be authors or artists. When veterans are consciously aware of the act, the performance of their individual veteran identity is its own work of art.

Yellow Birds and the Evolution of Veteran Identity

Kevin Powers's novel *The Yellow Birds* (2013) differs from Crane's in that the audience's search for evidence of cowardice is replaced with a search for evidence of war trauma. These rituals are a way of objectifying veterans, of seeing how they stack up within hierarchies of military masculinity. In my reading of Powers's novel, the tools of literary analysis are brought to bear on this problem in a way that sometimes seems as though I am addressing craft when my hope is that every analysis serves the larger phenomenological exploration of post-9/11 homecoming. For a novelist such as Powers, how does the act of storytelling intersect with his audience's views of veteran identity? In what ways are his characters constrained? And what limitations do readers place on the narrative structure due to stereotypical conceptions of veteran identity?

The desire to discern which veterans are heroes, victims, and cowards functions as part of America's "therapeutic culture," shaping war novels in the same way that stereotypical notions of feminine weakness shaped Crane's representation of war. In Crane's novel, Henry Fleming's fear of becoming a coward plays to readers interested in conceptions of veteran identity rooted in ideal forms of masculinity. Similarly, Powers attends to a readership invested in maintaining the notion that veterans are monolithically and irrecoverably traumatized by their experiences.

Shortly after the release of *Yellow Birds* in 2012, Benjamin Percy, writing for the *New York Times*, hailed the novel as "compact and powerful as a footlocker full of ammo."[71] Similar to James Jones, Powers enlisted in the US Army at the age of seventeen and went on to deploy to Iraq, later telling his story through the remove of fictional characters. The protagonist, twenty-one-year-old Private Bartle, befriends a seventeen-year-old Private Murph not long before deploying in 2004 to Al Tafar, Iraq. Stories that feature a veteran character working through trauma are so ubiquitous—perpetuated through a combination of market forces, veteran negotiations with historical memory, patriotic narratives, and of course the lives of veterans impacted psychologically by war—that they can be expected before ever opening the cover of a book about war. Bartle's story is no exception.

Again, the post-9/11 generation exists in a "therapeutic culture" in which identity is transactional, explaining why the dynamic in *Yellow Birds*, a novel that illustrates the transformation of an active duty soldier into a "veteran," requires audience participation. Illouz engages with social theorists who recognize that "modernity and capitalism . . . created a form of emotional numbness which separated people from one another, from their community and from their own deep selves."[72] Indeed, these divisions are what Aubry and Travis reveal in describing the appropriating effects of "therapeutic culture." Illouz complicates this argument and shows how, despite numbness and divisions, shared emotions are intrinsic parts of capitalism that follow "the logic of economic relations and exchange."[73] The framework guiding these relations intertwines victimhood with self-help, fostering an environment where the individual is free to both create and cure their own misery. Individuals need only to find some physical referent, some "red badge of courage" through which to explain invisible wounds.

How does Powers tap into the audience's expectations? A "traumatic assumption" is first employed in describing the character Sergeant Sterling, an experienced veteran who "had been to Iraq already, on the first push north out of Kuwait, and had been decorated, so even the higher-ups looked at him with admiration."[74] Sterling, as Powers implies through his backstory and demeanor, is already haunted by war, and his behavior is subject to its influence. The implicit question of the novel is this: "Will Bartle's experiences in Iraq result in his ending up like Sterling?" Post-traumatic symptoms haunt the plot of *Yellow Birds* as anticipation for an answer to this question.

Percy addresses that anticipation in his *New York Times* review as he comments on Powers's leaving the audience to guess about the circumstances of Murph's death: "This serves the story in two ways. First, it turns readers into active participants, enlisting them in a sense as co-authors who fit together the many memories and guess at what terrible secret lies in wait, the truth behind Murph's death. Because they lean forward instead of back, because they participate in piecing together the puzzle, they are made more culpable."[75] Percy claims that *Yellow Birds* requires readers to recognize their own culpability for war. Take this line of argument one step further. War and veteran identity and inseparable. There will always be recruits who enlist to prove they are heroes. There will always be recruits who enlist in search of a "red badge of courage." They will not seek out death or dismemberment, but a violent experience that grants them symbolic authority. When readers "piece together the puzzle" in Powers's novel, they are doing the work of maintaining stereotypical conceptions of veteran identity that perpetuate these calls to war.

The first chapter of *Yellow Birds* is a traditional, *in medias res* telling of a combat mission, and by the third chapter Murph hasn't survived. He hovers like a ghost over the plot, a ghost whose backstory is filled in through the psychological symptoms of grief, loss, and post-traumatic stress often found among those who survive war. Bartle's story must conform to the audience's expectation that trauma will emerge as a foundational part of his identity. Bartle's foil is Sterling, who exists at a different stage of self-definition. On the other hand, Bartle struggles to craft his own subjectivity in the face of similar trauma, even as that trauma is alluded to during the plot's development. An audience lacking knowledge about his wartime experiences expects Bartle to endure trauma. In *Yellow Birds* that trauma is guaranteed.

Sergeant Sterling is defined by a lack of feminine attributes—care, compassion, empathy, self-awareness. Illouz associates these traits with psychological resilience. This lack also positions Sterling as Bartle's antagonist. Not long after Bartle is introduced to combat in the first chapter, Sergeant Sterling creates a human manifestation of war: "I hated him. I hated the way he excelled in death and brutality and domination. But more than that, I hated the way he was necessary, how I needed him to jar me into action even when they were trying to kill me."[76] When Sergeant Sterling reappears in the second chapter, which takes place in 2003, before the deployment, he dresses down the two privates, especially the seventeen-year-old Murph. Bartle promises Murph's mother that he will bring her son home alive. Then, a switch flips in the sergeant and he knocks Bartle to the ground, striking him twice in the face, saying, "Report me if you want. I don't fucking care anymore."[77] Sergeant Sterling refuses to accept the realigned emotional culture required of him, one in which masculinity might exist as something more dynamic. His actions are excused, however, because he is only capable of achieving what is possible for popular stereotypes like Walt Kowalski and other "wounded warriors."

In *Yellow Birds*'s third chapter, Bartle and Sterling, along with their unit, stop in Germany on their way home. Though restricted to base for acclimation, Bartle decides to go AWOL (absent without leave) for the evening to explore the nearby town of Kaiserslautern. He takes a cab, experiencing during the ride what can only be described as a panic attack:

> As I looked out onto the trees that edged the road, my muscles tensed and I began to sweat. I knew where I was: a road in Germany, AWOL, waiting for the flight back to the States. But my body did not: a road, the edge of it, and another day. My fingers closed around a rifle that was not there. I told them the rifle was not supposed to be there, but my fingers would not listen, and they kept closing around the space where my rifle was supposed to be and I continued to sweat and my heart was beating much faster than I thought reasonable.[78]

In the cab ride sequence lie all the hallmarks of combat, minus the actual combat. Bartle's struggle is a psychological one. But his conditioned behavior, reacting to uncertain terrain passing by in the window by gripping the imagined rifle as though readying himself for combat, is performative. The imaginary rifle is helpful to Bartle because its real presence in combat once provided him with a sense of security and agency.[79] Just because the rifle is imagined and just because Bartle's behavior is performative, it does not mean that his psychological turmoil during the cab ride is any less real.

Bartle's pain is clear to a priest he encounters in a church after his cab ride. The priest tells Bartle he looks "troubled," and offers to listen should the soldier want to talk. Bartle avoids the conversation, leaving with the priest's advice: "You are only as sick as your secrets."[80] It should come as no surprise that this saying is commonly used in Alcoholics Anonymous meetings. The priest suggests two things: first, Bartle is a veteran (a likely scenario, given his age, speech, demeanor, and location in Germany); and second, Bartle could be an alcoholic (*much* less likely, unless the priest works from the assumption that all veterans are alcoholics). Bartle's silence perpetuates the lie, but his silence also allows him to avoid further reminiscences of war. The traumatic narrative forming around Bartle is one that excuses both his negative emotions and his negative behaviors. The priest, it would seem, picks up on this fact and offers the young soldier a warning about the road he is traveling. In effect, the priest warns Bartle not to give in to the forces compelling him toward silence and self-destruction.

Somehow, somewhere in his first deployment, the gifts of empathy and introspection were taken away from Sterling. At least, this much is implied by the fact that Sterling is a war veteran. The "wounded warrior" subjectivity forming around Bartle has an example to draw on. It is clear, before trauma emerges in the narrative, that those characteristics missing in Sterling will be those that Bartle struggles to maintain. Those "feminine attributes" anchoring him to home and peace are also at stake because Sergeant Sterling, his leader, views them as a threat. Interestingly, Crane's protagonist retreats to nature, a feminized sanctuary in the novel that shields the young boy from war. There, Henry Fleming finds solace and time to reflect. Bartle and Sterling find themselves in a different sort of feminized sanctuary, a brothel, and military masculinity is exposed as violent and dangerous.

Bartle makes his way to the brothel after his interaction with the priest, and Sterling emerges with a crash: "Coming down the steps, careening from wall to wall, was Sergeant Sterling. . . . He was shirtless and bleeding from the side of his mouth."[81] He tells Bartle that he's "[l]iving the fucking dream" as he proceeds to assault the woman working the bar, intimidating her to the point of crying because she has threatened to report Bartle as AWOL. If, as Illouz indicates, "identity is found and expressed in the experience of suffering and in the understanding of emotions gained in the telling of the story,"[82] then Sterling's flaws are predictable in *Yellow Birds*'s third chapter.

Both Bartle and Sterling are off base in opposition to the standing orders of their superiors. They try, briefly, to escape the military, to escape memory. But the first thing the sergeant wants to talk about is the look on Murph's face when "that hajji blew herself up in the DFAC," or dining facility.[83] Hidden in this short line is Sterling's attempt to take control of the chaotic memories haunting him. "Hajji" is a wartime slur used by soldiers to refer to people of Middle Eastern descent. Ultimately, wartime epithets are semantically pejorative. They allow the speaker to appropriate a word or cultural touchstone and control it by broadening or narrowing its meaning. Usually, wartime epithets are morphologically formed through clipping, eponymity, or coinage; phonetically, they are usually one or two syllables, and the longer they are used the more speech sounds they lose. The epithet above refers to Islamic pilgrimage to Mecca in Saudi Arabia. Of course, it means something different when distorted by a nonbeliever carrying a machine gun. As a slur, Sterling uses the word to try to gain a sense of control over his memory of the suicide bomber. Clearly, it is not very effective. He's in a bad way. And it has everything to do with Murph, the preordained topic of conversation between Sterling and his soldier. The subject of their deceased comrade must inform every conversation between the two. There's no "traumatic assumption," just a fact: Murph has already died.

The plot functions by inserting a real trauma where previously the audience had only an assumption. Also preordained, however, is Sterling's inability to be anything other than a "wounded warrior." Though Powers has revealed very little of their war at this point in the novel, the "negative emotions" and attributes of Bartle and Sterling are more than accepted, they're accounted for as parts of a "therapeutic narrative." Again, Bartle's struggle will be to avoid the trap that has already ensnared Sterling; his trauma will either result in personal growth or he will give in to the pressures of silence and conformity that inform a "wounded warrior" identity.

Ultimately, the reader has the power to excuse the behavior of these two soldiers. Further, granting this power to the reader mimics how another form of power is taken away from veterans in the real world. *Yellow Birds* is a story of catharsis. But it engages its civilian readers in the same way the Wounded Warrior Project engages potential donors. *Yellow Birds* pressures its civilian readers to anticipate Bartle's trauma, just as donors to the nonprofit organization anticipate the wounds of soldiers their donations are meant to help. The expectation is that Bartle will discover a wound—a referent for the symbolic position the young veteran occupies in their minds. Civilian readers need Bartle's silence so that they can imagine a war narrative they deem appropriate. In other words, readers of the novel perceive Bartle's mental state, make their own assessment, and then imagine Murph's death as violent on a scale which corresponds with their preconceived notions. It's a circular way of defining veteran identity, one which omits the actual veteran. Again, when veterans allow themselves to be stereotyped in this way, they forgo their rights to self-definition, continued growth, and an individualized identity. They even lose ownership of their memories.

4

The Veteran Storytellers

Román Baca may be the only classically trained ballet dancer to have served as a marine in Fallujah during the Iraq War. He founded the Exit12 Dance Company, "which tells veterans' stories choreographically, to increase cross-cultural understanding and heal divisions."[1] Specifically, the cultural divides explored in Exit12 performances are those between veterans and civilians, but also the common humanity these groups share with citizens of countries where American soldiers deploy. Baca's troupe gave a performance at Eastern Kentucky University in 2012. Veterans, faculty, and students sat on stone seats circling our outdoor amphitheater—The Ravine. We watched a surreal confluence of ballet infused with military movements and emotion. Each dance told a story: transformation from child to soldier, leaving behind loved ones to serve in war, moral and spiritual injuries, just to name a few.[2] I thought it fitting that it was 100 degrees on that humid Kentucky day. It made the choreography depicting war that much more impactful.

Baca's life and body of work is emblematic of what I refer to in this book as the veteran "storyteller." He harnesses his talent and military experience to construct a self that cannot exist within the artificial boundaries assigned to "heroes" and "wounded warriors." As a veteran, I recognized the intentional way Exit12's dancers held their mock M16s in the performance. They had taken great care to learn about soldiering and combat movements. Baca taught the dancers in his troupe these things the way any veteran might teach something learned in service. He found a way to make his military experience matter. And those willing to listen were able to converse—to create a unique form of art, a fusion of ballet and veteran iconography found nowhere else.

In any given Exit12 performance, a spectator might see a low crawl transform into an assemblé or an act of violence trigger a pirouette. There's something simultaneously beautiful and profane about every minute. The Exit12 Dance Company forces its audiences to sacrifice, to let in the ugliness of a larger truth that allows the beauty they cherish to exist. The performances undermine stereotypes and silencing mechanisms. Román Baca combines talent with his military experience to tell the stories he wants to tell. He harnesses his symbolic authority to educate and inspire. More recently, his work has grown into an outreach to help veterans struggling with reassimilation. He is equipping fellow veterans the way one soldier might help another tighten a shot group at the firing range, only the target is a coherent sense of self. Baca self-actualized, becoming an individualized model of veteran identity for other veterans to follow.

Veteran storytellers determine what their service means to them and explain to others why it should matter. Their identities are rooted in resilience and post-traumatic growth. For many veterans, and not just combatants, the process of sorting through memories associated with service is painful. They bleed onto a page or canvas, or they tell their stories through actions. In the previous chapter, I shared the story of Erick Millette, a veteran who lent his symbolic authority to a nonprofit organization only to feel betrayed when that power was misused. His identity was misappropriated, and he took it back when he publicly spoke out. Veteran storytellers do not allow themselves to be defined by others. They can certainly lend their authority to causes that encompass social groups—that is their right—but they maintain the agency to walk away. Veteran storytellers complicate veteran identity, individualizing it, providing models capable of the successes that elude veterans who adopt the "hero" or "wounded warrior" stereotypes.

Writing About War in College

On the first day of class my sophomore year, the sociology professor announced that he was from Baghdad, Iraq. It was 2008, and I'd been out of the army a little over a year. I mostly felt guilt when I thought of Operation Iraqi Freedom—memories of bombed-out buildings, sewage-filled streets, bodies on the side of the road. My experience wasn't representative of all veterans, and my vantage was limited, but I personally hadn't witnessed a lot of progress during my two deployments. How did Dr. Hassan regard the American presence in his home country? Did he view us as *liberators* or *perpetrators*? Did he even care about my veteran status?

I lived in Kentucky, a part of the country that tends to align itself politically with the architects of that war. To most of my fellow students it was nation building—noble and just. Still, I remembered devastation, and I felt like my professor could peer inside and see all of my insecurities and doubts. My behavior, willingness to interact with others, and perceptions of myself as a veteran were entirely based on *my assumptions* about Dr. Hassan's view of veterans who had served in Iraq. As with Cooley's "looking glass self," I was what I thought Dr. Hassan thought I was.

As a transportation soldier, I'd spent days and weeks on the road with Jordanian and Iraqi truck drivers. It was often my task to wake them and get their trucks lined up prior to departing the base. I'd been dismayed by how some were treated. In 2003, during my first deployment, I remember a man crying because he wanted to leave the base to go be with his wife. He wasn't allowed because it was a security concern. No one spoke enough of his language to calm him, and I imagine this experience made him feel like a prisoner. I wondered if he saw me as another armed guard. Not long after, insurgents sneaked into the little camp adjacent to our base near Balad and murdered a large number of those drivers for being "collaborators." It was no secret why we contracted the drivers. When an IED struck one of their vehicles and killed the occupant, it didn't get added to the death count scrolling across the bottom of the screen on CNN back home. I wanted to show some respect, so I bought a book about the country and tried to learn a few Arabic phrases. The drivers' faces lit up when they heard a young nineteen-year-old running up and down the truck line, repeating phrases from the book, butchering the dialect. Dr. Hassan's face also lit up when I said "shukran" instead of "thank you" one day in class.

He'd lived through the terrors of Saddam Hussein and hadn't been home for more than a decade. There were people and places he missed. He asked me to describe Tikrit in detail. He asked me about the Bedouins in southern Iraq who swarmed our convoys to sell worthless currency and bootleg DVDs. He gave me extra credit to write short stories about sitting around campfires with Jordanian truck drivers—trading snuff for bootlegged approximations of whiskey. I'd stay after class or visit his office. We would talk for as long as his schedule permitted. He contextualized my limited vantage with lived experience, historical background, and sociological perspectives. Over time, I began to feel more kinship than guilt during our conversations. In many ways, telling those stories helped me overcome a stereotype I had created for myself. They helped me rediscover part of my humanity.

A few years later, I found myself standing in front of a college classroom. I'd been tasked with designing and implementing an orientation course specifically for veterans. Thinking back to my experiences with Dr. Hassan, but also my scholarly interests in autobiography and identity formation, I decided to offer optional writing assignments. My students had not gone through affluent MFA programs or learned to speak the coded languages of publishing presses. They were not motivated by profit or fame. Rather, they came to me seeking help with the work of organizing memories, articulating thoughts, and putting their best foot forward to express themselves to their families. I wanted to give them the opportunity Dr. Hassan had given me to see through self-imposed stereotypes. I wanted them to think of military service as a foundation on which to begin writing the *next* chapter in their lives.

The *Journal of Military Experience* (JME) emerged from those classes. A year later, that peer-to-peer work grew into an event, the 2012 Military Experience & the Arts (MEA) Symposium, funded by the Kentucky Department of Veterans Affairs. More than 130 veterans and family members flew in from across the country to take part in workshops, listen to lectures, watch performances, and hone the art of crafting selves. It was at this event that I first saw an Exit12 performance. We borrowed blankets from a local army depot and crashed in an empty dorm. Community members and university staff created potlucks. It was a beautiful confluence of creativity and altruism. Veterans were ready to tell their stories. Civilians were eager to listen.

Suzanne Rancourt was one of those veterans ready to tell a story. She says she learned to "swim underwater at an extremely young age," and that she "had to be resuscitated numerous times," resulting in out-of-body experiences that became "second nature." These were the types of anecdotes she shared when I asked if I could use her as an example in this chapter. The group that attended the 2012 symposium was predominantly comprised of post-9/11 veterans. Rancourt strode in barefooted, wearing the flowing skirt of a 1960s flower child, unmistakably proud of the tightly bound gray braid extending the length of her back. But it wasn't her appearance that made me follow her work closely in the years that followed. Rancourt's poetry and prose are structurally and lyrically exceptional, and her writing presents military identity as fluid, as something informed by the veteran's life before service and after. As such, her work is accessible to both veterans and nonveterans; it invites genuine dialogue between both parties by refusing to acknowledge the existence of "civilian" experience or "veteran" experience, instead replacing both with "human" experience.

Publishers can serve as gatekeepers, rejecting works that do not conform to their criteria. Veterans willing and able to share their stories quickly find that not fitting a certain mold precludes them from contributing to national dialogue on the very military they experienced firsthand. Criteria for *exclusion* could be eschewing particular forms of prose predominant in MFA programs, the market mindset of agents catering to a "war weary" audience (at least, that was the excuse given to me on several occasions), but mostly mainstream publishing venues demanding only those stories that fit into the "hero" and "wounded warrior" molds. It often feels as though publishers of veterans' writing want three things: war porn, victimization narratives, and feel-good stories. It took several years of working with MEA's editors, but Rancourt eventually produced a story about her service that was none of these things.

"The Bear That Stands"—her work of nonfiction that details her rape by a navy sailor, the deaths of lovers and family, and her acknowledgment to herself that she needed to work through these things—begins with her standing at her kitchen table wondering why "some people don't understand the word no."[3] Fed up with a stalker's intrusions, threats, and acts of vandalism on her property, Rancourt finds herself in a closet, fumbling through the dark in order to locate "the familiar," a weapon—which awakens a military identity she'd struggled for years to bury: "There are dark places that I have done my best to cap over with tombstones. Places that I simply don't want to visit anymore. Or places that I thought had been thoroughly buried and mulched. Then something happens, catches me off guard. Me, off guard!"[4] Rancourt loads the weapon, "creating a solid plan" in the two kitchen table sequences that bookend the story.[5] At first, it appears as though "The Bear That Stands" will be one of the veteran returning to violence. But Rancourt is above such stereotypes. She nuances the story, locating in the weapon both the strength and the pain she sought to bury along with her military past.

"The Bear That Stands" is less about violence and more about learning to separate strength from the pain. Between the decisions made at that kitchen table are a number of flashbacks. She describes Terry, a boyfriend whose death resulted in her decision to join the Marine Corps: "My first love was my first loss. I still have every letter that he sent to me from Marine Corps Recruit Depot, Parris Island, S.C. Let's call him Williams, Terry E. [referencing the military's unaffectionate use of names] DOB 24 April 1958."[6] Terry is "the third of six" sudden deaths endured by Rancourt before she decides to enlist.[7] She's assigned to "an 81 mm mortar platoon as a photojournalist," describing both camaraderie and the difficulty of serving in a military just beginning to open itself to women.[8] Along with mentions of racial strife and drug use, it's clear Rancourt is not interested in whitewashing the military's imperfections.

A short time after enlisting, she wakes up to a man raping her: "His narrow, bony hips pumped a frenetic rhythm and pressure. Pressure from his pelvis, pressure from his abdomen, chest, and shoulders, pressure from his mouth on my face . . . I was mumbling . . . and pushing with my forearms at his throat."[9] It's not clear in the story whether Rancourt was drugged or clubbed over the head and dragged back to that barracks room. But "his face, black eyebrows too close together, his bony-ass rabbit-pumping pelvis, smells, and the pounding on the door" are vividly accounted for in the story.[10] The "pounding on the door" is the frantic effort of "two Marine brothers." And as the story continues, their concern exists in stark contrast to a military institution indifferent to the crime inflicted on Rancourt.

Her rape is traumatic in two stages, with the first being the rape itself and the second being the treatment she receives because of it. Rancourt's ostracism begins when a new officer arrives at her unit after her assault. He repeatedly makes sexual advances, and after lodging a formal complaint Rancourt is given the choice of remaining silent or fighting against cultural norms much larger than herself. The officer accuses her first of stealing, then of malingering. But Rancourt stands her ground. And her decision to fight ends with the male officer's early retirement.

Unfortunately, the events also force Rancourt out of the military, a separation she likens to the deaths in her story. In addition to Terry, Rancourt discusses her mother's death and that of Jaime, "a Vietnam vet, 101st Airborne, combat wounded. He always said, 'If you didn't have a drug problem before you went through Phang Rang hospital, you did when you left.'"[11] In dealing with each death, Rancourt's identity takes shape. Her military experience influences the way she comes to interpret the death of her mother. That death influences the way she understands the deaths of Terry and Jaime. And the rape which results in her discharge from the military, which Rancourt considers a form of death, is worked through in a story. In return, Rancourt is capable of understanding the death and birth of the identity she forges through the painstaking, years-long process of writing "The Bear That Stands."

"Heroes" and "wounded warriors" do not get the opportunity to reimagine themselves. In accepting silence in exchange for comfort and patriotic narratives of the state, they limit themselves to existing only as they were in the past. They deprive themselves of the kind of catharsis present in "The Bear That Stands." The story itself undermines traditional notions of military identity, masculinity, and culture. Its protagonist's positionality is more "human" than "veteran." Like Baca's ballet, Rancourt's writing harnesses her veteran identity, forcing the audience to acknowledge ugly truths about crimes committed against women in uniform. Her pain is transformed into something instructional. It is not put onto a pedestal and hermetically sealed off as the trauma experienced by veterans who "don't like to talk about it." Rancourt, as a veteran storyteller, invites her readers into a story about the present. She refuses to be confined to the past.

The steady progression forward to that kitchen table in 2011 suggests that Rancourt is capable of charting her own future. She's not a victim, a hero, or a bystander. She is Suzanne Rancourt: an individual. The weapon Rancourt pulls from the closet is a form of self-protection. But it represents the intricate weaving of strength and pain associated with her past. First, she explains how, after her discharge from the Marines, she was beaten daily by her first husband. Rancourt explains how she stood up to that abuser, just as she stood up to the male military officer in the Marine Corps, and finally she applies those experiences to her present problem with a stalker: "He thought he had found a victim, easy prey, but had woken a sleeping bear. The rage, indignation, memories, flooded my mind."[12] Then, as Rancourt steps out of her front door the "world shift[s] like Code Red alarms, flashing lights: OUT OF CONTEXT!!! OUT OF CONTEXT!!! I stopped. What was I doing?!"[13] In this moment of clarity Rancourt recognizes that the indoctrination and training that taught her to respond to threats with deadly violence has no place in the civilized world. But the threat itself is not entirely what awakened the bear. It is that her stalker, even in the civilized world, more closely resembles the rapist from her past.

Military and civilian cultures are not sealed off from each other. So what, then, is "OUT OF CONTEXT"? American exceptionalism holds that America has a special role in human history and its future. Rancourt's reaction itself is not out of context. Idealized notions of America, veterans, and reassimilation are out of context. The stalker would be "easy prey" for someone with Rancourt's training. But silence is more insidious: "There are only so many casket flags a person can receive before closing the heart to the various vulnerabilities of daily living some folks call 'normal.' I thought I had removed myself from the arduous exposures of emotional contact with others."[14] Recognizing that veterans do not stop living after military service is essential to Rancourt's survival. Eventually, she turns to the veteran community for help: "I began writing again, connected with other female vets, participated in Art Reach: Project America, attended expressive arts experiential retreats and Military Experience & the Arts conferences. And I began to remember. I chose people and groups wisely, people who understood the harsh dichotomies of military and civilian cultures."[15] A clear dichotomy between "sick" and "better" does not exist. In her story, Rancourt taps into her military past as a form of strength. In her life, she allows herself to be vulnerable, opening herself up to the veteran community that had once betrayed her.

Rancourt's story doesn't present writing as a panacea. At the end, that "something" which Rancourt recognizes as "not correct" within herself remains. She finds community. She becomes aware of both the strengths and traumas wrapped up in her military identity. But her story remains open-ended: "I refuse to forget. I refuse to drink the waters of Lethe because my survival is proof of existence. Atrocities happened, horror happened, and it is my duty to speak, to defend and protect, my family, my home, myself. Warriors have not died in vain."[16] Her veteran identity is not silent. Her future is not written off as an eventual reassimilation that will never come. The veteran in "The Bear That Stands" exists now, learning, growing, and asking her readers to do the same.

Negotiating Narratives and Veteran Safe Spaces

Bradley Johnson is another example of a veteran storyteller. He was among the few contributors to the first *JME* who was not one of my students. He found out about the publication from someone in my class and sought me out. His short story "My Life as a Soldier in the 'War on Terror'" explores his decision to enlist in the National Guard, his homecoming after a deployment to Iraq, and his subsequent struggles in the areas of marriage, work, and education.[17] If anything, the story succeeds because of its simplicity: a snapshot of life before war, a stark contrast to life after.

There are allusions to combat, but Johnson provides few details: "This isn't the part of my story where I give a play-by-play of my time in Iraq."[18] As Johnson's editor, I read these words and casually suggested during the revision process that he elaborate on what he did during the war. He added the words, "Iraq sucked, people died, people shot at me, and I shot back" in a subsequent draft. There was a power differential between us. I was the editor. He was the contributor. In many situations, that dynamic lends itself to gatekeeping, to individuals other than the veteran dictating which parts of a veteran's story get told and how. Editors are one example. But even fellow veterans can serve as gatekeepers when they assert the dominance of a particular type or era of service.

The process unfolds in conversations, consciously and unconsciously. I previously shared a story about a veteran from the Korean War telling me not to thank a veteran from the Vietnam War because "they lost." But it is not uncommon among veterans of the same generation to silence each other. As a transportation soldier, combat arms soldiers would refer to me as a "POG," or a person other than a grunt. Usually this is good-natured ribbing. Sometimes it is more than that, such as when a veteran storyteller is told that their service did not matter enough to serve as a tool to instruct others. Johnson likely wanted to sidestep this sort of gatekeeping; he felt that what happened *after* his experience in war was more important than what happened *during*.

In "Combat in the Classroom," an article I wrote for UC-Davis's *Writing on the Edge*, I discuss the progression of the *JME* from an extra credit assignment to a journal built on an intentional peer-to-peer editing process.[19] Johnson and the other authors were vulnerable, their stories raw. I cried after reading about one student's friend dying in Iraq, and again when another told the story of a girl tossed into a mass grave in Bosnia. These veterans, who became students, then writers, showed me a lot of trust. And I did my best to help them express themselves in print. At the same time, I became curious about the confidence and sense of camaraderie I saw emerging.

Birgitte Refslund Sørensen refers to this sort of experience as a "social becoming."[20] Exploring homecoming, Sørensen explains that the experience is influenced by practical considerations (for example, professions and access to health care), but also by the symbolic limitations placed on veterans' prevailing narratives. My student authors, in addition to their own stories, told a collective story of homecoming; each contribution to the *Journal of Military Experience* was one in a chorus. They were going through the process of identity formation, and although the act of writing took place with me one-on-one, sharing those stories was a social act.

Jonathan Shay comments on the importance of community in the healing of psychological wounds: "The answer does not lie in something that is new or expensive, or once it is said, surprising: it lies in *community.* Vietnam veterans came home *alone.* The most significant community for a combat veteran is that of his surviving comrades."[21] On the individual level, writing brings order to chaotic, fragmented memories. It puts emotions into context. And survivors of trauma—not just war veterans—have turned to writing and art throughout recorded history to work through their experiences. It is particularly popular among patients who either refuse or who do not respond well to traditional therapies.[22] Authors like Sebastian Junger point to the absence of community to explain the alienation of post-9/11 veterans. Karl Marlantes believes soldiers are ill-prepared for the experience of war, and that medical professionals and veterans themselves underestimate the impact of moral and spiritual wounds. I have blamed the silencing power of stereotypes. Storytelling, or the act of consciously examining, revising, and sharing one's conception of self, holds promise in all of these areas.

But where does one draw the line between doing something with a group of people that is *therapeutic* and providing actual therapy? Rhetoric and composition scholars Alexis Hart and Roger Thompson expressed this concern in a response to the article I shared about my students.[23] They'd received a grant from the Conference on College Composition & Communication to conduct site visits and interview writing faculty. My own interview took place in the outdoor amphitheater where Román Baca and the Exit12 Dance Company gave their performance. We shouted over the sound of a pulverizer belonging to another veteran artist, Drew Cameron, who founded the "Combat Paper" workshop that teaches veterans how to make paper from their uniforms.[24] Baca uses ballet, my students use writing, and Cameron uses papermaking to help veterans shape their identities into something new.

Hart and Thompson worried that asking veterans to produce personal narratives could provoke mental health issues. They wondered if college educators were prepared when only about 8 percent of academic departments reported any specialized training working with military veterans.[25] Their article claimed the problems I had uncovered in my classes were "complex" and dealing with them was "not without cost."[26] I shared these concerns, but my overriding belief has always been that veterans should be unfettered by fears of instability when they choose to tell their stories. I did my best to balance my classes. A great deal of the content focused on metacognition and harnessing the strengths veterans bring with them out of uniform. In fact, the only explicit instructions I gave the journal contributors was to attempt to tie who they had been in uniform to who they hoped to become by earning a college degree.

Hart and Thompson speculated about "transference" and "parallel processing"—attempts to work through my own issues.[27] They weren't wrong. All educators benefit—personally and professionally—when they respect the diversity of perspectives students bring to the classroom. Homecoming is a lifelong experience, and I was undergoing the process of identity formation alongside students who were often older, more seasoned veterans than me. My transformation as a veteran coincided and intertwined with my evolution as an educator. Likewise, the stories my students shared in word and deed likely remain parts of their identities. Given these facts, it would be disingenuous to claim myself capable of an intellectual remove, especially when empathy is an editor's most valuable tool.

From 2010 to 2013, veteran storytellers were inventing new ways—inside and outside academia—to share their experiences every day. One leader in the space, Ron Capps, founder of the Veterans Writing Project and author of *Writing War* (2011), asks veterans to consider the human condition in their stories. He suggests, "The theme of a book or a story, whether it's fiction or nonfiction, is the principal idea you the author are trying to get across to the reader. It is the real reason you're writing the story in the first place: You have something worth saying about the human experience. The story is the vehicle you use to expose what you want to say about the human condition, the theme."[28] Later in the book, Capps advises his veteran authors that "[m]aturing as a writer means becoming more one's self."[29] My argument in this chapter is not that veterans would be better served by writing autobiographically than by writing fiction. Nor is it that all veterans should express themselves creatively. Rather, I view interpersonal communication—the work of crafting memoir, fiction, or art—and service *synonymously* as acts of identify formation. My claim is that veterans need to be taught to recognize and subvert the conscious and unconscious pressures that prevent them from expressing themselves authentically. Creative works simply reveal these pressures plainly.

I look back at the last decade of veterans' creative communities in this chapter because they hold promise for future generations of veterans. The Great War poets—Sassoon, Owen, Graves—found solace and healing in sharing their works. Groups like the Deadly Writers Patrol emerged after the Vietnam War. It seems like each generation must reinvent the wheel, and what gets lost are healthy models of veteran identity in the cultural milieu for returning veterans to draw on and model in the process of homecoming. I want to emphasize these examples of veterans "maturing" and "becoming more one's self" in order to preserve them.

The stigma of mental illness is probably the biggest threat to veteran creative expression. In higher education, administrators often express concern about veterans writing within the context of a college classroom. Even Hart and Thompson, well-known for their support of veterans in higher education, worried in their article that there are not enough instructors like me who are able "consistently to create the type of space that our veterans need as they return to civilian life as students . . . the greatest work we can do as writing instructors is to ensure that our students are aware of the services and other safe spaces."[30] However, colleges are major sites of transformation for veterans exiting the service, and "safe spaces" are problematic for those who need to engage in self-exploration.

Instead of handing our veterans a microphone, our colleges section off veterans from the rest of the student population. They are provided with resource centers, lounges, personalized graduation ceremonies, and the sorts of cohort classes I was asked to design. These gestures are well-meaning, but they can also function as silencing mechanisms. I am not attempting to malign or describe some sort of conscious effort to disenfranchise veterans. And concerns like those expressed by Hart and Thompson are rooted every bit in genuine care and compassion for the veteran community. Still, veterans are not a victim class. Sharing stories about war and service is not *necessarily* psychologically damaging. And it is not the role of the college educator to deny veterans their right to testimony or to diagnose mental illness. Staying vigilant and responding to veterans' needs is the best recourse. Avoiding difficult conversations and sectioning off veterans from the larger campus population is not.

On Difference and Disability

Reflecting on his interactions with the VA health care system, Bradley Johnson asks, "Are they paying me so that I can walk away or so that they can? . . . Even now, years later, my best friends in the world tell me that I'm different . . . that I am any number of things that are . . . *different.*"[31] Johnson's emphasis on the word "*different*" indicates a special meaning. He doesn't mean "*different*" in the sense that going to war "turns boys into men." Instead, in his own words, he lists the perceptions others have of him: "Supposedly, I am violent, aggressive, loud, agitated, and not very nice. These are the descriptions that tend to top the list."[32] These are also the descriptions associated with stereotypically "disgruntled" veterans—with "wounded warriors" who keep people at a distance.

Either Johnson sees through others' efforts to stereotype him, or he recognizes his own avoidance mechanism. "*Difference*," in Johnson's parlance, refers to the personality changes others see in him. In order to receive benefits, these changes must be worked into a coherent disability narrative for the VA. It is paradoxical in that veterans receive exceptional treatment through official channels and in patriotic rhetoric. Yet, they must exist within a hierarchy of disabilities, one in which they are labeled and ranked according to how much or how little they suffer.

Severo and Milford describe the government as a "slippery insurance company," and war as an arrangement in which "soldiers were lured into service with offers of generous pay, bonuses, and benefits, only to be scorned as mercenaries and social parasites."[33] Similarly, Johnson asks his reader to consider commercials they might've seen: "'Veterans are a priority,' and 'helping them' is our job. . . . I have a chest full of medals, some that you can only get from being in combat. But to get the care I needed I still had to prove to the VA through letters from my peers that I was in combat."[34] Johnson lives daily with evidence of his combat experience—in his mind, on his body, as medals, and in the "*difference*" described to him by others. However, when he chooses to make use of the pact made between soldier and society, the one that promises health care and respect, he is asked repeatedly to *prove* himself. Johnson describes his frustration, echoed by many veterans, about a system in which the first priority is to root out potential frauds and malingerers. Maintaining the integrity of these systems is important, but not more important than the first duty of providing compassionate care.

Taylor Rugg conducted interviews and qualitative research to better understand how veterans move in and out of hero/civilian symbolic positions. The author claims, "positionality can create identities that overlap and contradict one another, and the identity of veteran does just that . . . [the veteran] occupies the civilian identity and the military identity simultaneously, and this is why she must continually negotiate her identity through discourse."[35] Similarly, Judith Butler argues that subjecting people to existence within categories defines who they are in the moment and well into the future.[36] I have discussed three institutions along with Johnson's story: the family, higher education, and the VA. Johnson claims his family and friends see him as a stereotype—a "wounded warrior." These perceptions are damaging because, as shown in the story, he must wage a constant war not to see himself in the same way. Meanwhile, he is a student at a higher education institution where self-definition can take place. Yet a critical response to the edited collection containing his work deemed his testimony a threat to higher education's larger safe spaces—efforts to section veterans off in gilded cages. Finally, the VA constantly casts doubt on his testimony, pathologizes it, and assigns value to it only if it is framed in negative terms. Johnson, along with many veteran storytellers, faces an uphill battle when it comes to self-definition.

Why have post-9/11 veterans begun to balk at the phrase "thank you for your service"? When asked, they will tell you they feel civilians conveying gratitude in this way are being sincere. They acknowledge that their generation is treated far better than the generation that served in Vietnam. Yet, the phrase is experienced by many as though it is a *microaggression*.[37] Of course, microaggressions and outright aggression differ in that the former is usually unintentional, a gesture that reminds a member of a social group that they are *truly* among the minority. For example, telling a non-native speaker that they speak the language well is intended as a compliment, yet the message also reminds the individual that they are perceived as "non-native." Derald Sue Wing describes microaggressions as invisible, subtle acts that reinforce the "otherness" of nondominant social groups. Microaggressions are perpetrated consciously and unconsciously by individuals in positions of power and privilege.[38] The phrase "thank you for your service" reminds veterans that they are "others," strangers in a strange land, undermining their attempts to feel at home.

The returning veteran is vulnerable, what Guy Standing would refer to as a precariat,[39] or someone whose lack of agency makes them susceptible

Román Baca and Exit12 Dance Company. Photograph by Andy Hart.
Courtesy of Román Baca.

Exit12 Dance Company. Photograph by Rachel Neville. Courtesy of Román Baca.

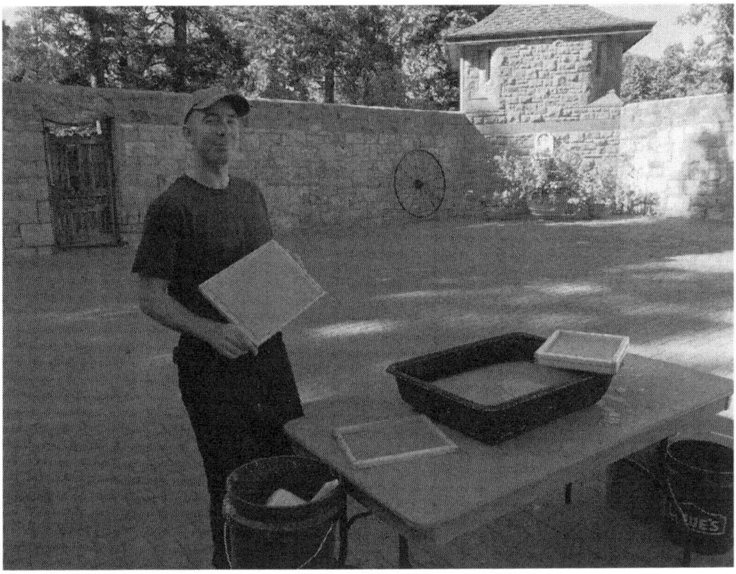

Drew Cameron leading a Combat Paper papermaking workshop. Courtesy of Drew Cameron.

Prisoner of War (2013). Composite photograph with digital drawing by Tif Holmes. Courtesy of Tif Holmes.

Tea Time (2012). Digital photograph by Giuseppe Pellicano. Courtesy of Giuseppe Pellicano.

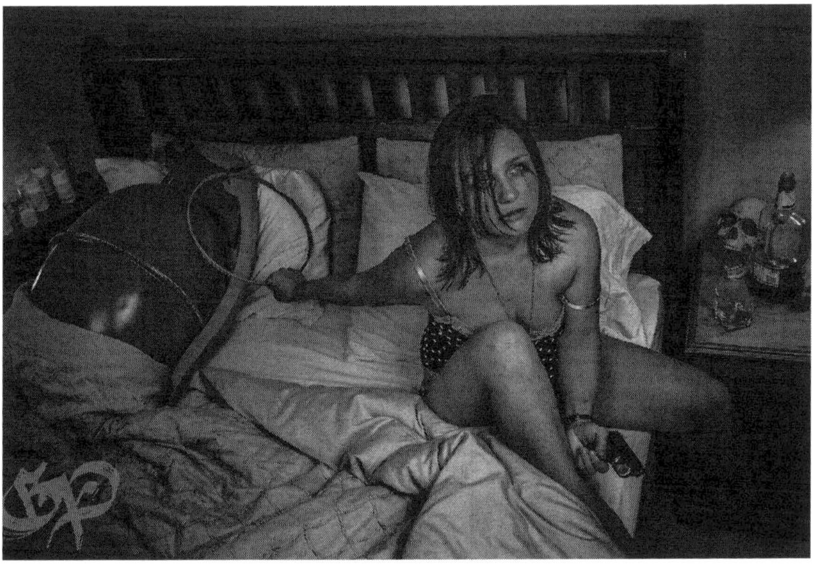

Oh Happy Day (2012). Digital photograph by Giuseppe Pellicano. Courtesy of Giuseppe Pellicano.

to the judgment of nation states. Veterans moving from the military institution to the care of the VA institution exist only within the boundaries of being sick or not sick enough. They do not give medals for recovery; they take away benefits. Critics of the VA's disability compensation system, such as Junger, suggest that existence within these boundaries prevents veterans from healing and evolving beyond them.

Johnson's description of the VA certainly reflects a "social conditioning process."[40] Scott Parrott, David Albright, and their colleagues (2020) worry that "[f]or many Americans, veterans are not real—they are screen images" controlled by a "shrinking number of corporate entities."[41] The authors find that while the public generally conceives of veterans as "heroes," using a similar definition of the stereotype that I have used in this book, this label could be problematic for veterans with injuries that make them feel as though they cannot live up to that standard.[42] I'd been surprised that my students and other contributors to the *JME* overwhelmingly wrote about trauma. They rarely discussed boredom, humor, or even machismo. It was as though they felt that combat trauma lent their stories ethos, that no one would care about their struggles with readjusting if their stories weren't steeped in violence.

I grappled with this same decision when writing the introduction to this book. Ultimately, I decided that beginning with a vignette about my experiences in Iraq would lend credibility to what I had to say about veteran identity in the pages that followed. In particular, I wanted to illustrate why asking a veteran "Did you ever kill anyone?" is problematic, even for veterans like myself who do not have to live with that sort of burden. I could have relied on statistics, or testimony, or literary/film examples. I spent years doing the prerequisite research necessary to write this book. I've spent even more years serving veterans in the nonprofit and higher education sectors. Yet, that personal experience—my veteran testimony—of war and the life that came after is where I feel I have the most credibility. It is also where I feel the most is at stake. My experiences are wound into my personal history, which informs my identity and my relationship with both the real world and my imagined readers. Importantly, I chose to share that story in order to advance a narrative that is my own, that serves my needs and the veterans I serve.

Johnson, on the other hand, uses the word "*difference*" to describe a confluence of social pressures to conform to a false narrative. The pressure comes from family, higher education, and the VA health care system. The written story, however, provides Johnson with an opportunity to speak openly and define his postwar self on his own terms. He uses *Predator* (1987) and *Braveheart* (1995), films portraying hypermasculine warrior archetypes, to describe the simplicity of existing in a constant state of anger while deployed. He says, "You'd rather not fight, but as long as you have to, you are going to rain down hell on the enemy. I realize this all sounds cruel and illogical, but so is war. You truly stop caring. You don't want to shoot, but you will. And you won't think about it, until you get home that is."[43] In his hypermasculine examples, Johnson draws on touchstones corresponding to a veteran identity he feels readers will recognize. He is experimenting with the sort of positionality explored by Rugg, who found that veterans can move between the liminal spaces separating veteran and civilian identities.[44] Like Rugg's subject, who undermines stereotypical conceptions of veteran identity by recognizing and playing to their tune as needed, Johnson taps into his "*difference*" and juxtaposes it alongside caricatures and conflicting narratives of apathy and passion to show that he is in control.

MEA's community edits grammar and punctuation while listening, bringing complete strangers—some veteran, some civilian—together to focus on veterans' creative works. This collaborative environment results in a convergence of writing and teaching methods. And sometimes styles clash. In those instances of disagreement, two or three professionals come together with their respective skills and motivations to truly *engage* with veterans' works, and, by extension, veterans' issues. Editing is a form of conversation. It normalizes rather than pathologizes discussions of military and wartime service. The work helps veterans articulate their thoughts and ambitions, but it also educates each volunteer, editor, or discussion moderator. Hart and Thompson's claim that writing can be a triggering event may hold true in individual cases, but the serious revision required to complete a story results in dialogue, repeated returns to the site of trauma, and always the freedom to walk away.

Engaging Fiction: MEA's Blue Falcons

Daniel Buckman, a former infantryman and the author of four novels featuring veteran characters and themes, wrote in the introduction to MEA's first fiction journal about Virginia Woolf's finding "a space of her own": "Military veterans, like women writers in the 1920s, need a room of their own in a civilian-dominated literary establishment. Over the last months, I believe we created a room and the stories written in this room are good enough to keep Virginia Woolf dancing for a good long time."[45] *The Blue Falcon Review* (BFR) consisted of works developed in online writing workshops. Like the *JME*'s authors, each contributor received the opportunity to experiment and tell their story with the support of an experienced author.

It's no fiction that the military gets carried away with acronyms. A meal, ready to eat, becomes an "MRE." Push-ups, sit-ups, and running are forms of physical training, so they become "PT." The list goes on. Sometimes, young soldiers take up the mantle of acronymizing things for themselves, and often with humorous effects. Someone particularly prone to getting a group into trouble, for example, is referred to as a "Buddy Fucker," which acronymizes to "BF." In turn, in military/veteran colloquial usage "BF" has become a "Blue Falcon" for reasons unbeknownst to me. The title of MEA's first fiction publication, *The Blue Falcon Review* (BFR), is a dig at civilian ignorance of veteran language. It's also a deceptive title, granting those readers *in the know* an advantage over those who are not. I felt it was a push back against the notion that all military-themed literature must be about the dark, the macabre, or hyper-violent. Like many people forced to confront boredom and hardship, veterans use humor to cope. The complexity of veteran identity was something we hoped to capture.

Fiction writers must travel a more winding path than that of the memoirist when challenging the prevailing narratives of veteran identity. The authors in *BFR* could not rely on wartime service as ethos. Rather, veteran fiction writers must deal in the subtlety of language, with veteran identity as a social construct, not something experienced. In using fiction to develop a personal identity, they must change the meaning of the word "veteran" so that it better represents them as individuals. Few of MEA's authors are as skilled in this craft as Jerad W. Alexander.

Alexander's contribution, "Cold Day in Bridgewater," opens with a toothache. It is a pain that follows a bartender as he goes about his day-to-day duties, including after a veteran comes in out of the cold looking for a drink: "The light shifts around him, or maybe it's just me. I don't know what it is. We don't get too many around here, but when you find out someone is a serviceman, I tell you, it's like the scenery changes. At least it does for me, I guess anyway. To hell what you think if you don't believe that."[46] Immediately, the veteran character is put onto a pedestal. The bartender, after offering his patron two free drinks, uses the phrase "thank you for your service." The character will be asked to pay for these drinks, not with cash, but conformity.

The veteran character in the story, Steve, is one of several "others." The bartender, on different occasions, makes disparaging remarks about individuals of Mexican and Middle Eastern descent. The pain in the narrator's tooth is always at the forefront of his narration, outweighing any serious considerations of identity or individuality. He has strong opinions about veterans: "Ahh, hell. I figure any guy that goes over there is a hero, I don't care what they did."[47] This comment carries double meaning: regardless of what the soldier did, he's a "hero," but it also suggests the speaker truly does not care what soldiers have done or, at least, that he doesn't want to hear about it. It is another example of how some veterans view the phrase "thank you for your service" as a microaggression. Essentially, it elicits a conversation about service only to end the conversation before it can start. The civilian has done their part without even having to think about what the veteran endured on their behalf.

The bartender displays his skill in giving career advice: "You a 20-year man?" he asks before adding, "Good benefits to be had in the military. Retirement, medical, dental, all that. Stuff don't come cheap. . . . And hell, it's a damn job in this country that ain't been taken up by some illegal."[48] In his every attempt to praise military service, the bartender merely manages to be offensive, reducing his patron's service to "a damn job." Further, he reduces the character's motivations for serving to "benefits," all while attempting to elicit the veteran's agreement with a racist worldview.

So far, the bartender has subtly told the veteran that the nature of his service is something he has the privilege not to care about. He has stated his assumption that veterans are mostly mercenaries who sign up for benefits. And he has suggested that service members—those who serve in the Middle East, in particular—ascribe to racist worldviews. For the reader, the tension in "Cold Day in Bridgewater" is palpable at this point in the story.

The climax involves Steve baiting the bartender into a hypothetical discussion. The bartender, along with his reductionist views of policies toward the Middle East, offers the following suggestion, "We oughta just bomb them all back to the Stone Age. Every last one of them. We're gonna have to eventually anyway."[49] The veteran butters his potato, beginning his meal, and a tense scene develops in which Steve suggests increasingly vile and inhumane acts of war to satiate a warmongering bartender.

"Where do you wanna start?" Steve asks, drawing the bartender into his trap: "We might have trouble at first with their army, but my boys are good. I mean, we can do some real damage. I'm talking total destruction, and we don't miss much, either. Oh sure, we might get a civilian here and there, maybe a kid, which sucks, but to hell with it, right? What difference does it make, right?"[50] The narrator becomes uncomfortable, attempting to backtrack on his prior assertions by ruling out the murder of children. Steve does not relent: "Don't worry, we'll pay them. In a lot of those countries a dead goat costs more than a dead person, anyway . . . I mean, they're not really people. Not in God's eyes, anyway, right?"[51] His tone is that of mockery. His words are vitriolic.

The veteran in "Cold Day in Bridgewater" sees through the bartender's chest-thumping: "We'll go over there in rotations, just like we do now. Seven months over, seven months back. I dunno, maybe some guys will have to stay there longer, but we'll build big bases with McDonalds and Burger Kings with shopping malls and swimming pools and Wednesday night salsa dance lessons. Ship over Toby Keith and we'll have concerts. Keith is still touring, right?"[52] Steve lists a number of offerings from consumer culture meant to ease the discomfort of deployed soldiers, revealing them as nothing more than paltry compensation for the sacrifices required in war. The beers and slogan offered at the start of the story are the same.

Each elevation in the veteran's tone corresponds with an earlier moment of silence. Alexander provides example after example of how veterans experience feelings of alienation when acclimating to civilian life. Veteran identity intertwines with a larger national identity, which each American experiences subjectively. By extension, veterans exist as characters in a larger fiction—what Parrot, Albright, and their colleagues refer to as "screen images." Alexander presents a veteran character aware of appropriation and the symbolic role of veterans in society. He presents a character willing to fight back.

Earlier in the story, between the narrator's racist tirades, the work of an "Arab" technician, as the narrator calls him, intrudes on the conversation between Steve and the bartender. Later, after both parties reveal themselves, the veteran's reality begins to intrude on the civilian's fiction: "My tooth pounds. I rub in more Orajel. I turn to face the Marine. He looks at me, eyes wide and alive, clicking fires. The corners of his mouth are turned down in a smirk, maybe. Or maybe he's just sick, or about to get sick. The light vanishes from his eyes, like maybe he's sad or something."[53] Interestingly, the narrator proves incapable of empathy, of understanding what the veteran feels on any level. His toothache—or, his physical pain—mirrors a psychological wound carried by the veteran, yet he repeatedly returns to his own feelings: "I never asked for all that. Who wants to hear all that? I don't want to hear all that. I look back at the television. He saws off another piece of steak."[54] How does the civilian narrator respond? How does he deescalate the situation? After *provoking* Steve, he merely *ignores* him. Offering only bits of replies, tonguing his tooth, hoping the next shift will arrive soon. In short, the narrator exercises his privilege and shrugs him off.

Ignored, Steve asks for the bill and offers the words, "thank you for your service." He evokes the irony of the bartender thanking him for a thing he knows nothing about. Steve holds up a mirror for his antagonist, reflecting his carelessness to prove a point. The phrase evolves from a way of avoiding conversations about war into a sense of agency in "Cold Day in Bridgewater" because it is the veteran who uses the words like a weapon or shield. Veterans hoping to exist as more than stereotypes do not have the privilege of ignoring their veteran identities. Veterans are required to self-identify in exchange for entitlements, such as VA benefits. In addition, individuals like the bartender provoke veterans into self-identifying through protest. "Cold Day in Bridgewater" provides evidence of both veteran "difference" and the stereotypes leveled on veterans. However, it is also a story about agency and the ability to recognize fictions before they become one's source of self-definition.

It is important to point out that Alexander's civilian bartender is also a stereotype. Of course, not all civilians project racism or dismissive attitudes toward military culture on veterans. The two main characters in "Cold Day in Bridgewater" speak the same language. But they do not share the same brand of patriotism. The bartender expects the veteran to behave rudely toward the Middle Eastern technician, as he did himself in a previous scene; he expects him to share his vile thoughts of bombing Muslim countries; he expects Steve's silence. This silence, which will linger so long as the veteran allows himself to be passively defined by others, is the echo chamber in which "heroes" and "wounded warriors" live. The climax of the story results in Steve subverting the narrator's privilege, asserting his *individuality* and preventing the appropriation of his postwar identity. "Cold Day in Bridgewater" portrays a fictional world, but it also provides veterans with guidance about how to behave when stereotyped. It provides an alternative form of veteran identity.

Further Complicating Veteran Identity: MEA's Veteran Artists

The fiction and nonfiction authors of the previous sections combine storytelling with innate resilience to avoid victimized "wounded warrior" and trivialized "hero" stereotypes. For Rancourt, the military was the site of ultimate betrayal—sexual assault by a fellow service member. However, the author refuses to let that event define her, tapping into veteran identity to locate strength and a new community in which to heal. Johnson uses storytelling to revise the narrative prescribed to him by loved ones and the government he served. Alexander, through the guise of a fictional bartender, teaches veteran readers how to avoid becoming mere extensions of civilian racism and angst. The veterans in these stories do not remain silent. What do veteran *artists* do once they have broken through society's prevailing stereotypes regarding veterans?

Tif Holmes lends her skill to the work of combating military sexual trauma (MST). Sadly, many veterans deny the existence of MST. They do not deny that it happens, but that there's anything uniquely "military" about it. As Rancourt's story showed, soldiers—male, female, and nonbinary alike—who are assaulted usually have to contend with superior officers and a situation impossible to escape. Holmes was a member of the US Army Reserve Band when she experienced her own assault. A classically trained musician, the traumas of being sexually assaulted, stalked, and ignored left her unable to play her instrument without being triggered. That aspect of her veteran identity was inescapable, so she turned to a new artistic medium in the visual arts.

In *Prisoner of War* (2013) Holmes depicts a female soldier held silent. Camouflage melts into the red, white, and blue of the American flag to disguise an unspeakable crime. In her description of the piece, Holmes explains that the "black shadow-figure standing . . . represents . . . something or someone keep[ing] us prisoner beyond the battlefield." Holmes continues, "On my own very personal level, it represents a physical being—a comrade—who betrayed my trust and sexually assaulted me repeatedly during my military service."[55] The level of bravery involved in the creation of a work like this cannot be overstated. The legal and military institutions failed Holmes, and hidden in *Prisoner of War* is an amalgamated image of the artist and her perpetrator. The artist never got to see the perpetrator face repercussions, and when that "black shadow-figure" and the symptoms of her PTSD tried to silence her, she used her art to subvert both. She takes a series of her most traumatic memories and repurposes them, transforming art into protest, wounds into weapons.

For Holmes and Rancourt, rape is not the last transgression; it is the first of many, a starting point in a series of denials, a pattern of ostracizing, and continued sexual harassment, which ultimately brings careers to an early end. The message of works like "The Bear That Stands" and *Prisoner of War* is one of urgency: 28–33 percent of women and 1–12 percent of men will experience sexual assault at some point during their military careers.[56] Those percentages are reality; soldiers like Holmes and Rancourt hope to dispel society's larger fictions: idealized notions of veteran identity and calls for reassimilation by a public that has refused to recognize MST.

The harm inflicted on families by war was a recurring theme when I served as MEA's editor-in-chief. Giuseppe Pellicano's *Tea Time* (2012) adorns the cover of *JME*'s third volume. It is part of a larger "Grenade Series" that the artist views as "a soldier's attempt at re-familiarizing him or herself as the father/mother figure within the family."[57] In the work, a young girl sits at a table with a plastic tea set. The bright colors and oversized teddy bear create a playful atmosphere, one shattered by her playmate: an ominous instrument of death, the grenade. The scene is striking, of course, due to the close proximity of a child to a weapon. The grenade, which represents the girl's father, is both a stereotype and a real acknowledgment of the psychological struggles many veterans face.

The bartender's failure (one of his many failures) in Alexander's "Cold Day in Bridgewater" is that he attempts to assert *his* voice in place of the *veteran's*. Hence, the veteran usurps the bartender's voice by saying "thank you for your service" on the way out of the bar. It's not that nonveterans shouldn't discuss the topic of PTSD, the horrors of war, or the roles of veterans in their postwar lives; those are things civilians *must* discuss. However, when these conversations are relegated to the superficial, and when veterans are politicized and alienated, the ramifications on veterans and their families move from a problem of rhetoric to problems of physical and psychological well-being. Authors like Johnson, Rancourt, and Alexander, as well as artists who share the motivations of Holmes and Pellicano, want to be included in the conversation. They want to complicate veteran identity and provide models for other veterans to follow. They take ownership of their symbolic authority to comment on issues impacting past, current, and future generations of veterans.

Tea Time, a work of photography dealing heavily in stereotypes and symbolism, conveys a message that can be sent best by a veteran. Pellicano turns the notion of "invisible wounds of war" on its head, externalizing the dark, often violent thoughts and memories that can accompany the condition. The work shows that there's nothing literally dark about PTSD. Instead, the artist uses bright colors that emphasize the impulses and intrusive thoughts common to the condition. The "ticking time bomb" character referenced by the grenade is present at the little girl's table, but that character is not in control. Of course, the grenade could also be interpreted as someone who knows something about the fragility of life. The skull on the floor beside the table represents the unspeakable, the horrors of war, the loss of innocence, or perhaps the veteran wrestling with the theme of mortality. Pellicano's act of testimony begs a deeper questioning of the "time bomb" stereotype, but not at the expense of pretending all is well with returning veterans. It is a work that, rhetorically, and in the wrong context, would likely be perceived as derogatory if produced by a civilian.

By depicting a domestic, interior scene, Pellicano shows the intrusion of PTSD into the homecoming, not media spectacles such as "Returning Veteran Greeted by Loving Dog" or "Deployed Veteran Surprises Child in Classroom" with a million likes on social media. Popular media showers the public with images and video snippets of veterans returning home to tearful embraces. But that is where those stories end. There's rarely, if ever, any follow-up, and Pellicano shines a light on the long struggle that awaits military families after the honeymoon period ends. Pellicano doesn't invent the "wounded warrior," or the violence and instability attributed to veterans; he recognizes them as perceptions held by others and deals with them through extreme depictions. He shocks his audience the way Alexander's bartender was shocked when presented with his racist worldview taken to its logical conclusion.

The "Grenade Series" uses imagery usually (and blatantly) associated with veteran stereotypes: a grenade as a ticking time bomb, the veteran addicted to pills, a family within close proximity to danger. Pellicano's vantage as a veteran allows him to deal with stereotypes in a way that does not subject other veterans to the appropriating effect found in dominant narratives. As a whole, the "Grenade Series" succeeds because of the authority granted to the artist by his veteran status. Some stories, in instances when prevailing fictions converge on uncomfortable truths, *need* to be told by a veteran. Representations of veterans created by civilians, such as Stephen Crane's Henry Fleming, can at times capture the truth of military experience, but evaluations of veteran identity by veterans themselves keep these representations grounded in reality.

Pellicano and Crane are both examples of authenticity—in their works and in their efforts to understand veteran identity. Authenticity serves as a bridge that allows for further empathy, for mutual understanding to emerge where previously ritual defined the rhetorical situation. This exchange is not limited to civilians better understanding veterans. It works both ways. *Oh Happy Day* (2012) is another work from Pellicano's "Grenade Series." In it, a young, distraught woman (the artist's wife) sits on the edge of a bed with a pistol. Pellicano, the veteran, is attempting to see the pain caused by PTSD through the eyes of a military spouse. He claims that *Oh Happy Day* "provides a glimpse of the desperation of the other half in coping with the soldier's disabilities. . . . They can feel helpless in providing support and understanding to their returning soldier or they are unintentionally abused and suffer alongside them."[58] "Secondary PTSD" is the name of the condition described by Pellicano. To be in a relationship with someone suffering from mental illness can result in feelings of guilt. The partner may wonder if they "said something wrong" when the condition takes a turn for the worse. They may come to devalue their own well-being in hopes of focusing more on the partner with a diagnosis. Conditions like PTSD impact the whole family. In Pellicano's work, the child is shown as largely unaware of the father's condition in *Tea Time.* In *Oh Happy Day*, the symbolism of the alcohol bottle mirrors the pills, and the spouse has also become dangerous, holding a gun, and latching onto the pin that can set off the grenade. One interpretation could be that she has come to blame and see herself as the trigger.

Anxiety, depression, hypervigilance, anger attacks, and flashbacks are bound to have effects that extend beyond the veteran and into the lives of those people who care for them. How often do spouses blame themselves for these changes? And how often do they internalize and experience the symptoms themselves as a form of transference? Finding answers to these questions and others was one reason why military spouses became contributors to MEA publications. Once again, veteran storytellers invented a space that expanded to create a community based on healing and growth.

Oh Happy Day depicts a tearful woman holding onto a pistol and grenade pin. Pulling the pin, of course, will set off the grenade, and this fact has, presumably, brought the woman to tears. Perhaps she has come to blame herself for the condition suffered by her spouse. The focus of *Tea Time* is the daughter. In *Oh Happy Day* it is the wife. Earlier, I described the grenade as a "ticking time bomb." If, as this stereotype suggests, it is just *a matter of time* before the veteran turns violent, it is the woman in the image who perceives herself as the trigger. The woman photographed is literally the artist's wife. The work itself is an attempt to see through the spouse's eyes. *She* is the one dealing with the unspeakable, the horrors of war, or mortality. Both drugs—the pills on one side, the alcohol on the other—are ways of self-medicating. But few stop to consider how military spouses endure their own traumas, some having little to do with the military. Pellicano's attempts to engage with spouses, to understand what he sees as guilt, and to show them that they are not alone reflect the humanity of veterans—their ability to empathize and see themselves through the eyes of others. Life as a "ticking time bomb" is no life at all. Pellicano's work shows that neither is a life lived in fear of that bomb's explosion.

While homecoming is the most common theme in works published by MEA, the majority of the submissions I worked with over a period of five years were predicated on altruism, a trait I've attributed to veterans throughout this book. This fact should be the prevailing narrative surrounding military veterans: They retain the sense of collective responsibility instilled in them through training and combat experience. The future of veteran literature and art, if MEA is any indication, will be one in which veteran storytellers use their skills to engage with more than veterans' issues. Imagine what authors like Rancourt, Johnson, and Alexander could do if their talents were so employed. Imagine artists such as Holmes and Pellicano tackling rape and family strife on a national stage, for all Americans. It is possible to get to that point, but only if veteran identity is allowed to exist beyond the symbolic domain of stereotypes.

Belonging and Growth

David Ervin, a memoirist and fellow Iraq War veteran, emerged as the ideal candidate to replace me as MEA's president in 2015. He'd recently finished a memoir about the Iraq War, *Leaving the Wire: An Infantryman's Iraq* (2013), a book that he "felt the need to write because somebody needs to tell the average grunt's story."[59] When he came to MEA, he began experimenting with fiction because he wanted to delve deeper into human experience by looking at it from different angles, from perspectives other than his own. He began volunteering as an editor and repeatedly expressed that he found meaning in the work.

In 2015, we held our second national symposium in Lawton, Oklahoma. I handed over the passwords, tax documents, and contracts necessary to run the organization. Then, I took part in the event like any other veteran participant. MEA is still chugging along years later. Their flagship publication is a biannual magazine, *As You Were.* I'd worked with more than five hundred authors and artists on eight edited collections in my five years. David has since surpassed that number.

In 2021, David visited my Intro to Veterans Studies class to talk to my students about the topic of veteran identity. He texted me a few weeks before his visit: "The more I think about veteran identity the more I realize it isn't an identity at all. At least, it isn't supposed to be." I told him about some of the work I had been doing, including work on this book, and explained that a lot of veterans were waking up to just how limiting it can be to exist as a veteran. I'll paraphrase an example David gave to my students:

> One summer, I showed up at a historical event in full period costume. I had gotten into historical fiction, and to better understand what it felt like to live as a militiaman in the early nineteenth century, I had to do research. I tromped around through the hills, taking in the sights and sounds and smells. I looked up the clothing of the period, the minutia: types of wool used, stitching patterns, colorings. I learned to make moccasins and coats by hand. When I showed up to the event that day, the coat I was wearing had buttonholes that took twenty minutes each to make. I had put weeks, if not months into my work, hoping to talk with young people about history. Then, a guy walks up to me and says, "I heard you served in the Iraq War." Someone else had told him I'd written a book about my deployment in 2005, so I responded in the affirmative. He then proceeded to ask me questions about Iraq for no less than an hour. And it didn't have anything to do with me or my book. He just wanted me to confirm what he already believed. I wanted to be anywhere else in that moment.

David described to my class a situation similar to what the character in Alexander's story experienced. The problem with the encounter, David explained to my students, was that the interaction reduced the knowledge and experience he could share to a very narrow, four-year snapshot of his life. He had gone to great lengths to become what he referred to as "a more well-rounded human being." He had come to the event that day to educate children, but his veteran identity prevented it.

An avid reader, David had been reading a book about yoga in the week leading up to his class visit, Deborah Adele's *The Yamas and Niyamas: Exploring Yoga's Ethical Practice* (2009). He said, to the best of his knowledge, the book had nothing to do with the topic of veteran identity. But he had found a passage that he thought imparted the wisdom he had hoped to share with my students: "Every group has its rules and belief systems. . . . [W]hen a conflict arises between the need to belong and the need to grow, we have to make a choice. We must either sacrifice a part of ourselves to maintain our belonging, or we must risk the approval and support of the group by growing" beyond it.[60] David tried to grow beyond his veteran identity and found himself being pulled back to a state of being in which only four years of his life mattered. MEA, he claims, allows him to hold onto his veteran identity but also compartmentalize it. He enjoys the camaraderie and helping veterans, but these days he prefers to focus his personal efforts on historical fiction and other endeavors.

The examples given in this chapter—Baca, Rancourt, Johnson, Alexander, Holmes, Pellicano, and Ervin—are among a growing cadre of veteran authors and artists finding means through which to express themselves. Future studies into the homecoming experiences of military veterans will, undoubtedly, focus on those instances in which veterans further complicate veteran identity, continuing to grow when existence within the group makes it difficult. As the opportunities for veterans to give testimony increase, and as more nuanced images of veteran identity rise to the surface, veterans will cease being viewed as a monolith. More importantly, future generations of veterans will find in veteran storytellers resilient, adaptable models of veteran identity to help them transition into civilian life. It is our collective duty to listen, provide opportunities for growth, and treat each veteran as an individual, not what we need or want them to be. Veterans served their nation in uniform. When they come home, they deserve the chance to continue growing.

Epilogue

The Rise of Veterans Studies

In this book, I have argued that veterans of the post-9/11 generation must not allow themselves to be stereotyped. To be called a "hero" can be flattering. To accept sympathy as a "wounded warrior" can be comforting. But these labels exist in the American unconscious to describe veterans monolithically, and often so that veteran identity might be harnessed to support causes and narratives other than the veteran's own. These stereotypes can also be limiting on an individual level because existing as someone else's ideal veteran is not to exist as oneself.

Those veterans I have referred to as storytellers recognize stereotypes, subvert them, and craft nuanced examples of veteran identity for other veterans to model. Veteran authors and artists study narrative structure, hone the craft of narrating self, and tap into the symbolic authority granted to them to make personal and political statements. However, in a phenomenological or Althusserian sense, veterans are *always already* storytellers. Their intersectional identities and experiences make them unique. And beyond creative expression, any veteran is capable of being a storyteller through impression management, their treatment of others, or service to their home community.

Of course, post-9/11 veterans can't tell the story of themselves in a vacuum. An audience is necessary to listen, reflect, and engage in dialogue about war and the life that comes after. Veterans are told to reassimilate, and to help them in that process society provides educational benefits and medical care. They are told that they have much to learn about "the civilian sector" if they want to be successful. But it's assumed veterans have nothing to teach society in return, and this assumption results in feelings of alienation.

Homecoming is not an experience. It is a lifelong process, one in which the veteran's knowledge should be assimilated into our collective understanding of the world. Each veteran returns home having completed a years-long practicum in the humanities; they possess knowledge about other cultures, historical movements, resilience, and service. However, and as I have shown, dialogue with civilians is often interrupted by stereotyping and mythmaking processes that result in veteran silence. I have suggested ways and shown examples of how to elicit veteran testimony. But there are also ways to enlist civilians and equip them with the skills and confidence needed to listen to what veterans have to say.

Jerad W. Alexander, the veteran whose short work "Cold Day in Bridgewater" was discussed in this book's fourth chapter, also wrote the memoir *Volunteers: Growing Up in the Forever War.*[1] He deals with such themes as media representations of veterans, the decision to serve, the whitewashing of war, and reassimilation. Alexander writes:

> This divide has grown from the elective experience of professional military service that has, by virtue of its volunteerism, created a class largely removed from the greater American culture, become a kingdom all its own . . . I would feel trapped between the kingdom I had left and the world I was attempting to be absorbed by, even desperately. But it was impossible. There are so few of us—about 7 percent of the population—and our stories so unusual compared to the relative safety of the American landscape that the terrors and virtues of military service will always set us apart. We become veterans: the avatars of patriotism, psychic wounds, presumptions of action-movie heroism, and sometimes even unspoken pity, all acknowledged with the guilty platitude "Thank you for your service."[2]

Alexander describes in this single paragraph most of the issues I have tried to touch upon in this book. The separateness and difference that veterans feel in relation to their civilian counterparts is amplified by the ways in which veterans and civilians communicate—through rituals and "platitudes." Though nonveterans sincerely want to express their gratitude, the separateness, when combined with superficial understandings of service members and the wars they fight, results in the phrase "thank you for your service" having a different meaning to veterans.

In his short story, Alexander used fiction to provide an example: a bartender projecting his meaning of the word "service" upon a veteran who held such a different view that it provoked him to anger. Clearly, it is important that veterans and nonveterans agree upon what it means to serve before gratitude can be both given by the civilian and received by the veteran. It isn't that civilians are not trying. Alexander says they are trying "desperately" in his memoir. Yet, my argument remains that the patriotic script that defines the *ritual* of giving thanks to veterans needs to be rewritten. What if instead of saying "thank you for your service" we asked veterans to "tell me about your service"? What if the presumption that testimony necessarily damages veterans psychologically disappeared and—not unlike the warriors in the tribes described by Sebastian Junger—veterans had defined roles as educators on the topic of the resilience of humanity? Alexander hid his anger in a work of fiction. Tif Holmes hid her pain in images layered upon one another to create a work of art that portrayed her as a prisoner to silence. We try to understand veterans through the prisms of mental illness and economics all the time. My claim is that we need to reevaluate the veteran's *symbolic position*—what it means to be a veteran. Civilians need to be taught new ways of expressing gratitude and engaging in dialogue, and veterans need to resist the feeling that "military service will always set us apart" and embrace the symbolic authority granted to them through military service.

We spend a lot of time and money creating "safe spaces" where veterans can speak freely among themselves or with a therapist. What if in addition to these efforts we did more to make the country that veterans return to inclusive of their perspectives? In 2010, I created the nation's first academic program in Veterans Studies at Eastern Kentucky University.[3] At the Kentucky Center for Veterans Studies we teach that veteran identity is intersectional and nonmonolithic. No two veterans are the same: social identities ranging from gender to race, socioeconomic class, religion, and ability shape veterans' perspectives before, during, and after service. In other words, "If you know a veteran, you know only one veteran."

Colleges are major sites of transformation for returning veterans. It is imperative that higher education professionals embrace veterans and aid them in the homecoming process. This work is not the sole responsibility of the Department of Veterans Affairs or veterans service organizations. Nor is it only the responsibility of offices that process VA benefits and provide other services. Veterans are discovering themselves in classrooms, in student organizations, and in interactions with students, staff, and faculty. Each member of the campus community plays a part in facilitating dialogue between veterans and their chosen tribes.

I taught a student nicknamed "Bingo" many years ago, in both my veteran orientation to college course and Intro to Veterans Studies. He was a bright, charismatic man who used humor to mask an inner sadness. As part of a literal mask-making exercise, he scrawled the words "death" and "end it" in black contrast on the inside of his white, art store theater mask. Underneath these words, in blood red, and repeated no less than three dozen times, were simple variations on the word for laughter: "Ha! Ha. HA." The outside of the mask represented how he felt the world viewed him; it was decorated with a smiling mouth, the word "war," and the type of striped-face camouflage you might find on a marine in a war movie.

Bingo was always exceptional in that he took it upon himself to help his peers by sharing what he learned. You would never guess that he was in pain because he was always telling jokes. For example, he made a quip about how my mask-making exercise reminded him of arts and crafts in grade school before throwing himself into it. He later told the class the meaning behind dark words on the inside of his mask: "We would laugh as loud as we could to drown out the gunfire—to drown out the sounds of killing them." He went on to express guilt and to describe how that same laughter continued to echo in his mind years later. I got the impression that he had never discussed the events or their consequences outside of a therapist's office.

Even though "death," "end it," and laughter filled the inside of his mask, not a speck of pain could be found on the outside. War, as Bingo felt civilians understood it, was clean and unmarred. On the inside of his mask, however, in the space where Bingo expressed how he continued to experience war in the present, war was profane, violent, true. Either inadvertently or by design, it was as though Bingo depicted the pressure to conform to a "hero" identity on the outside of his mask and the pressure to conform to the "wounded warrior" stereotype on the inside.

Frank, a former marine I taught in the same classes as Bingo, interpreted the mask similarly in one of the many times he stayed after class to chat. He was a highly intelligent student who also used humor to mask an inner sadness. Frank would add to his teacher's reading list, and he tried his best to find a community, serving, like Bingo, in the student veteran organization, even auditing my classes when they dealt with military culture or history. He told me several times that he felt ashamed of being injured in Iraq.

After my semester with Bingo and Frank ended, Frank stuck around and became my unofficial teaching assistant for the next crop of student veterans. When they arrived for their freshman year, he showed up early each Tuesday and Thursday morning, not for pay or course credit, just to give them advice about the road that lay ahead. Frank never lost sight of the altruism that led him to serve in the Marine Corps. He tried hard to find himself after experiencing war. He tried VA therapy and the onslaught of drugs that often goes along with it. He tried hard to "come home." He died by suicide in 2015.

At the Veterans Memorial located at the heart of campus, Frank's name is carved into a granite bench sitting adjacent to the Fallen Soldier Cross Memorial constructed in 2017. This memorial was designed by sculptor Allen Ferg, a Vietnam veteran who dedicated his work to his friend and platoonmate, Dr. Robert Topmiller. Topmiller was an EKU history professor who died by suicide in 2008. We use his textbook *Binding Their Wounds: America's Assault on Its Veterans* (2011) in our Veterans Studies courses. Another one of Topmiller's friends, a Vietnam veteran and peace activist, Peter Berres, is one of our primary instructors. I repeatedly remind our students that they are fortunate to be able to learn from veterans of that generation, as their numbers grow fewer every day.

As a result of teaching Veterans Studies, I have continued to grow as an educator, veteran, and human being. We convinced Peter to teach for us after he retired from a highly successful career at the University of Kentucky. He volunteered to serve during the Vietnam War out of a sense of duty and patriotism, later becoming an interrogator. The experience changed his outlook on war and led him to play prominent roles in international peace movements. He has joined advocacy groups and served among humanitarian delegations to places like Iran and Cuba. He took groups of students to Vietnam to show them the devastation that war and Agent Orange continue to have on the local population. He once told my class, "They have a different culture. I can honestly say I received a warmer welcome when I returned to Vietnam than when I returned to my own country all those years ago." Peter has helped me see the connection between veteran identity and war's cyclical nature. Yet, despite his experiences, he describes his military service as inherently positive. It helped him find a calling and a sense of purpose. He is a veteran storyteller in the truest sense, harnessing the symbolic authority available to him to try and prevent war for future generations. I learn something new from him each semester.

Currently, hundreds of students take Veterans Studies courses at EKU each year. We also confer Veterans Studies minors and certificates, and I am working toward a four-year degree. Students take our courses for personal and professional reasons, and informal surveys show the majority have veteran family members. Many of our students hope to someday work alongside or provide services to veterans as psychologists, social workers, nurses, business owners, or police officers. Each graduate goes out into the world equipped to undermine stereotypes and encourage veteran testimony. I ask, "Imagine yourself five to seven years after graduation. You are in your first leadership position, and you hire a recently discharged veteran. Are you going to draw on the types of stereotypes we've discussed this semester? Or are you going to find ways to tap into that veteran's resilience and leadership ability? How are you going to welcome them home?" Similarly, I teach those students in the "helping professions" to recognize that veteran identity represents only one aspect of an individual's life. Many veterans deal with the types of adversity and inequality faced by members of the other social groups with which their veteran identity intersects.

Starting with the introductory course in Veterans Studies, every student records at least one veteran's oral history, archiving it in the William H. Berge Oral History Center. It is an important project that helps nonveterans overcome unfounded fears of psychologically harming veterans by talking to them about service. Often, students will interview a parent, grandparent, or sibling. Sometimes they will happen upon veterans while working part-time jobs, or they'll realize they sit next to a veteran in another class. Students have repeatedly told me that these interviews were the first meaningful conversations they had had about the military with people they've known their whole lives. College freshmen—especially those born after 9/11—are shocked when they learn about the treatment of Vietnam veterans and about veterans who continue to suffer from Agent Orange, Gulf War Syndrome, nuclear exposure, and, more recently acknowledged, military sexual trauma. In discussion forums there are common refrains: "Why did the government wait so long to admit what happened?" and "Why does every veteran problem get blamed on PTSD?"

Mindful of the need to not perpetuate victimization narratives, I sandwich uncomfortable histories with examples of veterans who display post-traumatic growth and resilience. Students learn about veteran peace activists like Peter, humanitarians in groups like Team Rubicon, and entrepreneurs like those who started the Black Rifle Coffee Company.

Another one of our instructors, Elizabeth Barrs, recently completed a Ph.D. in history and was an active-duty army intelligence officer for twenty-one years. She served tours in Desert Storm, Iraq, Afghanistan, and the White House Situation Room. Each student she interacts with sees an example of a veteran who is a lifelong learner, one eager to discuss service and tap into her leadership experience to facilitate dialogue between veteran and nonveteran students. Student veterans who take our classes to contextualize and process their experiences are great examples of veteran identity; they tend to emerge as classroom leaders.

LaSheka Mason, a former army staff sergeant and business major, took my Intro to Veterans Studies class in 2021. Our class met synchronously online once a week, usually to go over current assignments and hear from guest speakers. One evening, someone with an unrecognizable username started causing distractions. It may have been a student. It may have been a Zoom "bomber." I'm not sure. I was too busy interviewing our guest to figure it out.

Mason grew agitated. The topic that week was combat and the physical, mental, and spiritual toll it takes on those who experience it. When I paused to ask for comments or questions, Mason unmuted her mic: "I want to say something to some of my fellow students. The stuff they are talking about is real. I have lived it. Until you have been in these command situations or seen what can happen to people downrange, you have no clue how serious this can be. That is why it bothers me when I see someone making a fool of themselves on camera when we are talking about people losing their lives. If you don't want to be in this class, hit the road. I am here to learn, and I know I am not the only one." I started assigning Mason to "guard duty" when we had guests, making her a co-host in our online forums so that she could show the door to anyone "making a fool of themselves."

I gladly "passed the mic" when Mason unmuted during our Veterans of Color module. Her identity, conviction, and willingness to be vulnerable provided insights and an immediate example of intersectionality that the class would not have been able to understand with as much significance. "You can't tell me you 'don't see color,' that you only see the world through a black and white lens," Mason told the class. "I had to hide injuries when I was in the military because I didn't want to be perceived as weak. There were people who saw me as 'less than,' either because I was a woman or the color of my skin. I've always pushed myself twice as hard, not because I wanted to, but because I had to."

For the module, I assigned a video recording of a December 2020 traffic stop in Virginia involving Caron Nazario, a Black lieutenant in the Virginia National Guard. The video contained troubling footage showing police officers needlessly pepper-spraying Nazario, and I assigned it because I wondered if the image of a soldier in uniform would elicit the sort of sympathy that many in our county refuse to give people of color. Our class discussion took place right after the Derek Chauvin trial in April 2021. Emotions were raw, and Mason's words left the two Veterans Studies professors humbled and her fellow students speechless. I asked Mason how she felt that particular intersection of veteran identity with race could yield deeper insights into both identities: "It hurts. That's all I can say. It hurts. It hurts when you are willing to go out, put your life on the line, and fight for this country and people still treat you like you aren't good enough. Not because of anything you did or didn't do. But just because you are you—because of the color of your skin."

Mason could have reacted with much more anger, and she later shared some disturbing stories of how she was mistreated because of her race and gender before, during, and after service. Recently, she told a group of our students that she had been stopped in a parking lot by a customer at Lowe's. The company offers privileged parking spaces for veterans. But because Mason is a Black woman, someone took it on himself to wait outside until she returned to her vehicle. The man called her "the worst kind of human being," knowing nothing about Mason's seven years of service and deployment to Afghanistan. He only knew that she didn't look like the white, male "heroes" available in his limited imagination. Mason told the nonveteran students, "So, I told him 'thank you for your service of pulling parking lot guard duty' and went about my day," to raucous applause. The Veterans Studies program provides these sorts of veteran-civilian interactions within a "laboratory of learning," where it is okay for civilians to ask questions and for veterans to learn the craft of impression management. Rather than veteran safe spaces and echo chambers, our colleges need more programs that allow veterans and nonveterans to interact authentically.

Over the past decade, academic programs in Veterans Studies have emerged on campuses across the country. The second program was founded at the University of Missouri-St. Louis by US Army Lieutenant Colonel (retired) Jim Craig. Craig improved on my original definition, describing the field as "an emerging, inherently multidisciplinary academic field devoted to developing a clearer understanding of veterans and the veteran experience in the past, the present, and the future."[4] Other academic programs have been established at Arizona State University, the University of California-Irvine, the University of Utah, and St. Leo University, where the first bachelor of arts in Veterans Studies was established in fall 2021 by Ernest McClees and Karen Hannel. In addition to serving nonveterans, McClees hopes his program will help former service members "fully understand their experience . . . and their place in a larger society."[5]

Those with established programs in Veterans Studies have worked together and shared best practices. Jim Craig and I workshopped curriculum designs when we were establishing our respective programs a decade ago. Ernest McClees taught at EKU prior to moving to St. Leo. In fact, we recently convened representatives from every existing program in the country. Our goal is to establish a national center for excellence in Veterans Studies. It is my hope that we can provide mentoring for program founders and advocate for the exponential growth of Veterans Studies on campuses nationwide. It is uplifting to know that we are part of a group that naturally eschews the territorialism so common in higher education.

Academic programs like the Kentucky Center for Veterans Studies tend to be infused with an activist component. Of course, researchers and philosophers have been writing about veterans' issues dating back to Homer. Sigmund Freud wrote about World War I veterans and the collective unconscious. Willard Walter Waller applied sociological concepts to the "veteran problem" he perceived in the 1940s. Paul Fussell, Jonathan Shay, Sebastian Junger, and Karl Marlantes are all thinkers who perceived of veteran identity as a distinct topic worthy of scholarship. In tandem with the growth of academic programs in Veterans Studies, researchers have forged groups. There are established research programs at the Veterans & Media Lab at the University of Alabama,[6] the Institute for Veterans & Military Families at Syracuse University,[7] and Ohio State's Suicide & Trauma Reduction Initiative for Veterans (STRIVE).[8] Meanwhile, the Air Force Academy has led the way in veteran and war-related humanities scholarship with *War, Literature & the Arts* for more than thirty years.[9] I was proud to present on EKU's new Veterans Studies program at the first Veterans in Society Conference hosted by Virginia Tech in 2013.[10] And I serve on the editorial board for the independently run, open-access *Journal of Veterans Studies* that has become a hub for interdisciplinary scholars throughout the world.[11] In fact, the founder of that publication, Mariana Grohowski, served for several years as a leader in the group Military Experience & the Arts discussed in the last chapter of this book.

Students like LaSheka Mason, Bingo, and Frank are what drive me to continue growing our program at EKU. I am also inspired by nonveteran students like Katie Andrews, who said, "Having veterans in the class and a veteran-instructor allowed me to learn from people who had actually experienced what we were discussing—instead of just reading from a book. It was a bit intimidating trying to understand things that are pretty much impossible to understand unless you have lived them."[12] More recently, our students formed a group—the Veterans Studies Alliance—intended to be a place for both nonveterans and veterans to communicate and collaborate on service projects.

Nonveteran students have shown me that civilians have so much to offer the veteran community when veterans give them the permission to grow and learn about military service. Many have taken the lead on a number of service and professionalization initiatives. Jatana Boggs, a psychology major, worked with the Veterans Affairs hospital in Lexington, Kentucky, to establish a mentoring program for students who want to go into careers serving veterans. Another student, Lora Scott, has developed a "virtual visits" outreach that will let EKU student volunteers visit with veterans in assisted living facilities remotely. Samuel Lewis now runs a podcast called "Service to Service" dedicated to showcasing examples of veterans who break with stereotypical conceptions of veteran identity, but also nonveterans who are coming up with innovative ways to serve the veteran community.

Officially, the Fallen Soldier Cross Memorial at Eastern Kentucky University recognizes "all those who lost their lives because of their service, but not while in active service." A casting of the upside-down rifle, boots, and helmet used to memorialize fallen comrades at war sits at the center of a stainless steel sphere. Brett Morris, who helped me start the Veterans Studies program at EKU, explained that the sphere "symbolizes that PTSD is not unique to America, and represents the global nature of the problems facing all warriors after they leave service."[13] Dog tags hang from inside the sphere, each with the name, date of birth, and date of death of a member of the campus veteran community. As the wind hits the dog tags, they tap against the steel, creating a wind chime effect that, in a way, gives a voice to the fallen. Through Veterans Studies, I hope to amplify that voice and use higher education to transform veteran homecoming into a communal process that includes us all.

Acknowledgments

I am largely in the debt of remarkable women who have shared compassion, knowledge, and wisdom with me throughout my personal and professional life. So, I will start there.

First, and without even a close second, I want to thank my partner, Lisa Day. Her love has been constant, her patience unwavering. She has read everything I have ever written and knows me better than anyone ever will. I love her as a companion and an intellectual equal. I respect her independence, and I cherish her intuition.

Lisa tells me my mother, Sylvia Roberts, was the first feminist in my life, the one who taught me to respect women and engage in life as a moral being. She woke up every morning at 5 a.m. and filled notebooks with math, trying to think of ways to make ends meet as a single parent. Watching her repeatedly bounce back from adversity taught me resilience and self-reliance. Thank you, Tim, for making the second half of her life better than the first, as well as for your mentorship.

Thank you also to those women-scholars who played roles in shaping my trajectory. Professor Lynn Shearer inspired me to study literature. The poet Wanda Fries encouraged me to pursue my passion for writing. Dr. Deborah Core was the first to encourage me to apply my military experience in readings of American literature. Dr. Virginia Blum, who hooded me in 2017, pushed me to my intellectual limits and helped me understand social theory. Dr. Pearl James's mentorship made me a better writer. Dr. Sara Zeigler has provided guidance and supported my efforts to build a distinctive program in Veterans Studies over the past decade.

Work on this book would not have concluded without the help of Dr. Abigail Prang. She dragged me across the finish line, providing precision peer review, expert knowledge, and kindness when I complained about trying to find time to write while working two jobs. Of course, teamwork makes the dream work with Starr Wentzel and Donna Jones, friends and colleagues who covered down for me and championed my work every step of the way.

I also want to acknowledge veterans who made this work possible. Dr. Brett Morris gave me my first job serving veterans in higher education. He encouraged me to pursue my outlandish ideas, opened doors, and got people to listen. After finishing my Ph.D., it was Dr. Eugene Palka who guided me to my first academic appointment, enabling me to "officially" start my career. Dr. David Albright persuaded me to finish this book and mentored me during the process of proposing the project to publishers.

It has been invaluable to converse with my younger brother, Joshua Roberts. I often pictured him as my "imaginary reader," picking up the book the day after his enlistment ended. During the writing of this book, he evolved from a young navy recruit to an experienced submariner and noncommissioned officer. I am exceedingly proud of what he has accomplished in uniform and as a father. I am excited to see what he does next.

Thanks must go to David Ervin for letting me tell some of his story, but more for the selflessness he has shown leading Military Experience & the Arts since 2015. I know it is a labor of love, and it has been amazing to see him keep the dream alive. Tif Holmes and Giuseppe Pellicano were gracious enough to allow me to use their amazing works of art. Román Baca shared pictures and gave me the opportunity to tell the story of the Exit12 Dance Company. Drew Cameron has always inspired me with Combat Paper, and I look forward to our next workshop. I discussed the works of several authors I met through my involvement in the veterans' creative communities: Suzanne Rancourt, Jerad Alexander, and Bradley Johnson. I hope I did them justice and I encourage my readers to seek out their more recent works, because they are truly remarkable authors.

Finally, thanks must go to the friends I made in uniform: the "Turley Boys," the noncommissioned officers who molded me, and a platoon leader who taught me self-respect. I am proud of everyone I served alongside in the 51st Transportation Company "Steel Knights" (Mannheim, Germany). Rest in peace Corporal Kevin M. Jones. You are missed.

Notes

Introduction

1. Maribel Aponte et al., *Minority Veterans Report: Military Service History and VA Benefit Utilization Statistics*, PDF file, March 2017, Department of Veterans Affairs and National Center for Veterans Analysis and Statistics, https://www.va.gov/vetdata/docs/SpecialReports/Minority_Veterans_Report.pdf.

2. "Facts and Statistics About Women Veterans," Women Veterans Healthcare, US Department of Veterans Affairs, December 17, 2013, https://www.womenshealth.va.gov/womenshealth/latestinformation/facts.asp.

3. Kim Parker et al., "The American Veteran Experience and the Post-9/11 Generation," Pew Research Center: Social and Demographic Trends, Pew Research Center, September 10, 2019, https://www.pewresearch.org/social-trends/2019/09/10/the-american-veteran-experience-and-the-post-9-11-generation/.

4. Daniel Milton and Andrew Mines, "'This Is War': Examining Military Experience Among the Capitol Hill Siege Participants," PDF file, April 12, 2021, Program on Extremism, 8, https://ctc.usma.edu/wp-content/uploads/2021/04/This-is-War_Final.pdf.

5. Scott Parrott et al., "Mental Representations of Military Veterans: Pictures (and Words) in Our Heads," *Journal of Veteran Studies* 6, no. 3 (December 2020): 61–71, http://doi.org/10.21061/jvs.v6i3.207.

6. Tim O'Brien, *The Things They Carried* (New York: Broadway, 1990), 85.

7. Karl Marlantes, *What It Is Like to Go to War* (New York: Atlantic Monthly Press, 2011), 213.

8. Paul Fussell, *The Great War and Modern Memory* (New York: Sterling, 1975), 37.

1. A Theory of Veteran Identity

1. "Paid Patriotism at NFL Games?" *VFW Magazine* 102, no. 10 (2015): 8.

2. Abraham Lincoln, Abraham Lincoln papers: Series 3, General Correspondence, 1837 to 1897: Abraham Lincoln, March 4, 1865 Second Inaugural

Address; endorsed by Lincoln, March 4, 1865, Manuscript/Mixed Material, http://hdl.loc.gov/loc.mss/ms000001.mss30189a.4361300.

3. Terry Eagleton, *Literary Theory: An Introduction* (Minneapolis: Univ. of Minnesota Press, 2008), viii.

4. Dennis Sobolev, *The Concepts Used to Analyze Culture: A Critique of Twentieth-Century Ways of Thinking* (Lewiston, N.Y.: Edwin Mellen, 2010), 2.

5. Robert C. Fuller, *Americans and the Unconscious* (Oxford: Oxford Univ. Press, 1986), 5.

6. Seymour Martin Lipset, *American Exceptionalism: A Double-Edged Sword* (New York: Norton, 1996), 18.

7. Arthur Asa Berger, *Cultural Criticism: A Primer of Key Concepts* (Thousand Oaks, Calif.: Sage, 1995), 15–16.

8. Ibid., 355.

9. Yves Winter, "*The Prince* and His Art of War: Machiavelli's Military Populism," *Social Research* 81, no. 1 (2014): 177, Academia.edu.

10. Giorgio Agamben, *The Coming Community* (Minneapolis: Univ. of Minnesota Press, 1993), n.p.

11. Stanley Kubrick, dir., *Full Metal Jacket* (1987; Burbank, Calif.: Warner Brothers, 2007), Blu-ray.

12. John W. Copeland and David W. Sutherland, "Sea of Goodwill: Matching the Donor to the Need," Office of the Chairman of the Joint Chiefs of Staff Warrior and Family Support, Council on Foundations, May 17, 2010, 1.

13. Smedley D. Butler, *War Is a Racket: The Antiwar Classic by America's Most Decorated Soldier* (1935; reprint, Scotts Valley, Calif.: CreateSpace Independent Publishing, 2014).

14. "William T. Sherman: Major General," Civil War Trust, accessed 2014, https://www.battlefields.org/learn/biographies/william-t-sherman.

15. Paul John Eakin, *Living Autobiographically: How We Create Identity in Narrative* (Ithaca, N.Y.: Cornell Univ. Press, 2008), xiv.

16. Ibid., 152.

17. Sheldon Rampton and John Stauber, *Weapons of Mass Deception: The Uses of Propaganda in Bush's War on Iraq* (New York: Tarcher/Penguin, 2003), 192–93.

18. Ronald Reagan, "National Security and SDI," l, March 23, 1983, Washington, D.C., transcript, *American Experience*, accessed 2014, https://www.pbs.org/wgbh/americanexperience/features/reagan-security/.

19. Winter, "*The Prince* and His Art of War," 164–65.

20. *Rightwing Extremism: Current Economic and Political Climate Fueling Resurgence in Radicalization and Recruitment*, PDF file, April 7, 2009, US Department of Homeland Security, 7, https://fas.org/irp/eprint/rightwing.pdf.

21. Daniel Milton and Andrew Mines, "'This Is War': Examining Military Experience Among the Capitol Hill Siege Participants," PDF file, April 12, 2021, Program on Extremism, 8, https://ctc.usma.edu/wp-content/uploads/2021/04/This-is-War_Final.pdf.

22. Willard Walter Waller, *The Veteran Comes Back* (New York: Dryden Press, 1944), 187, https://archive.org/details/veterancomesback00wallrich/page/16/mode/2up.

23. Ibid., 124.

24. Reuben L. Hill, "Works by Waller," *International Encyclopedia of the Social Sciences*, August 8, 2016, https://www.encyclopedia.com/people/social-sciences-and-law/sociology-biographies/willard-w-waller.

25. Eric Hodges, Nancy Dallett, Jim Dubinsky, Jim Craig, and Bruce Pencek, "Waller's The Veteran Comes Back at 77," online panel presentation, "Conversations in Veteran Studies," Veterans Studies Association, May 18, 2021.

26. Michael Robinson and Kori Schake, "The Military's Extremism Problem Is Our Problem," *New York Times*, March 2, 2021, https://www.nytimes.com/2021/03/02/opinion/veterans-capitol-attack.html.

27. Jennifer Bronson, E. Ann Carson, Margaret Noonan, and Marcus Berzofsky, *Veterans in Prison and Jail, 2011–12*, PDF file, December 2015, US Department of Justice, https://justiceforvets.org/wp-content/uploads/2017/03/BJS-Report.pdf.

28. D. Mark Anderson and Daniel I. Rees, "Deployments, Combat Exposure, and Crime," *IZA Discussion Papers* 7761 (2013).

29. Sonya Norman, Eric B. Elbogen, and Paula P. Schnurr, "Research Findings on PTSD and Violence," US Department of Veterans Affairs, https://www.ptsd.va.gov/professional/treat/cooccurring/research_violence.asp#three.

30. Sean Illing, "Is Civilization Good for Us? Sebastian Junger on the Dangers of Social Fragmentation," *Vox*, October 27, 2016, https://www.vox.com/2016/9/13/12842400/sebastian-junger-tribe-interview.

31. Sebastian Junger, *Tribe: On Homecoming and Belonging* (New York: Twelve, 2016), 101.

32. Waller, *The Veteran Comes Back*, 247.

33. Jonathan Shay, *Odysseus in America: Combat Trauma and the Trials of Homecoming* (New York: Scribner, 2002), 12.

34. Ibid., 243.

35. Ibid., 244.

36. Eric J. Leed, "Fateful Memories: Industrialized War and Traumatic Neuroses," *Journal of Contemporary History* 35, no. 1 (2000): 88.

37. Junger, *Tribe*, 79.

38. Ibid.

39. Ibid.

40. Matthew R. Zefferman and Sarah Mathew, "Combat Stress in a Small-Scale Society Suggests Divergent Evolutionary Roots for Posttraumatic Stress Disorder Symptoms," *Proceedings of the National Academy of Sciences* 118, no. 15 (April 2021): 7, e2020430118; DOI: 10.1073/pnas.2020430118.

41. Ibid., 8.

42. Richard Severo and Lewis Milford, *The Wages of War: When America's Soldiers Came Home—From Valley Forge to Vietnam* (New York: Simon and Schuster, 1989), 358.

43. *National Veteran Suicide Prevention Annual Report*, PDF file, 2019, US Department of Veterans Affairs, https://www.mentalhealth.va.gov/docs/data-sheets/2019/2019_National_Veteran_Suicide_Prevention_Annual_Report_508.pdf.

44. Waller, *The Veteran Comes Back*, 247.

45. Junger, *Tribe*, 102.

46. Steve Wahle, "PhDs Who Can Win a Bar Fight," online panel presentation, University of South Carolina, March 23, 2021.

47. Sam Levin, "Army Veterans Return to Standing Rock to Form a Human Shield against Police," *The Guardian*, February 11, 2017, https://www.theguardian.com/us-news/2017/feb/11/standing-rock-army-veterans-camp.

48. Ibid.

49. Ibid.

50. Ibid.

51. "Mission," Team RWB, accessed April 2021, https://www.teamrwb.org/about-us/mission/.

52. "Enriching the Lives of America's Veterans," PDF file, September 8, 2014, Team RWB, https://teamrwb.org/wp-content/uploads/2017/11/TRWB-Study_ImpactMetricsForWebsite.pdf?_ga=2.70276880.1071987360.1622070155–111700387.1622070155.

53. "The Story of Team Rubicon," Team Rubicon, accessed May 2021, https://teamrubiconusa.org/story/.

54. "Veterans Empowered to Protect African Wildlife," VETPAW, accessed May 2021, https://vetpaw.org/.

55. "About SVA," Student Veterans of America, accessed May 2021, https://studentveterans.org/about/.

56. Jennifer Steinhauer, "Veterans' Groups Compete with Each Other, and Struggle with the V.A.," *New York Times*, January 4, 2019, https://www.nytimes.com/2019/01/04/us/politics/veterans-service-organizations.html.

2. Our Nation's Heroes

1. Erving Goffman, *The Presentation of Self in Everyday Life* (New York: Anchor, 1959).

2. Ibid., 2–3.

3. Tony Scott, dir., *Top Gun* (1986; Los Angeles: Paramount Pictures, 1998), DVD.

4. William A. Wellman and Harry d'Abbadie d'Arrast, dir., *Wings* (1927; Los Angeles: Paramount Famous Lasky Corporation, 2012), DVD.

5. Philip Kaufman, dir., *The Right Stuff* (1983; Hollywood, Calif.: Ladd Company, 1997), DVD.

6. Linda R. Robertson, *Dream of Civilized Warfare: World War I Flying Aces and the American Imagination* (Minneapolis: Univ. of Minnesota Press, 2003).

7. Ibid., 88.

8. Kevin L. Ferguson, "Aviation Cinema," *Criticism* 57, no. 2 (2015): 319–20.

9. Marc Webb, dir., *The Ghost of You*, performed by My Chemical Romance (Los Angeles, Calif.: DNA, 2005), music video.

10. Ibid.

11. Wilfred Owen, "Dulce et Decorum Est," in *The Norton Anthology of English Literature*, ed. Stephen Greenblatt (New York: Norton, 2006), 1974.

12. *Top Gun*, dir. Tony Scott.

13. Ferguson, "Aviation Cinema," 310.

14. Ibid.

15. Amy Nicholson, "Tom Cruise Was Brilliant in *Top Gun*, You Just Might Not Remember," *LA Weekly* (Los Angeles, Calif.), December 16, 2014, 3.

16. *Top Gun*, dir. Tony Scott.

17. Ibid.

18. Nicholson, "Tom Cruise Was Brilliant," 6.

19. Ibid.

20. *Top Gun*, dir. Tony Scott.

21. *The Ghost of You*, dir. Marc Webb.

22. G. Thomas Couser, *Altered Egos: Authority in American Autobiography* (New York: Oxford, 1989), 16–17.

23. Leo Braudy, *From Chivalry to Terrorism: War and the Changing Nature of Masculinity* (New York: Vintage, 2005), xv.

24. Ferguson, "Aviation Cinema," 310.

25. Victoria L. Bromley, *Feminisms Matter: Debates, Theories, Activism* (Toronto: Univ. of Toronto Press, 2012), 153.

26. Jack Halberstam, *Female Masculinity* (Durham: Duke Univ. Press, 1998), 1.

27. Ibid.

28. Brenda Boyle, “Rescuing Masculinity: Captivity, Rescue and Gender in American War Narratives,” *Journal of American Culture* 34, no. 2 (2011): 149, EBSCO.

29. Kirk Savage, *Standing Soldiers, Kneeling Slaves: Race, War, and Monument in Nineteenth-Century America* (Princeton: Princeton Univ. Press, 1997), 97.

30. Annessa Stagner, “Recovering the Masculine Hero: Post-World War I Shell Shock in American Culture,” UCLA Center for the Study of Women, 2009, 1, https://escholarship.org/uc/item/4jt5g1q2.

31. Ibid., 7.

32. *Top Gun*, dir. Tony Scott.

33. *The Ghost of You*, dir. Marc Webb.

34. *Top Gun*, dir. Tony Scott.

35. Halberstam, *Female Masculinity*, 2.

36. Braudy, *From Chivalry to Terrorism*, xv.

37. Brian Mockenhaupt, “I Miss Iraq. I Miss My Gun. I Miss My War,” *Esquire*, June 26, 2007, 2, https://www.esquire.com/news-politics/a26372/esq0307essay/.

38. Ibid., 3.

39. Ibid., 5.

40. Ibid., 6.

41. Ibid., 18–19.

42. Cathy Caruth, *Unclaimed Experience: Trauma, Narrative, and History* (Baltimore: Johns Hopkins Univ. Press, 1996), 4.

43. Braudy, *From Chivalry to Terrorism*, 29.

44. “The Army Values,” US Army, accessed 2016, https://www.army.mil/values/.

45. Leo Braudy, *The Frenzy of Renown: Fame and Its History* (New York: Vintage, 1997), 556.

46. Braudy, *From Chivalry to Terrorism*, 552.

47. Anthony Swofford, *Jarhead: A Marine's Chronicle of the Gulf War and Other Battles* (New York: Scribner, 2003).

48. “Ninety Percent of U.S. Wounded Survive: In Iraq, Firepower Increases, Deaths Decrease,” *ScienceDaily*, January 28, 2005, 1, https://www.sciencedaily.com/releases/2005/01/050127234012.htm.

49. Lewis Milestone, dir., *All Quiet on the Western Front* (1930; Universal City, Calif.: Universal Pictures, 1999), DVD.

50. Ibid.

51. Modris Eksteins, *Rites of Spring: The Great War and the Birth of the Modern Age* (Boston: Mariner Books, 2000), 254.

52. Braudy, *From Chivalry to Terrorism*, 29.

53. Lesley L. Coffin, *Lew Ayres: Hollywood's Conscientious Objector* (Jackson: Univ. of Mississippi Press, 2012), ix.

54. Ibid., 131.

55. Ibid., 128.

56. Ibid., 133.

57. Jay Winter, *Remembering War: The Great War between Memory and History in the 20th Century* (New Haven, Conn.: Yale Univ. Press, 2006), 19.

58. Ibid., 12.

59. Peter Karsten, *Encyclopedia of War and American Society* (Thousand Oaks, Calif.: Sage, 2005), 412.

60. Congressional Medal of Honor Society, 2017, last modified 2021, https://www.cmohs.org/.

61. Thomas D. Beamish, Harvey Molotch, and Richard Flacks, "Who Supports the Troops? Vietnam, the Gulf War, and the Making of Collective Memory," *Social Problems* 42, no. 3 (1995): 344–360. https://doi.org/10.2307/3096852.

62. *Oxford English Dictionary*, s.v. "hero," accessed 2017, oed.com.

63. "Alvin C. York," Congressional Medal of Honor Society, 2017, https://www.cmohs.org/recipients/alvin-c-york.

64. Howard Hanks, dir., *Sergeant York* (1941; Burbank, Calif.: Warner Brothers, 2006), DVD.

65. David D. Lee, *Sergeant York: An American Hero* (Lexington: Univ. Press of Kentucky, 1985), 1.

66. *Sergeant York*, dir. Howard Hanks.

67. Ibid.

68. Ibid.

69. "Alvin C. York," Congressional Medal of Honor Society.

70. *Sergeant York*, dir. Howard Hanks.

71. Joe Johnson, dir., *Captain America: The First Avenger* (2011; Los Angeles: Paramount Pictures, 2011), DVD.

72. Jake Miller, "Obama Awards Medal of Honor to Marine Kyle Carpenter," CBS News, last modified June 19, 2014, https://www.cbsnews.com/news/obama-awards-medal-of-honor-to-marine-kyle-carpenter/.

73. Paul Szoldra, "Medal of Honor Recipient Kyle Carpenter Is Coming Out with a Book He Says 'Will Truly Help People,'" *Task and Purpose*, last modified May 4, 2019, https://taskandpurpose.com/news/kyle-carpenter-book/.

74. Mark Straw, "Traumatized Masculinity and American National Identity in Hollywood's Gulf War," *Journal of Contemporary Film* 6, no. 2 (2008): 129.

75. *Sergeant York*, dir. Howard Hanks.

76. Straw, "Traumatized," 135.

77. Owen, "Dulce et Decorum Est."

78. "Donald Gilbert Cook," Congressional Medal of Honor Society, 2017, https://www.cmohs.org/recipients/donald-g-cook.

79. Ashley Southall, "Medals of Honor, Denied Because of Prejudice, to Be Belatedly Awarded," *New York Times*, February 21, 2014, https://www.nytimes.com/2014/02/22/us/medals-of-honor-denied-because-of-prejudice-to-be-belatedly-awarded.html.

80. "Dakota Meyer," Congressional Medal of Honor Society, 2017, https://www.cmohs.org/recipients/dakota-l-meyer.

81. Jesse Hibbs, dir., *To Hell and Back* (1955; Universal City, Calif.: Universal International Pictures, 2004), DVD.

82. William A. Wellman, dir., *Heroes for Sale* (1933; Burbank, Calif.: Warner Brothers, 2009), DVD.

83. Ibid.

84. Ibid.

85. Ibid.

86. Mel Gussow, "FILM: Darryl F. Zanuck, Action Hero of the Studio Era," *New York Times*, September 1, 2002, https://www.nytimes.com/2002/09/01/movies/film-darryl-f-zanuck-action-hero-of-the-studio-era.html.

87. James Wingate to Darryl F. Zanuck et al., May 1933, *Studio Letters and Censorship Reports*, the Academy of Motion Picture and Arts Sciences, Margaret Herrick Library, Beverly Hills, California.

88. *Heroes for Sale*, dir. William A. Wellman.

89. Gussow, "FILM."

90. Philip Hanson, *This Side of Despair: How the Movies and American Life Intersected during the Great Depression* (Madison, Wisc.: Associated University Presses, 2008), 40.

91. *Heroes for Sale*, dir. William A. Wellman.

92. W. B. Yeats, ed., *Oxford Book of Modern Verse 1892–1935* (Oxford: Oxford Univ. Press, 1936).

93. Fred Crawford, *British Poets of the Great War* (Selinsgrove, Pa.: Susquehanna Univ. Press, 1988), 24.

94. Caroline Cox, "Invisible Wounds: The American Legion, Shell-Shocked Veterans, and American Society, 1919–1924," *Traumatic Pasts: History, Psychiatry, and Trauma in the Modern Age, 1870–1930*, ed. Mark S. Micale and Paul Frederick Lerner (Cambridge: Cambridge Univ. Press, 2001), n.p.

3. Our Wounded Warriors

1. Chip Reid and Jennifer Janisch, "Wounded Warrior Project Accused of Wasting Donation Money," CBS News, last modified January 26, 2016, 5, https://www.cbsnews.com/news/wounded-warrior-project-accused-of-wasting-donation-money/.

2. "Warriors Speak: Sharing the Impact of a Generation," Wounded Warrior Project, 2017, https://www.woundedwarriorproject.org/mission/warriors-speak.

3. Judith Butler, *The Psychic Life of Power: Theories in Subjection* (Stanford, Calif.: Stanford Univ. Press, 1997), 11.

4. Reid and Janisch, "Wounded Warrior Project," 16.

5. Ibid., 3.

6. Chip Reid, "Reforms at Wounded Warrior Project after CBS News Investigation," CBS News, last modified September 2, 2016, 9, https://www.cbsnews.com/news/reforms-at-wounded-warrior-project-after-cbs-news-investigation/.

7. Ibid., 2.

8. "Wounded Warrior Project," *Charity Navigator*, 2021, https://www.charitynavigator.org/index.cfm?bay=search.summary&orgid=12842.

9. Richard Severo and Lewis Milford, *The Wages of War: When America's Soldiers Came Home—From Valley Forge to Vietnam* (New York: Simon and Schuster, 1989), 16.

10. Vincent Sherry, *The Great War and the Language of Modernism* (New York: Oxford Univ. Press, 2003), 193.

11. Caroline Cox, "Invisible Wounds: The American Legion, Shell-Shocked Veterans, and American Society, 1919–1924," *Traumatic Pasts: History, Psychiatry, and Trauma in the Modern Age, 1870–1930*, ed. Mark S. Micale and Paul Frederick Lerner (Cambridge: Cambridge Univ. Press, 2001), 291.

12. Eric J. Leed, *No Man's Land: Combat and Identity in WWI* (Cambridge: Cambridge Univ. Press, 1979), 196.

13. Ibid., 281.

14. Tom Brokaw, *The Greatest Generation* (New York: Random House, 1997), xxxviii.

15. Cox, "Invisible Wounds," 334.

16. Kendrick Oliver, *The My Lai Massacre in American History and Memory* (Manchester, UK: Manchester Univ. Press, 2006), 9.

17. Ibid., 11.

18. Eva Illouz, *Cold Intimacies: The Making of Emotional Capitalism* (Cambridge, UK: Polity, 2007).

19. Ibid., 8, 10.

20. Ibid., 25.

21. Ibid., 15–16.

22. Ibid., 17.

23. Ibid., 23.

24. Eric Solomon, "A Definition of the War Novel," in *The Red Badge of Courage*, ed. Donald Pizer and Eric Carl Link (New York: Norton, 2008), 181.

25. George Wyndham, "A Remarkable Book," in *The Red Badge of Courage*, ed. Donald Pizer and Eric Carl Link (New York: Norton, 2008), 241.

26. James Jones, *The Thin Red Line: A Novel* (1962; reprint, New York: Delta Books, 1998), 23.

27. Stephen Crane, *The Red Badge of Courage*, ed. Donald Pizer and Eric Carl Link (New York: Norton, 2008), 22.

28. Charlie Savage, "Bowe Bergdahl, Facing Desertion Trial, Asks Obama for Pardon," *New York Times*, December 2, 2016, 4, https://www.nytimes.com/2016/12/02/us/politics/bowe-bergdahl-asks-obama-for-pardon.html.

29. Nancy Montgomery, "Command Sergeant Major: No Troops Died Searching for Bergdahl," *Stars and Stripes*, March 31, 2016, https://www.stripes.com/news/command-sergeant-major-no-troops-died-searching-for-bergdahl-1.402016.

30. Stephen Crane, "The Veteran," in *The Red Badge of Courage*, ed. Donald Pizer and Eric Carl Link (New York: Norton, 2008), 230.

31. Ibid.

32. Crane, *The Red Badge of Courage*, 33.

33. Ibid.

34. Anthony Rotundo, *American Manhood: Transformations in Masculinity from the Revolution to the Modern Era* (New York: Basic, 1993), 21.

35. Braudy, *From Chivalry to Terrorism*, xviii.

36. Ibid.

37. Ibid., 27.

38. Ibid., 26.

39. Donald Pizer, "Henry Behind the Lines and the Concept of Manhood in *The Red Badge of Courage*," *Stephen Crane Studies* 10, no. 1 (2001): 2–7.

40. Joel Meyerson, ed., *Transcendentalism: A Reader* (Oxford: Oxford Univ. Press, 2000).

41. Crane, *The Red Badge of Courage*, 35.

42. Ibid., 43.

43. Ibid., 60.

44. Rotundo, *American Manhood*, 20–22.

45. Pizer, "Henry," 2.

46. Owen, "Dulce et Decorum Est," 1974, lines 25–28.

47. Glenn Altschuler and Stuart Blumin, *The GI Bill: The New Deal for Veterans* (Oxford: Oxford Univ. Press, 2009), 24.

48. Modris Eksteins, *Rites of Spring: The Great War and the Birth of the Modern Age* (Boston: Mariner Books, 2000), 254.

49. Leslie Midkiff DeBauche, *Reel Patriotism: The Movies and World War* (Madison: Univ. of Wisconsin Press, 1997), 165.

50. Severo and Milford, *The Wages of War*, 288.

51. Ibid., 291.

52. J. E. Smyth, *Reconstructing American Historical Cinema: From* Cimarron *to* Citizen Kane (Lexington: Univ. Press of Kentucky, 2006), 236.

53. Kaja Silverman, *Male Subjectivity at the Margins* (New York: Routledge, 1992), 53.

54. Ibid., 106.

55. Ibid., 121.

56. Tim Aubry and Trysh Travis, "What Is 'Therapeutic Culture,' and Why Do We Need to 'Rethink' It?" in *Rethinking Therapeutic Culture*, ed. Tim Aubry and Trysh Travis (Chicago: Univ. of Chicago Press, 2015), 1.

57. Ibid., 2–3.

58. Ibid., 4.

59. Payton J. Jones, Benjamin W. Bellet, and Richard J. McNally, "Helping or Harming? The Effect of Trigger Warnings on Individuals with Trauma Histories," *Clinical Psychological Science* 8, no. 5 (September 2020): 905–17. https://doi.org/10.1177/2167702620921341.

60. Aubry and Travis, "What Is 'Therapeutic Culture,'" 7.

61. Stevan Weine, "What Happens—and Who Benefits—When Trauma Victims Are Encouraged to Tell Their Stories?" in *Rethinking Therapeutic Culture*, ed. Tim Aubry and Trysh Travis (Chicago: Univ. of Chicago Press, 2015), 143.

62. Paul John Eakin, *How Our Lives Become Stories: Making Selves* (Ithaca, N.Y.: Cornell Univ. Press, 1999).

63. Stevan Weine, "What Happens," 147.

64. Sebastian Junger, *Tribe: On Homecoming and Belonging* (New York: Twelve, 2016), 88.

65. Ibid.

66. Sebastian Junger, "Our Lonely Society Makes It Hard to Come Home from War," YouTube video, June 10, 2016, https://www.youtube.com/watch?v=o9DNWK6WfQw.

67. Ibid.

68. Junger, *Tribe*, 90.

69. Ibid.

70. Clint Eastwood, dir., *Gran Torino* (2008; Burbank, Calif.: Warner Brothers, 2009), DVD.

71. Benjamin Percy, "On the Ground," review of *The Yellow Birds*, by Kevin Powers, *New York Times*, October 4, 2012, https://www.nytimes.com/2012/10/07/books/review/the-yellow-birds-by-kevin-powers.html.

72. Illouz, *Cold Intimacies*, 1.

73. Ibid., 5.

74. Kevin Powers, *The Yellow Birds* (New York: Back Bay Books, 2012), 33.

75. Percy, "On the Ground," 4.

76. Powers, *Yellow Birds*, 19.

77. Ibid., 48.

78. Ibid., 53–54.

79. Travis L. Martin, "Phantom Weapon Syndrome," *American Imago* 72, no. 1 (2015): 63–88.

80. Ibid., 54.

81. Powers, *Yellow Birds*, 66.

82. Illouz, *Cold Intimacies*, 53.

83. Ibid., 67.

4. The Veteran Storytellers

1. "Román Baca: Artistic Director," Exit 12 Dance Company, accessed May 21, 2021, https://exit12danceco.org/bios.

2. "Exit 12: Moved by War," Vimeo, January 22, 2019, https://vimeo.com/312834658.

3. Suzanne S. Rancourt, "The Bear That Stands," *Journal of Military Experience* 3 (2013): 29.

4. Ibid., 30.

5. Ibid., 47.

6. Ibid., 31.

7. Ibid., 33.

8. Ibid.

9. Ibid., 34–35.

10. Ibid., 35.

11. Ibid., 40.

12. Ibid., 47.

13. Ibid., 48.

14. Ibid., 31.
15. Ibid., 46.
16. Ibid., 48.
17. Bradley Johnson, "My Life as a Soldier in the 'War on Terror,'" *Journal of Military Experience* 1, no. 1 (2012): 50–55, https://encompass.eku.edu/jme/vol1/iss1/10/.
18. Ibid., 51.
19. Travis L. Martin, "Combat in the Classroom: A Writing and Healing Approach to Teaching Student Veterans," *Writing on the Edge* 22 (2012): 27–35.
20. Birgitte Refslund Sørensen, "Veterans' Homecomings: Secrecy and Post-deployment Social Becoming, *Cultural Anthropology* 56, no. 12 (2015): 231–40.
21. Jonathan Shay, *Odysseus in America: Combat Trauma and the Trials of Homecoming* (New York: Scribner, 2002), 33.
22. Deborah Dysart-Gale, "Lost in Translation: Bibliotherapy and Evidence-Based Medicine," *Journal of Medical Humanities* 29, no. 1 (2008): 33–43.
23. Alexis Hart and Roger Thompson, "War, Trauma, and the Writing Classroom: A Response to Travis Martin's 'Combat in the Classroom,'" *Writing on the Edge* 23 (2013): 37–47.
24. "Combat Paper," 2021, https://www.combatpaper.org/.
25. Hart and Thompson, "War, Trauma, and the Writing Classroom," 39.
26. Ibid., 40.
27. Ibid., 41.
28. Ron Capps, *Writing War: A Guide to Telling Your Own Story* (The Veterans Writing Project, 2011), 68.
29. Ibid., 116.
30. Ibid., 46.
31. Johnson, "My Life as a Soldier in the 'War on Terror,'" 53.
32. Ibid.
33. Richard Severo and Lewis Milford, *The Wages of War: When America's Soldiers Came Home—From Valley Forge to Vietnam* (New York: Simon and Schuster, 1989), 16.
34. Johnson, "My Life as a Soldier in the 'War on Terror,'" 53.
35. Taylor Elizabeth Rugg, "Identity Negotiation in Military Service Members," *Young Scholars in Writing* 15 (July 2019): 20–30, https://youngscholarsinwriting.org/index.php/ysiw/article/view/260.
36. Judith Butler, *The Psychic Life of Power: Theories in Subjection* (Stanford, Calif.: Stanford Univ. Press, 1997), 11.
37. Derald Wing Sue, *Microaggressions in Everyday Life: Race, Gender, and Sexual Orientation* (Hoboken, N.J.: Wiley, 2010), 5.

38. Ibid., xv.

39. Guy Standing, *The Precariat: The New Dangerous Class* (London: Bloomsbury, 2014), 174.

40. Ibid.

41. Scott Parrott et al., "Mental Representations of Military Veterans: Pictures (and Words) in Our Heads," *Journal of Veteran Studies* 6, no. 3 (December 2020): 68, http://doi.org/10.21061/jvs.v6i3.207.

42. Ibid.

43. Johnson, "My Life as a Soldier in the 'War on Terror,'" 52–53.

44. Rugg, "Identity Negotiation in Military Service Members," 28.

45. Daniel Buckman, "From the Managing Editor," *The Blue Falcon Review: A Journal of Military Fiction* 1 (2013): 5, https://militaryexperience.org/the-blue-falcon-review-vol-1/.

46. Jerad W. Alexander, "Cold Day in Bridgewater," *The Blue Falcon Review: A Journal of Military Fiction* 1 (2013): 62–63.

47. Ibid., 64.

48. Ibid., 65.

49. Ibid., 67.

50. Ibid.

51. Ibid., 67–68.

52. Ibid., 68.

53. Ibid.

54. Ibid.

55. Tif Holmes, *Prisoner of War*, in *Journal of Military Experience* 3 (2013): 295.

56. Carl Andrew Castro et al., "Sexual Assault in the Military," *Current Psychiatry Reports* 17, no. 7 (2015): 54.

57. Giuseppe Pellicano, *Tea Time*, in *Journal of Military Experience* 3 (2013): 343.

58. Giuseppe Pellicano, *Oh Happy Day*, in *Journal of Military Experience* 3 (2013): 344.

59. David Ervin, guest speaker, online, Eastern Kentucky University, Richmond, Kentucky, March 26, 2021.

60. Deborah Adele, *The Yamas and Niyamas: Exploring Yoga's Ethical Practice* (Duluth, Minn.: On-Word Bound Books, 2009), 48.

Epilogue

1. Jerad W. Alexander, *Volunteers: Growing Up in the Forever War* (Chapel Hill, N.C.: Algonquin, 2021).

2. Ibid., 291.

3. "History," Kentucky Center for Veterans Studies, 2021, https://www.eku.edu/kcvs/history.html.

4. Jim Craig, "Bounding Veterans Studies: A Review of the Field," paper presented at the Veterans in Society Conference, Virginia Tech, Roanoke, Virginia, November 12, 2015, https://vtechworks.lib.vt.edu/bitstream/handle/10919/72924/Craig_Bounding_Veterans_Studies.pdf?sequence=1.

5. Selene San Felice, "Tampa-area university to offer the country's first 4-year veterans' studies degree," *Axios*, May 28, 2021, https://www.axios.com/st-leo-university-veterans-studies-program-5ced69d7-db2e-4ebc-8412-596ccae1cd2d.html.

6. "Veterans & Media Lab," University of Alabama, accessed May 2021, https://cis.ua.edu/research/veterans-and-media-lab/.

7. "Institute for Veterans & Military Families," Syracuse University, accessed May 2021, https://ivmf.syracuse.edu/.

8. "STRIVE," Ohio State University, accessed May 2021, https://medicine.osu.edu/departments/psychiatry-and-behavioral-health/strive.

9. "War, Literature & the Arts," accessed May 2021, https://www.wlajournal.com/.

10. "Veterans in Society," Virginia Tech, accessed May 2021, https://vtechworks.lib.vt.edu/handle/10919/56348.

11. *Journal of Veterans Studies*, accessed May 2021, https://journal-veterans-studies.org/.

12. Travis L. Martin, "Finding Common Ground," *Veterans of Foreign Wars Magazine*, September 2013, http://digitaledition.qwinc.com/article/Finding+Common+Ground%3A+Vets+And+Non-Vets+Collaborate+On+Campus++/1482342/171767/article.html.

13. "Sculpture Added to Veterans Memorial," Eastern Kentucky University, Richmond, Kentucky, November 13, 2017, https://stories.eku.edu/events/sculpture-added-veterans-memorial.

Bibliography

"38 CFR Book C, Schedule for Rating Disabilities: Mental Disorders." US Department of Veteran Affairs, 2015. https://www.benefits.va.gov/WARMS/bookc.asp.

2019 National Veteran Suicide Prevention Annual Report. PDF file. 2019. US Department of Veterans Affairs. https://www.mentalhealth.va.gov/docs/data-sheets/2019/2019_National_Veteran_Suicide_Prevention_Annual_Report_508.pdf.

"About SVA." Student Veterans of America. Accessed May 2021. https://studentveterans.org/about/.

Adele, Deborah. *The Yamas and Niyamas: Exploring Yoga's Ethical Practice.* Duluth, Minn.: On-Word Bound Books, 2009.

Agamben, Giorgio. *The Coming Community.* Minneapolis: Univ. of Minnesota Press, 1993.

Alexander, Jerad W. "Cold Day in Bridgewater." *The Blue Falcon Review: A Journal of Military Fiction* 1 (2013): 61–69.

———. *Volunteers: Growing Up in the Forever War.* Chapel Hill, N.C.: Algonquin, 2021.

Altschuler, Glenn, and Stuart Blumin. *The GI Bill: The New Deal for Veterans.* Oxford: Oxford Univ. Press, 2009.

"Alvin C. York." Congressional Medal of Honor Society. 2017. https://www.cmohs.org/recipients/alvin-c-york.

Anderson, D. Mark, and Daniel I. Rees. "Deployments, Combat Exposure, and Crime." *IZA Discussion Papers* 7761 (2013).

Aponte, Maribel, Tom Garin, Dorothy Glasgow, Tamara Lee, Earl Newsome III, Eddie Thomas, and Barbara Ward. *Minority Veterans Report: Military Service History and VA Benefit Utilization Statistics.* PDF file. March 2017. Department of Veterans Affairs and National Center for Veterans Analysis and Statistics. https://www.va.gov/vetdata/docs/SpecialReports/Minority_Veterans_Report.pdf.

"Army Approves Purple Hearts for Fort Hood Shooting." US Department of Defense, February 6, 2015. https://www.defense.gov/News/News-Stories/Article/Article/604063/.

"The Army Values." US Army. Accessed 2016. https://www.army.mil/values/.

Atkin, Albert. "Peirce's Theory of Signs." In *Stanford Encyclopedia of Philosophy*, edited by Edward N. Zalta. Palo Alto, Calif.: Stanford University, 2013.

Aubry, Tim, and Trysh Travis. "What Is 'Therapeutic Culture,' and Why Do We Need to 'Rethink' It?" In *Rethinking Therapeutic Culture*, edited by Tim Aubry and Trysh Travis, 1–23. Chicago: Univ. of Chicago Press, 2015.

Beamish, Thomas D., Harvey Molotch, and Richard Flacks. "Who Supports the Troops? Vietnam, the Gulf War, and the Making of Collective Memory." *Social Problems* 42, no. 3 (1995): 344–60. https://doi.org/10.2307/3096852.

Belau, Linda, and Petar Ramadanovic, eds. *Topologies of Trauma: Essays on the Limit of Knowledge and Memory*. New York: Other Press, 2002.

Bell, J. L. "George Washington on 'Veterans of Earlier Wars'?" *Boston 1775*. Last modified August 16, 2012. http://boston1775.blogspot.com/2012/08/george-washington-on-veterans-of.html.

Berger, Arthur Asa. *Cultural Criticism: A Primer of Key Concepts*. Thousand Oaks, Calif.: Sage, 1995.

Bigelow, Kathryn. *The Hurt Locker*. 2008. Los Angeles: Voltage Pictures, 2010. DVD.

Boyle, Brenda. "Rescuing Masculinity: Captivity, Rescue and Gender in American War Narratives." *Journal of American Culture* 34, no. 2 (2011): 149–60. EBSCO.

Braudy, Leo. *The Frenzy of Renown: Fame and Its History*. New York: Vintage, 1997.

———. *From Chivalry to Terrorism: War and the Changing Nature of Masculinity*. New York: Vintage, 2005.

Brokaw, Tom. *The Greatest Generation*. New York: Random House, 1997.

Bromley, Victoria L. *Feminisms Matter: Debates, Theories, Activism*. Toronto: Univ. of Toronto Press, 2012.

Bronson, Jennifer, E. Ann Carson, Margaret Noonan, and Marcus Berzofsky. *Veterans in Prison and Jail, 2011–12*. PDF file. December 2015. US Department of Justice. https://justiceforvets.org/wp-content/uploads/2017/03/BJS-Report.pdf.

Brown, Randy. "We Are the Stories." In *Welcome to FOB Haiku: War Poems from Inside the Wire*, edited by Randy Brown, 52. Johnston, Iowa: Middle West Press, 2015.

Buckman, Daniel. "From the Managing Editor." *The Blue Falcon Review: A Journal of Military Fiction* 1 (2013): 5. https://militaryexperience.org/the-blue-falcon-review-vol-1/.

Butler, Judith. *The Psychic Life of Power: Theories in Subjection.* Stanford, Calif.: Stanford Univ. Press, 1997.

Butler, Smedley D. *War Is a Racket: The Antiwar Classic by America's Most Decorated Soldier.* 1935. Reprint, Scotts Valley, Calif.: CreateSpace Independent Publishing, 2014.

Campbell, Andy. "Medal of Honor Recipient Arrested on Hit-and-Run Charge." *Huffington Post.* Last modified January 10 2017. https://www.huffpost.com/entry/kyle-carpenter-arrest-medal-of-honor_n_5685607ce4b014efe0da61e4.

Capra, Frank, dir. *It's a Wonderful Life.* 1946; Burbank, Calif.: Liberty Films, 2001. DVD.

Capps, Ron. *Writing War: A Guide to Telling Your Own Story.* The Veterans Writing Project, 2011.

Caruth, Cathy. *Unclaimed Experience: Trauma, Narrative, and History.* Baltimore: Johns Hopkins Univ. Press, 1996.

Castro, Carl Andrew, et al. "Sexual Assault in the Military." *Current Psychiatry Reports* 17, no. 7 (2015): 54.

"Cessation of Military Recruiting in Public Elementary and Secondary Schools." *American Public Health Association Policy Statement Database*, American Public Health Association, October 30, 2012. https://www.apha.org/policies-and-advocacy/public-health-policy-statements/policy-database/2014/07/23/11/19/cessation-of-military-recruiting-in-public-elementary-and-secondary-schools.

Chomsky, Marvin J. *Tank.* 1984. Culver City, Calif.: Lorimar Film Entertainment, 2004. DVD.

Coffin, Lesley L. *Lew Ayres: Hollywood's Conscientious Objector.* Jackson: Univ. of Mississippi Press, 2012.

Cohen, Leah Hager. "Point of Return." Review of *Home* by Toni Morrison. *The New York Times*, May 17, 2012. https://www.nytimes.com/2012/05/20/books/review/home-a-novel-by-toni-morrison.html.

Collins, Patricia Hill, and Sirma Bilge. *Intersectionality.* Cambridge, UK: Polity, 2016.

"Combat Paper." 2021. https://www.combatpaper.org/.

Congressional Medal of Honor Society. 2017. Last modified 2021. https://www.cmohs.org/.

Copeland, John W., and David W. Sutherland. "Sea of Goodwill: Matching the Donor to the Need." Office of the Chairman of the Joint Chiefs of Staff Warrior and Family Support, Council on Foundations, May 17, 2010.

Cornum, Rhonda. *She Went to War: The Rhonda Cornum Story.* New York: Ballantine, 2003.

Couser, G. Thomas. *Altered Egos: Authority in American Autobiography*. New York: Oxford, 1989.

Cox, Caroline. "Invisible Wounds: The American Legion, Shell-Shocked Veterans, and American Society, 1919–1924." *Traumatic Pasts: History, Psychiatry, and Trauma in the Modern Age, 1870–1930*, edited by Mark S. Micale and Paul Frederick Lerner, n.p. Cambridge: Cambridge Univ. Press, 2001.

Crane, Stephen. *Maggie: A Girl of the Streets*. 1893. Reprint, Scotts Valley, Calif.: CreateSpace Independent Publishing, 2017.

———. *The Red Badge of Courage*, edited by Donald Pizer and Eric Carl Link. New York: Norton, 2008.

———. "The Veteran." In *The Red Badge of Courage*, edited by Donald Pizer and Eric Carl Link, 229–33. New York: Norton, 2008.

Craig, Jim. "Bounding Veterans Studies: A Review of the Field." Paper presented at the Veterans in Society Conference, Virginia Tech, Roanoke, Virginia, November 12, 2015. https://vtechworks.lib.vt.edu/bitstream/handle/10919/72924/Craig_Bounding_Veterans_Studies.pdf?sequence=1.

Crawford, Fred. *British Poets of the Great War*. Selinsgrove, Pa.: Susquehanna Univ. Press, 1988.

"Dakota Meyer." Congressional Medal of Honor Society. 2017. https://www.cmohs.org/recipients/dakota-l-meyer.

Dao, James. "A Million Strong: Helping Them Through." *New York Times*, February 3, 2013. https://www.nytimes.com/2013/02/03/education/edlife/the-complicated-world-of-higher-education-for-troops-and-veterans.html.

Davis, Charles. "The US Military Is Collecting Data on Millions of High School Students." *Vice*, April 24, 2014. https://www.vice.com/en/article/gq85mm/how-the-military-collects-data-on-millions-of-high-school-students.

DeBauche, Leslie Midkiff. *Reel Patriotism: The Movies and World War*. Madison: Univ. of Wisconsin Press, 1997.

Doherty, Thomas. *Pre-Code Hollywood: Sex, Immorality, and Insurrection in American Cinema, 1930–1934*. New York: Columbia Univ. Press, 1999.

"Donald Gilbert Cook." Congressional Medal of Honor Society. 2017. https://www.cmohs.org/recipients/donald-g-cook.

DuBois, W. E. B. *The Souls of Black Folk*. 1903. Reprint, Mineola, N.Y.: Dover, 1994.

Dysart-Gale, Deborah. "Lost in Translation: Bibliotherapy and Evidence-Based Medicine." *Journal of Medical Humanities* 29, no. 1 (2008): 33–43.

Eagleton, Terry. *Literary Theory: An Introduction*. Minneapolis: Univ. of Minnesota Press, 2008.

Eakin, Paul John. *How Our Lives Become Stories: Making Selves*. Ithaca, N.Y.: Cornell Univ. Press, 1999.

———. *Living Autobiographically: How We Create Identity in Narrative.* Ithaca, N.Y.: Cornell Univ. Press, 2008.

Eastwood, Clint, dir. *Gran Torino.* 2008. Burbank, Calif.: Warner Brothers, 2009. DVD.

"Education and Training: History and Timeline." US Department of Veteran Affairs, March 18, 2013. https://www.benefits.va.gov/gibill/history.asp.

Eksteins, Modris. *Rites of Spring: The Great War and the Birth of the Modern Age.* Boston: Mariner Books, 2000.

Eliot, T.S. "The Hollow Men." *T. S. Eliot: Collected Poems, 1909–1962*, 77–82. New York: Harcourt, 1991.

Elsaesser, Thomas. "One Train May Be Hiding Another: History, Memory, Identity, and the Visual Image." In *Topologies of Trauma: Essays on the Limit of Knowledge and Memory*, edited by Linda Belau and Petar Ramadanovic, 61–72. New York: Other Press, 2002.

"Enriching the Lives of America's Veterans." PDF file. September 8, 2014. Team RWB. https://teamrwb.org/wp-content/uploads/2017/11/TRWB-Study_ImpactMetricsForWebsite.pdf?_ga=2.70276880.1071987360.1622070155-111700387.1622070155.

Ervin, David. Guest speaker, online. Eastern Kentucky University, Richmond, Kentucky. March 26, 2021.

"Exit 12: Moved by War." Vimeo. January 22, 2019. https://vimeo.com/312834658.

"Facts and Statistics About Women Veterans." Women Veterans Healthcare. US Department of Veterans Affairs, December 17, 2013. https://www.womenshealth.va.gov/womenshealth/latestinformation/facts.asp.

Faust, Gilpin Drew. *This Republic of Suffering: Death and the American Civil War.* New York: Knopf, 2008.

Felice, Selene San. "Tampa-area university to offer the country's first 4-year veterans' studies degree." *Axios*, May 28, 2021. https://www.axios.com/st-leo-university-veterans-studies-program-5ced69d7-db2e-4ebc-8412-596ccae1cd2d.html.

Felman, Shoshana, and Dori Laub, eds. *Testimony: Crises of Witnessing in Literature, Psychoanalysis and History.* New York: Routledge, 1992.

Ferguson, Kevin L. "Aviation Cinema." *Criticism* 57, no. 2 (2015): 309–31.

Frankenheimer, John. *The Manchurian Candidate.* 1962. Beverly Hills, Calif.: MGM, 2004. DVD.

Fuller, Robert C. *Americans and the Unconscious.* Oxford: Oxford Univ. Press, 1986.

Fussell, Paul. *The Great War and Modern Memory.* New York: Sterling, 1975.

Gates, Henry Louis, Jr. *The Signifying Monkey: A Theory of African American Literary Criticism.* 1979. Reprint, Oxford: Oxford Univ. Press, 2014.

Gibson, Mel, dir. *Braveheart.* 1995. Nashville: Icon Entertainment, 1995. DVD.

Goffman, Erving. *The Presentation of Self in Everyday Life.* New York: Anchor, 1959.

Grossman, Dave. *On Killing: The Psychological Cost of Learning to Kill in War and Society.* New York: Back Bay Books, 2009.

Gussow, Mel. "FILM: Darryl F. Zanuck, Action Hero of the Studio Era." *New York Times*, September, 1 2002. https://www.nytimes.com/2002/09/01/movies/film-darryl-f-zanuck-action-hero-of-the-studio-era.html.

Hagopian, Amy, and Kathy Barker. "Should We End Military Recruiting in High Schools as a Matter of Child Protection and Public Health?" *American Journal of Public Health* 101, no. 1 (2011): 19–23.

Halberstam, David. *The Coldest Winter: America and the Korean War.* New York: Hachette, 2008.

Halberstam, Jack Judith. *Female Masculinity.* Durham: Duke Univ. Press, 1998.

Hanks, Howard, dir. *Sergeant York.* 1941. Burbank, Calif.: Warner Brothers, 2006. DVD.

Hanson, Philip. *This Side of Despair: How the Movies and American Life Intersected during the Great Depression.* Madison, Wisc.: Associated University Presses, 2008.

Harkins, Gina. "The Marines Will Remove the Word 'Man' from These 19 Job Titles." *Marine Corps Times*, June 27 2016. https://www.marinecorpstimes.com/news/your-marine-corps/2016/06/27/the-marines-will-remove-the-word-man-from-these-19-job-titles/.

Hart, Alexis, and Roger Thompson. "War, Trauma, and the Writing Classroom: A Response to Travis Martin's 'Combat in the Classroom.'" *Writing on the Edge* 23 (2013): 37–47.

Herzog, Werner, dir. *Rescue Dawn.* 2007. Beverly Hills, Calif.: MGM, 2007. DVD.

Hetherington, Tim, and Sebastian Junger, dirs. *Restrepo.* 2010. San Francisco: Outpost Films, 2010. DVD.

Hibbs, Jesse, dir. *To Hell and Back.* 1955. Universal City, Calif.: Universal International Pictures, 2004. DVD.

Hill, Reuben L. "Works by Waller." *International Encyclopedia of the Social Sciences.* August 8, 2016. https://www.encyclopedia.com/people/social-sciences-and-law/sociology-biographies/willard-w-waller.

"History." Kentucky Center for Veterans Studies, 2021. https://www.eku.edu/kcvs/history.html.

Hodges, Eric, Nancy Dallett, Jim Dubinsky, Jim Craig, and Bruce Pencek. "Waller's The Veteran Comes Back at 77." Online panel presentation, "Conversations in Veteran Studies," Veterans Studies Association. May 18, 2021.

Hollinghurst, Alan. "The Fallen." Review of *Some Desperate Glory: The First World War the Poets Knew* by Max Egremont. *Harpers Magazine*, September 1, 2014, 82. https://harpers.org/archive/2014/09/the-fallen-2/2/.

Holmes, Tif. *Prisoner of War.* In *Journal of Military Experience* 3 (2013): 294–96.

Howell, Kellan. "Kyle Carpenter, Medal of Honor Recipient, Arrested for Hit and Run." *Washington Times*, December 31, 2015. https://www.washingtontimes.com/news/2015/dec/31/kyle-carpenter-medal-honor-recipient-arrested-hit-/.

"I Am Living Proof." *After Action Report: The Wounded Warrior Project*, 2017, 5. https://www.woundedwarriorproject.org/i-am-living-proof.

Illing, Sean. "Is Civilization Good for Us? Sebastian Junger on the Dangers of Social Fragmentation." *Vox*, October 27, 2016. https://www.vox.com/2016/9/13/12842400/sebastian-junger-tribe-interview.

Illouz, Eva. *Cold Intimacies: The Making of Emotional Capitalism.* Cambridge, UK: Polity, 2007.

"Institute for Veterans and Military Families." Syracuse University. Accessed May 2021. https://ivmf.syracuse.edu/.

Johnson, Bradley. "My Life as a Soldier in the 'War on Terror.'" *Journal of Military Experience* 1, no. 1 (2012): 50–55. https://encompass.eku.edu/jme/vol1/iss1/10/.

Johnson, Joe, dir. *Captain America: The First Avenger.* 2011. Los Angeles: Paramount Pictures, 2011. DVD.

Jones, David. *In Parenthesis.* 1937. Reprint, New York: New York Review Books, 2003.

Jones, James. *The Thin Red Line: A Novel.* 1962. New York: Delta Books, 1998.

Jones, Payton J., Benjamin W. Bellet, and Richard J. McNally. "Helping or Harming? The Effect of Trigger Warnings on Individuals with Trauma Histories." *Clinical Psychological Science* 8, no. 5 (September 2020): 905–17. https://doi.org/10.1177/2167702620921341.

Joseph, Stephen. *What Doesn't Kill Us: The New Psychology of Posttraumatic Growth.* New York: Basic Books, 2011.

Journal of Veterans Studies. Accessed May 2021. https://journal-veterans-studies.org/.

Junger, Sebastian. "Our Lonely Society Makes It Hard to Come Home from War." YouTube video, June 10, 2016. https://www.youtube.com/watch?v=o9DNWK6WfQw.

———. *Tribe: On Homecoming and Belonging.* New York: Twelve, 2016.

———. *War.* New York: Hachette, 2010.

Kane, Tim. "Who Bears the Burden? Demographic Characteristics of U.S. Military Recruits Before and After 9/11." The Heritage Foundation. November 7, 2005. https://www.heritage.org/defense/report/who-bears-the-burden-demographic-characteristics-us-military-recruits-and-after-911.

Karsten, Peter. *Encyclopedia of War and American Society.* Thousand Oaks, Calif.: Sage, 2005.

Kaufman, Philip, dir. *The Right Stuff.* 1983. Hollywood, Calif.: Ladd Company, 1997. DVD.

Keene, Jennifer D. *Doughboys, the Great War, and the Rethinking of America.* Baltimore: Johns Hopkins Univ. Press, 2003.

Kimmel, Michael. *The History of Men: Essays on the History of American and British Masculinities.* Albany, N.Y.: State Univ. of New York Press, 2005.

Kotcheff, Ted, dir. *First Blood.* 1982. Los Angeles: Orion Pictures, 2007. DVD.

Krammer, Arnold. *Prisoners of War: A Reference Handbook.* Westport, Conn.: Praeger, 2007.

Kubrick, Stanley, dir. *Full Metal Jacket.* 1987. Burbank, Calif.: Warner Brothers, 2007. Blu-ray.

Laub, Dori. "Bearing Witness, or the Vicissitudes of Listening." In *Testimony: Crises of Witnessing in Literature, Psychoanalysis and History,* edited by Shoshana Felman and Dori Laub, 57–74. New York: Routledge, 1992.

Lee, David D. *Sergeant York: An American Hero.* Lexington: Univ. Press of Kentucky, 1985.

Leed, Eric J. "Fateful Memories: Industrialized War and Traumatic Neuroses." *Journal of Contemporary History* 35, no. 1 (2000): 85–100.

———.. *No Man's Land: Combat and Identity in WWI.* Cambridge: Cambridge Univ. Press, 1979.

Levin, Sam. "Army Veterans Return to Standing Rock to Form a Human Shield against Police." *The Guardian,* February 11, 2017. https://www.theguardian.com/us-news/2017/feb/11/standing-rock-army-veterans-camp.

Lincoln, Abraham. Abraham Lincoln papers: Series 3. General Correspondence. 1837 to 1897: Abraham Lincoln, March 4, 1865 Second Inaugural Address; endorsed by Lincoln. March 4, 1865. Manuscript/Mixed Material. http://hdl.loc.gov/loc.mss/ms000001.mss30189a.4361300.

Lipset, Seymour Martin. *American Exceptionalism: A Double-Edged Sword.* New York: Norton, 1996.

Loggins, Kenny. "Danger Zone." Recorded 1986. *Top Gun* (soundtrack). Columbia.

Marlantes, Karl. *What It Is Like to Go to War.* New York: Atlantic Monthly Press, 2011.

Martin, Jacquelyn. *Obama Medal of Honor.* June 19, 2014. Associated Press. http://www.apimages.com/metadata/Index/Obama-Medal-of-Honor/599b7fcd7d7b4c9eb7cc7455506b13c5.

Martin, Travis L. "Combat in the Classroom: A Writing and Healing Approach to Teaching Student Veterans." *Writing on the Edge* 22 (2012): 27–35.

———. "Finding Common Ground." *Veterans of Foreign Wars Magazine.* September 2013. http://digitaledition.qwinc.com/article/Finding+Common+Ground%3A+Vets+And+Non-Vets+Collaborate+On+Campus++/1482342/171767/article.html.

———. "Introduction." *Journal of Military Experience* 1 (2011): i–iii.

———. "Phantom Weapon Syndrome." *American Imago* 72, no. 1 (2015): 63–88.

———. "Reality and Anti-Reality in WWI and WWII Memoirs." *War, Literature and the Arts* 24 (2012): 1–13.

McNeely, Judith. "'The War Was Easy . . . It Was the War of Words . . . That Was Tough': Countering Combat Trauma and Restoring Individual Identity through Twentieth- and Twenty-First Century Fiction." Ph.D. diss., Indiana University of Pennsylvania, 2013.

McTiernan, John, dir. *Predator.* 1987. Los Angeles: Amercent Films, 2000. DVD.

Mendes, Sam, dir. *Jarhead.* 2005. Universal City, Calif.: Universal Pictures, 2005. DVD.

Meyerson, Joel, ed. *Transcendentalism: A Reader.* Oxford: Oxford Univ. Press, 2000.

Milestone, Lewis, dir. *All Quiet on the Western Front.* 1930. Universal City, Calif.: Universal Pictures, 1999. DVD.

Miller, Jake. "Obama Awards Medal of Honor to Marine Kyle Carpenter." CBS News. Last modified June 19, 2014. https://www.cbsnews.com/news/obama-awards-medal-of-honor-to-marine-kyle-carpenter/.

Miller, Joseph R., ed. *Blue Nostalgia: A Journal of Post-Traumatic Growth* (2013). https://militaryexperience.org/blue-nostalgia-a-journal-of-post-traumatic-growth-vol-1/.

Milton, Daniel, and Andrew Mines. "'This Is War'": Examining Military Experience Among the Capitol Hill Siege Participants." PDF file. April 12, 2021. Program on Extremism. https://ctc.usma.edu/wp-content/uploads/2021/04/This-is-War_Final.pdf.

"Mission." Team RWB. Accessed April 2021. https://www.teamrwb.org/about-us/mission/.

Mockenhaupt, Brian. "I Miss Iraq. I Miss My Gun. I Miss My War." *Esquire,* June 26, 2007. https://www.esquire.com/news-politics/a26372/esq0307essay/.

Monsivais, Pablo Martinez. *President Barack Obama Awards the Medal of Honor to Former Marine Corps Cpl. Dakota Meyer.* Associated Press, September 15, 2011.

Montgomery, Nancy. "Command Sergeant Major: No Troops Died Searching for Bergdahl." Military.com, March 31, 2016. https://www.military.com/daily-news/2016/03/31/command-sergeant-major-no-troops-died-searching-for-bergdahl.html.

Morris, Brett. "A Bridge Program's Effect on Non-College Ready Student Veterans." Ed.D. diss., Eastern Kentucky University, 2013.

Morrison, Toni. *Beloved.* 1987. Reprint, New York: Vintage, 2004.

———. *The Bluest Eye.* 1970. Reprint, New York: Vintage, 2007.

———. *Home.* 2012. Reprint, New York: Vintage, 2003.

———. *Playing in the Dark: Whiteness and the Literary Imagination.* 1992. Reprint, New York: Vintage, 1993.

Nicholson, Amy. "Tom Cruise Was Brilliant in *Top Gun*, You Just Might Not Remember." *LA Weekly* (Los Angeles, Calif.), December 16, 2014.

"Ninety Percent of U.S. Wounded Survive: In Iraq, Firepower Increases, Deaths Decrease." *ScienceDaily*, January 28, 2005. https://www.sciencedaily.com/releases/2005/01/050127234012.htm.

Norman, Sonya, Eric B. Elbogen, and Paula P. Schnurr. "Research Findings on PTSD and Violence." US Department of Veterans Affairs. https://www.ptsd.va.gov/professional/treat/cooccurring/research_violence.asp#three.

O'Brien, Tim. *The Things They Carried.* New York: Broadway, 1990.

Oliver, Kendrick. *The My Lai Massacre in American History and Memory.* Manchester, UK: Manchester Univ. Press, 2006.

Orazem, Robert J., P. A. Frazier, P. P. Schnurr, H. E. Oleson, K. F. Carlson, B. T. Litz, and N. A. Sayer. "Identity Adjustment Among Afghanistan and Iraq War Veterans with Reintegration Difficulty." *Psychological Trauma: Theory, Research, Practice, and Policy*, Supp. 1 (November 2016): 4–11. doi: 10.1037/tra0000225.

Owen, Wilfred. "Dulce et Decorum Est." In *The Norton Anthology of English Literature*, edited by Stephen Greenblatt, 1974. New York: Norton, 2006.

Owen, Micah. "Put the Truck in Gear and Drive." *Journal of Military Experience* 1 (2011): 73–81.

"Paid Patriotism at NFL Games?" *VFW Magazine* 102, no. 10 (2015): 8.

Parker, Kim, Ruth Igielnik, Amanda Barroso, and Anthony Cilluffo. "The American Veteran Experience and the Post-9/11 Generation." Pew Research Center: Social and Demographic Trends. Pew Research Center, September 10, 2019. https://www.pewresearch.org/social-trends/2019/09/10/the-american-veteran-experience-and-the-post-9-11-generation/.

Parrott, Scott, David L. Albright, Nicholas Eckhart, and Kirsten Laha-Walsh. "Mental Representations of Military Veterans: Pictures (and Words) in Our Heads." *Journal of Veteran Studies* 6, no. 3 (December 2020): 61–71. http://doi.org/10.21061/jvs.v6i3.207.

Pellicano, Giuseppe. *Oh Happy Day.* In *Journal of Military Experience* 3 (2013): 344.

———. *Tea Time.* In *Journal of Military Experience* 3 (2013): 343.

Percy, Benjamin. "On the Ground." Review of *The Yellow Birds*, by Kevin Powers. *New York Times*, October 4, 2012. https://www.nytimes.com/2012/10/07/books/review/the-yellow-birds-by-kevin-powers.html.

Pizer, Donald. "Henry Behind the Lines and the Concept of Manhood in *The Red Badge of Courage.*" *Stephen Crane Studies* 10, no. 1 (2001): 2–7.

Powers, Kevin. *The Yellow Birds.* New York: Back Bay Books, 2012.

Rajamanickam, M. *Experimental Psychology with Advanced Experiments.* New Delhi: Concept Publishing, 1925.

Rall, Ted. "Poor and Uneducated, Like We Thought." *Boise Weekly*, August 1, 2007. https://mrgschicanoworld.files.wordpress.com/2015/04/14-poor-and-uneducated.pdf.

Ramadanovic, Petar. "In the Future . . . On Trauma and Literature." In *Topologies of Trauma: Essays on the Limit of Knowledge and Memory*, edited by Linda Belau and Petar Ramadanovic, 179–211. New York: Other Press, 2002.

Rampton, Sheldon, and John Stauber. *Weapons of Mass Deception: The Uses of Propaganda in Bush's War on Iraq.* New York: Tarcher/Penguin, 2003.

Rancourt, Suzanne S. "The Bear That Stands." *Journal of Military Experience* 3 (2013): 29–49.

Reagan, Ronald. "National Security and SDI." March 23, 1983. Washington, D.C. Transcript. *American Experience.* Accessed 2014. https://www.pbs.org/wgbh/americanexperience/features/reagan-security/.

Reid, Chip. "Reforms at Wounded Warrior Project after CBS News Investigation." CBS News. Last modified September 2, 2016. https://www.cbsnews.com/news/reforms-at-wounded-warrior-project-after-cbs-news-investigation/.

Reid, Chip, and Jennifer Janisch. "Wounded Warrior Project Accused of Wasting Donation Money." CBS News. Last modified January 26, 2016. https://www.cbsnews.com/news/wounded-warrior-project-accused-of-wasting-donation-money/.

Rightwing Extremism: Current Economic and Political Climate Fueling Resurgence in Radicalization and Recruitment. PDF file. April 7, 2009. US Department of Homeland Security. https://fas.org/irp/eprint/rightwing.pdf.

Robertson, Linda R. *Dream of Civilized Warfare: World War I Flying Aces and the American Imagination.* Minneapolis: Univ. of Minnesota Press, 2003.

Robinson, Michael, and Kori Schake. "The Military's Extremism Problem Is Our Problem." *New York Times*, March 2, 2021. https://www.nytimes.com/2021/03/02/opinion/veterans-capitol-attack.html.

"Román Baca: Artistic Director." Exit12 Dance Company. Accessed May 21, 2021. https://exit12danceco.org/bios.

Rossington, Michael. "Collective Memory." In *Theories of Memory: A Reader*, edited by Michael Rossington and Anne Whitehead, 133–38. Baltimore: Johns Hopkins Univ. Press, 2007.

Rossington, Michael, and Anne Whitehead, eds. *Theories of Memory: A Reader.* Baltimore: Johns Hopkins Univ. Press, 2007.

Rotundo, Anthony. *American Manhood: Transformations in Masculinity from the Revolution to the Modern Era.* New York: Basic, 1993.

Rugg, Taylor Elizabeth. "Identity Negotiation in Military Service Members." *Young Scholars in Writing* 15 (July 2019): 20–30. https://youngscholarsinwriting.org/index.php/ysiw/article/view/260.

Saussure, Ferdinand de. *Course in General Linguistics.* 1916. Reprint, Chicago: Open Court, 1998.

Savage, Charlie. "Bowe Bergdahl, Facing Desertion Trial, Asks Obama for Pardon." *New York Times*, December 2, 2016. https://www.nytimes.com/2016/12/02/us/politics/bowe-bergdahl-asks-obama-for-pardon.html.

Savage, Kirk. *Standing Soldiers, Kneeling Slaves: Race, War, and Monument in Nineteenth-Century America.* Princeton: Princeton Univ. Press, 1997.

Scott, Ridley, dir. *Blackhawk Down.* 2001. Los Angeles: Revolution Studios, 2001. DVD.

Scorsese, Martin, dir. *Taxi Driver.* 1976. Culver City, Calif.: Columbia Pictures, 1999. DVD.

Scott, Tony, dir. *Top Gun.* 1986. Los Angeles: Paramount Pictures, 1998. DVD.

"Sculpture Added to Veterans Memorial." Eastern Kentucky University, Richmond, Kentucky. November 13, 2017. https://stories.eku.edu/events/sculpture-added-veterans-memorial.

Seahorn, Janet J., and E. Anthony Seahorn. *Tears of a Warrior: A Family's Story of Combat and Living with PTSD.* Ft. Collins, Colo.: Team Pursuits, 2010.

Sengstock, Mary C. *Voices of Diversity: Multi-Culturalism in America.* Detroit: Springer, 2009.

Severo, Richard, and Lewis Milford. *The Wages of War: When America's Soldiers Came Home—From Valley Forge to Vietnam.* New York: Simon and Schuster, 1989.

Shay, Jonathan. *Odysseus in America: Combat Trauma and the Trials of Homecoming.* New York: Scribner, 2002.

Sherry, Vincent. *The Great War and the Language of Modernism.* New York: Oxford Univ. Press, 2003.

Shewring, Anne L. "We Didn't Do That Did We? Representation of the Veteran Experience." *Journal of American and Comparative Cultures* 23, no. 4 (2000): 51–66.

Showalter, Elaine. *The Female Malady: Women, Madness and English Culture, 1830–1980.* London: Virago Press, 1987.

Silverman, Kaja. *Male Subjectivity at the Margins.* New York: Routledge, 1992.

Simon, Cecilia Capuzzi. "Warrior Voices: Veterans Learn to Write the Words They Could Not Speak." *New York Times*, February 3, 2013. https://www.nytimes.com/2013/02/03/education/edlife/veterans-learn-to-write-and-heal.html.

Smyth, J. E. *Reconstructing American Historical Cinema: From* Cimarron *to* Citizen Kane. Lexington: Univ. Press of Kentucky, 2006.

Sobolev, Dennis. *The Concepts Used to Analyze Culture: A Critique of Twentieth-Century Ways of Thinking.* Lewiston, N.Y.: Edwin Mellen, 2010.

Solomon, Eric. "A Definition of the War Novel." In *The Red Badge of Courage*, edited by Donald Pizer and Eric Carl Link, 181–87. New York: Norton, 2008.

Sørensen, Birgitte Refslund. "Veterans' Homecomings: Secrecy and Postdeployment Social Becoming." *Cultural Anthropology* 56, no. 12 (2015): 231–40.

Southall, Ashley. "Medals of Honor, Denied Because of Prejudice, to Be Belatedly Awarded." *New York Times*, February 21, 2014. https://www.nytimes.com/2014/02/22/us/medals-of-honor-denied-because-of-prejudice-to-be-belatedly-awarded.html.

Spielberg, Steven, dir. *Saving Private Ryan.* 1998. Los Angeles: Paramount Pictures, 1999. DVD.

Stagner, Annessa. "Recovering the Masculine Hero: Post-World War I Shell Shock in American Culture." UCLA Center for the Study of Women. 2009. https://escholarship.org/uc/item/4jt5g1q2.

Standing, Guy. *The Precariat: The New Dangerous Class.* London: Bloomsbury, 2014.

Steinhauer, Jennifer. "Veterans' Groups Compete with Each Other, and Struggle with the V.A." *New York Times*, January 4, 2019. https://www.nytimes.com/2019/01/04/us/politics/veterans-service-organizations.html.

Stone, Oliver, dir. *Platoon.* 1986. Los Angeles: Hemdale, 1997. DVD.

"The Story of Team Rubicon." Team Rubicon. Accessed May 2021. https://teamrubiconusa.org/story/.

Straw, Mark. "Traumatized Masculinity and American National Identity in Hollywood's Gulf War." *Journal of Contemporary Film* 6, no. 2 (2008): 127–43.

"STRIVE." Ohio State University. Accessed May 2021. https://medicine.osu.edu/departments/psychiatry-and-behavioral-health/strive.

Sue, Derald Wing. *Microaggressions in Everyday Life: Race, Gender, and Sexual Orientation.* Hoboken, N.J.: Wiley, 2010.

Swofford, Anthony. *Jarhead: A Marine's Chronicle of the Gulf War and Other Battles.* New York: Scribner, 2003.

Szoldra, Paul. "Medal of Honor Recipient Kyle Carpenter Is Coming Out with a Book He Says 'Will Truly Help People.'" *Task and Purpose.* Last modified May 4, 2019. https://taskandpurpose.com/news/kyle-carpenter-book/.

Tappert, Tara Leigh. "Introduction: Artwork." *Journal of Military Experience* 3 (2013): 202–5.

Tocqueville, Alexis de. *Democracy in America.* 1835. Reprint, London: Penguin, 2003.

"VA Conducts Nation's Largest Analysis of Veteran Suicide." Office of Public and Governmental Affairs, US Department of Veteran Affairs. July 7, 2016. https://www.va.gov/opa/pressrel/pressrelease.cfm?id=2801.

"Veteran Finds Home, Hope as EKU Student." *Richmond Register*, September 30, 2013. https://www.richmondregister.com/news/veteran-finds-home-hope-at-eku/article_433f749c-6805-5dd4-af9f-d9437c833c74.html.

"Veterans & Media Lab." University of Alabama. Accessed May 2021. https://cis.ua.edu/research/veterans-and-media-lab/.

"Veterans Empowered to Protect African Wildlife." VETPAW. Accessed May 2021. https://vetpaw.org/.

"Veterans in Society." Virginia Tech. Accessed May 2021. https://vtechworks.lib.vt.edu/handle/10919/56348.

Vonnegut, Kurt. *Slaughterhouse Five, or The Children's Crusade.* New York: Delacorte Press, 1969.

Wahle, Steve. "PhDs Who Can Win a Bar Fight." Online panel presentation, University of South Carolina. March 23, 2021.

Waller, Willard Walter. *The Veteran Comes Back.* New York: Dryden Press, 1944. https://archive.org/details/veterancomesback00wallrich/page/16/mode/2up.

"War, Literature and the Arts." Accessed May 2021. https://www.wlajournal.com/.

"Warriors Speak: Sharing the Impact of a Generation." Wounded Warrior Project. 2017. https://www.woundedwarriorproject.org/mission/warriors-speak.

Webb, Marc, dir. *The Ghost of You.* By My Chemical Romance. Los Angeles, Calif.: DNA, 2005. Music video.

Weine, Stevan. "What Happens—and Who Benefits—When Trauma Victims Are Encouraged to Tell Their Stories?" In *Rethinking Therapeutic Culture,* edited by Tim Aubry and Trysh Travis, 145–53. Chicago: Univ. of Chicago Press, 2015.

Wellman, William A., dir. *Heroes for Sale.* 1933. Burbank, Calif.: Warner Brothers, 2009. DVD.

Wellman, William A., and Harry d'Abbadie d'Arrast, dirs. *Wings.* 1927. Los Angeles: Paramount Famous Lasky Corporation, 2012. DVD.

"Who We Are." Military Experience and the Arts. Accessed 2016. https://militaryexperience.org/mission-statement/.

"William Kyle Carpenter." Congressional Medal of Honor Society. 2017. https://www.cmohs.org/recipients/william-k-carpenter.

"William T. Sherman: Major General." Civil War Trust. Accessed 2014. https://www.battlefields.org/learn/biographies/william-t-sherman.

Wilson, Scott. "Obama to Award Medal of Honor to Two Dozen Veterans, Including 19 Discrimination Victims." *Washington Post*, February 21, 2014. https://www.washingtonpost.com/politics/obama-to-ward-medal-of-honor-to-19-soldiers-who-were-overlooked-because-of-their-ethnicity/2014/02/21/209594e8-9b10-11e3-975d-107dfef7b668_story.html.

Wingate, James, to Darryl F. Zanuck et al., May 1933. *Studio Letters and Censorship Reports.* The Academy of Motion Picture and Arts Sciences, Margaret Herrick Library, Beverly Hills, California.

Winter, Jay. *Remembering War: The Great War between Memory and History in the 20th Century.* New Haven, Conn.: Yale Univ. Press, 2006.

Winter, Yves. "*The Prince* and His Art of War: Machiavelli's Military Populism." *Social Research* 81, no. 1 (2014): 165–91. Academia.edu.

"Wounded Warrior Project." *Charity Navigator.* 2021. https://www.charitynavigator.org/index.cfm?bay=search.summary&orgid=12842.

Wyler, William, dir. *The Best Years of Our Lives.* 1946. Culver City, Calif.: Samuel Goldwyn Company, 1997. DVD.

Wyndham, George. "A Remarkable Book." In *The Red Badge of Courage*, edited by Donald Pizer and Eric Carl Link, 233–41. New York: Norton, 2008.

Yeats, W. B., ed. *Oxford Book of Modern Verse 1892–1935.* Oxford: Oxford Univ. Press, 1936.

Zefferman, Matthew R., and Sarah Mathew. "Combat Stress in a Small-Scale Society Suggests Divergent Evolutionary Roots for Posttraumatic Stress Disorder Symptoms." *Proceedings of the National Academy of Sciences* 118, no. 15 (April 2021). e2020430118; DOI: 10.1073/pnas.2020430118.

Index

About the Author

Travis L. Martin, Ph.D., is the founding director of the Kentucky Center for Veterans Studies at Eastern Kentucky University. He has established several nationally recognized programs to support returning veterans in higher education and the nonprofit sector. A scholar of American literature, psychoanalytic trauma theory, and social theory, Dr. Martin presents frequently at conferences and universities. He has published dozens of research articles and creative short works on veterans' issues. He resides in Richmond, Kentucky.

About the Cover Art

Some time ago I read a story about a poet who wrote about fire for several years straight. I don't recall specific details, or names, but this poet experienced a horrific fire and in order to heal, she had to write about it. When asked by a critic when she would stop writing about fire and return to her *normal* work, her response was, "I'll stop writing about fire when I don't *need* to write about it anymore."

I began my artistic career long before I ever pulled on a pair of combat boots. Back then I was primarily a musician who dabbled in nature photography. The eight years of my enlistment resulted in a *need* to express that experience that couldn't be filled by creating *normal* work. Thus began my conceptual photographic series. As I write this, I've been out of the army for as long as I was in, and I'm just beginning to return to *normal* work. Of course, *normal* is merely a social construct. Life does not follow rules, and neither does art. I am forever changed by my experiences. They have colored the tones of my artistic voice with a beauty, strength, and compassion that my previous work could not have known. My nature photography is more nuanced because of this, and I think the cover of this book is a fine example of that.

Tif Holmes